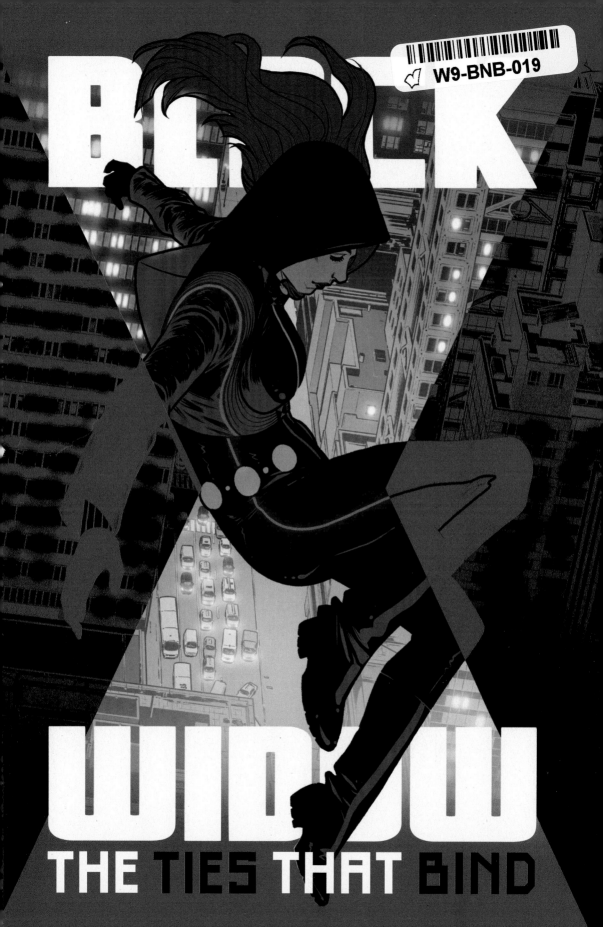

BLACK WIDOW

WIDOW
THE TIES THAT BIND

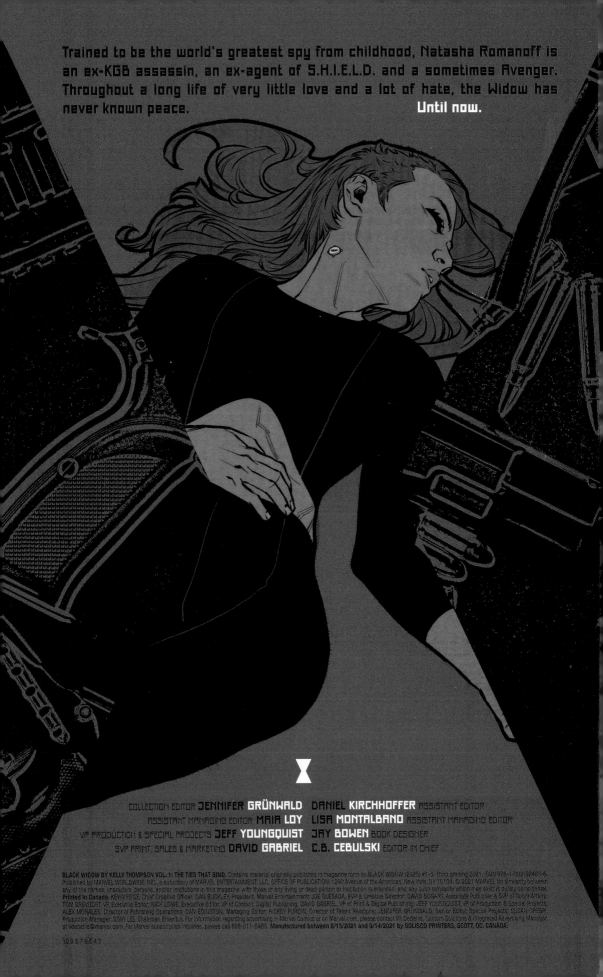

Trained to be the world's greatest spy from childhood, Natasha Romanoff is an ex-KGB assassin, an ex-agent of S.H.I.E.L.D. and a sometimes Avenger. Throughout a long life of very little love and a lot of hate, the Widow has never known peace. **Until now.**

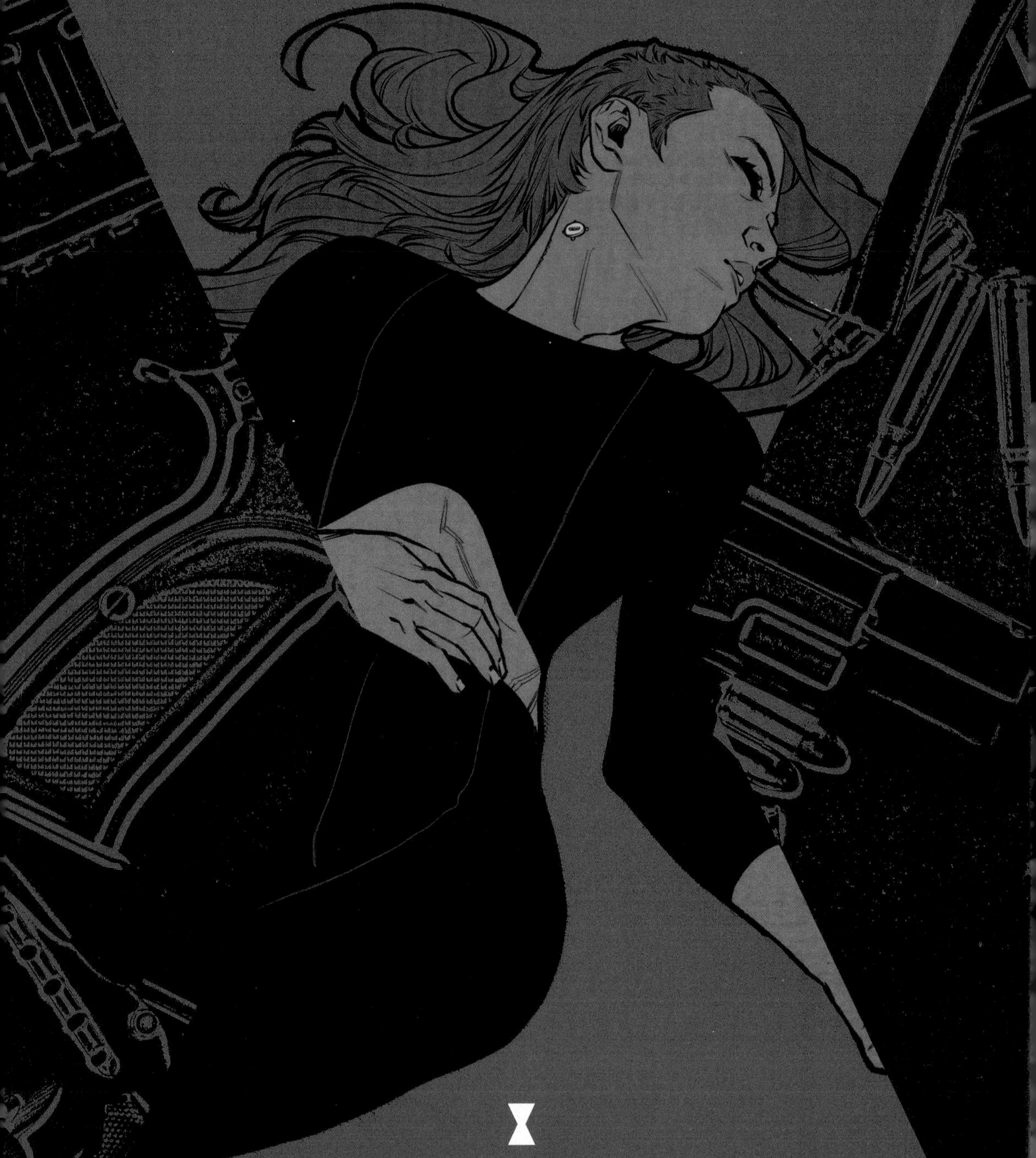

COLLECTION EDITOR JENNIFER GRÜNWALD
ASSISTANT MANAGING EDITOR MAIA LOY
VP PRODUCTION & SPECIAL PROJECTS JEFF YOUNGQUIST
SVP PRINT, SALES & MARKETING DAVID GABRIEL
DANIEL KIRCHHOFFER ASSISTANT EDITOR
LISA MONTALBANO ASSISTANT MANAGING EDITOR
JAY BOWEN BOOK DESIGNER
C.B. CEBULSKI EDITOR IN CHIEF

BLACK WIDOW BY KELLY THOMPSON VOL. 1: THE TIES THAT BIND. Contains material originally published in magazine form as BLACK WIDOW (2020) #1-5. Third printing 2021. ISBN 978-1-302-92483-6. Published by MARVEL WORLDWIDE, INC., a subsidiary of MARVEL ENTERTAINMENT, LLC. OFFICE OF PUBLICATION: 1290 Avenue of the Americas, New York, NY 10104. **Printed in Canada.** KEVIN FEIGE, Chief Creative Officer; DAN BUCKLEY, President, Marvel Entertainment; JOE QUESADA, EVP & Creative Director; DAVID BOGART, Associate Publisher & SVP of Talent Affairs; TOM BREVOORT, VP, Executive Editor; NICK LOWE, Executive Editor, VP of Content, Digital Publishing; DAVID GABRIEL, VP of Print & Digital Publishing; JEFF YOUNGQUIST, VP of Production & Special Projects; ALEX MORALES, Director of Publishing Operations; DAN EDINGTON, Managing Editor; RICKEY PURDIN, Director of Talent Relations; JENNIFER GRÜNWALD, Senior Editor, Special Projects; SUSAN CRESPI, Production Manager; STAN LEE, Chairman Emeritus. For information regarding advertising in Marvel Comics or on Marvel.com, please contact Vit DeBellis, Custom Solutions & Integrated Advertising Manager, at vdebellis@marvel.com. For Marvel subscription inquiries, please call 888-511-5480. **Manufactured between 8/13/2021 and 9/14/2021 by SOLISCO PRINTERS, SCOTT, QC, CANADA.**

10 9 8 7 6 5 4 3

BLACK
THE TIES THAT BIND

KELLY THOMPSON
WRITER

ELENA CASAGRANDE
WITH RAFAEL DE LATORRE (#5)
ARTISTS

JORDIE BELLAIRE
COLOR ARTIST

**CARLOS GÓMEZ &
FEDERICO BLEE**
FLASHBACK ART, #4

VC's CORY PETIT
LETTERER

ADAM HUGHES
COVER ART

SARAH BRUNSTAD
EDITOR

WIL MOSS
SENIOR EDITOR

TOM BREVOORT
EXECUTIVE EDITOR

WIDOW

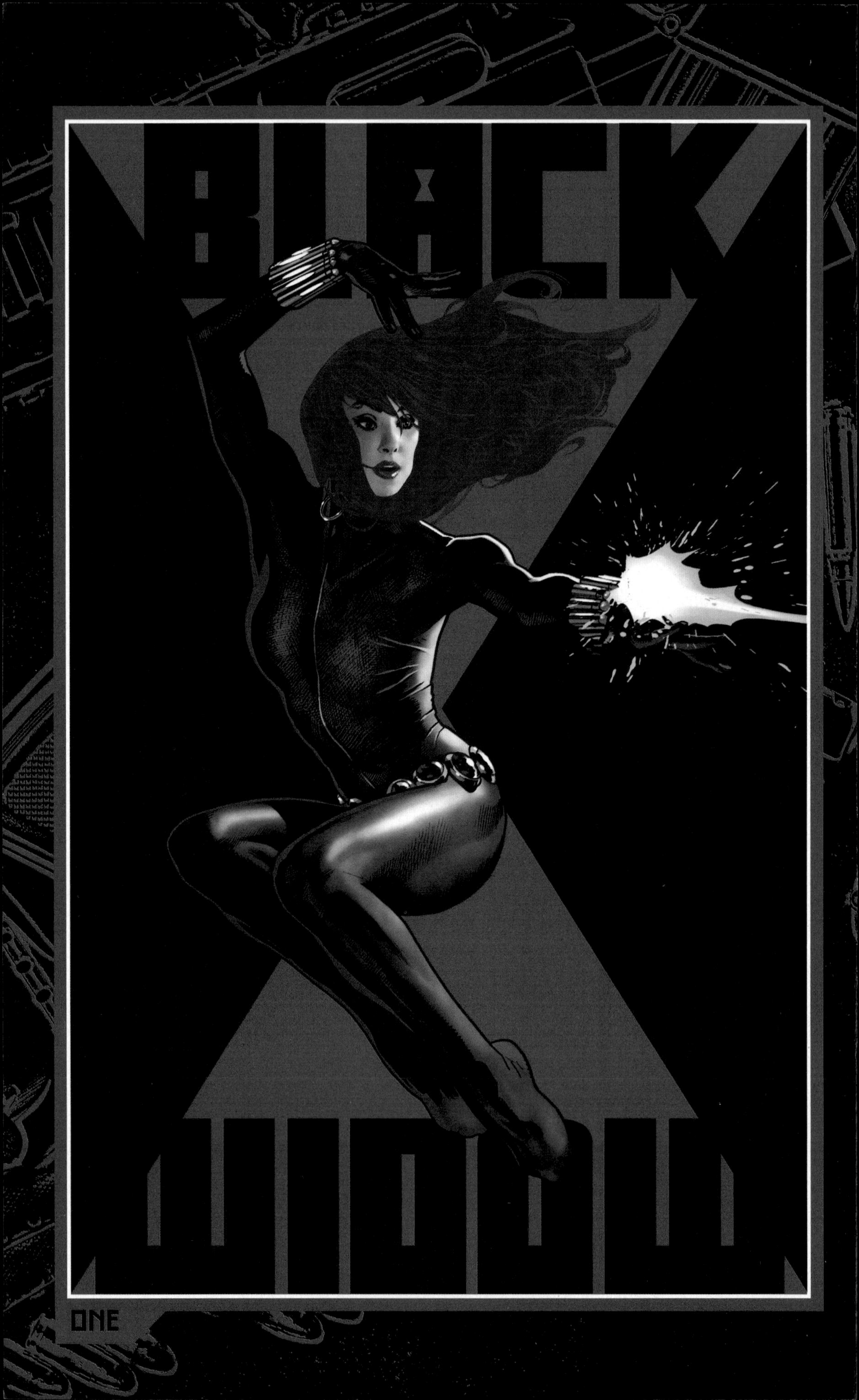
BLACK
WIDOW
ONE

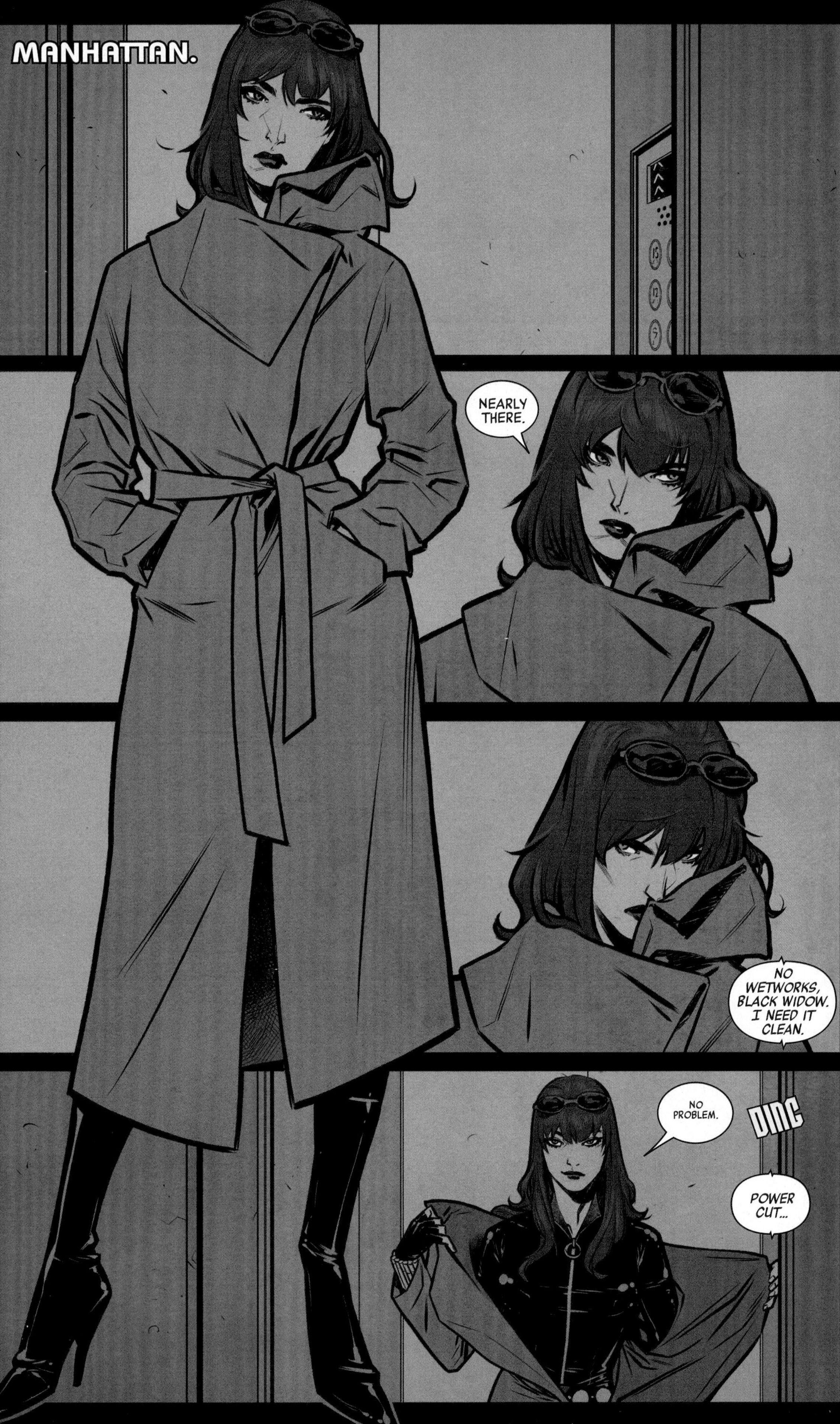
MANHATTAN.
NEARLY THERE.
NO WETWORKS, BLACK WIDOW. I NEED IT CLEAN.
NO PROBLEM.
DING
POWER CUT...

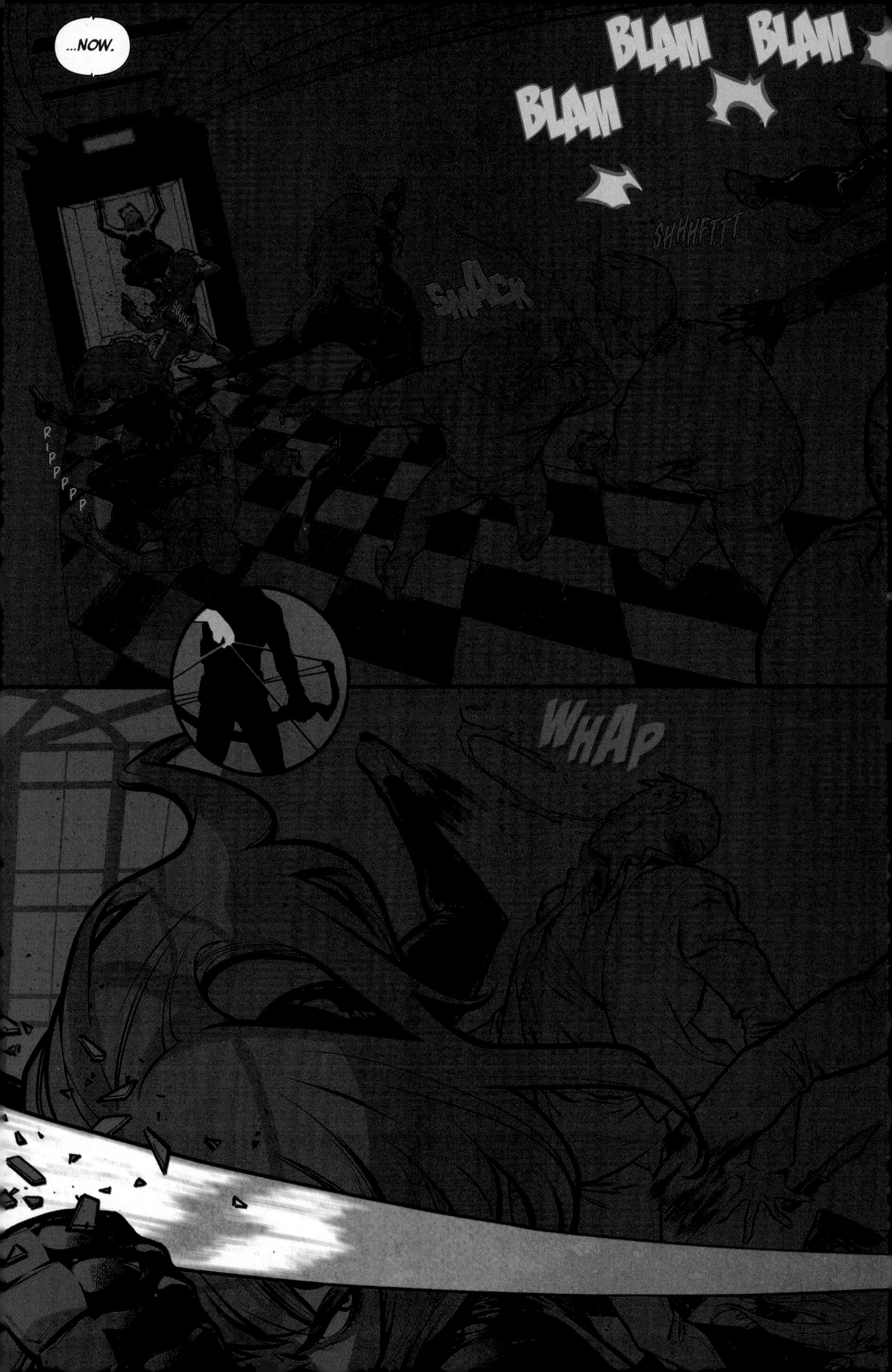
...NOW.
BLAM
BLAM
BLAM
SHHHFTTT
SMACK
SQUCH
RIPPPPPP
WHAP

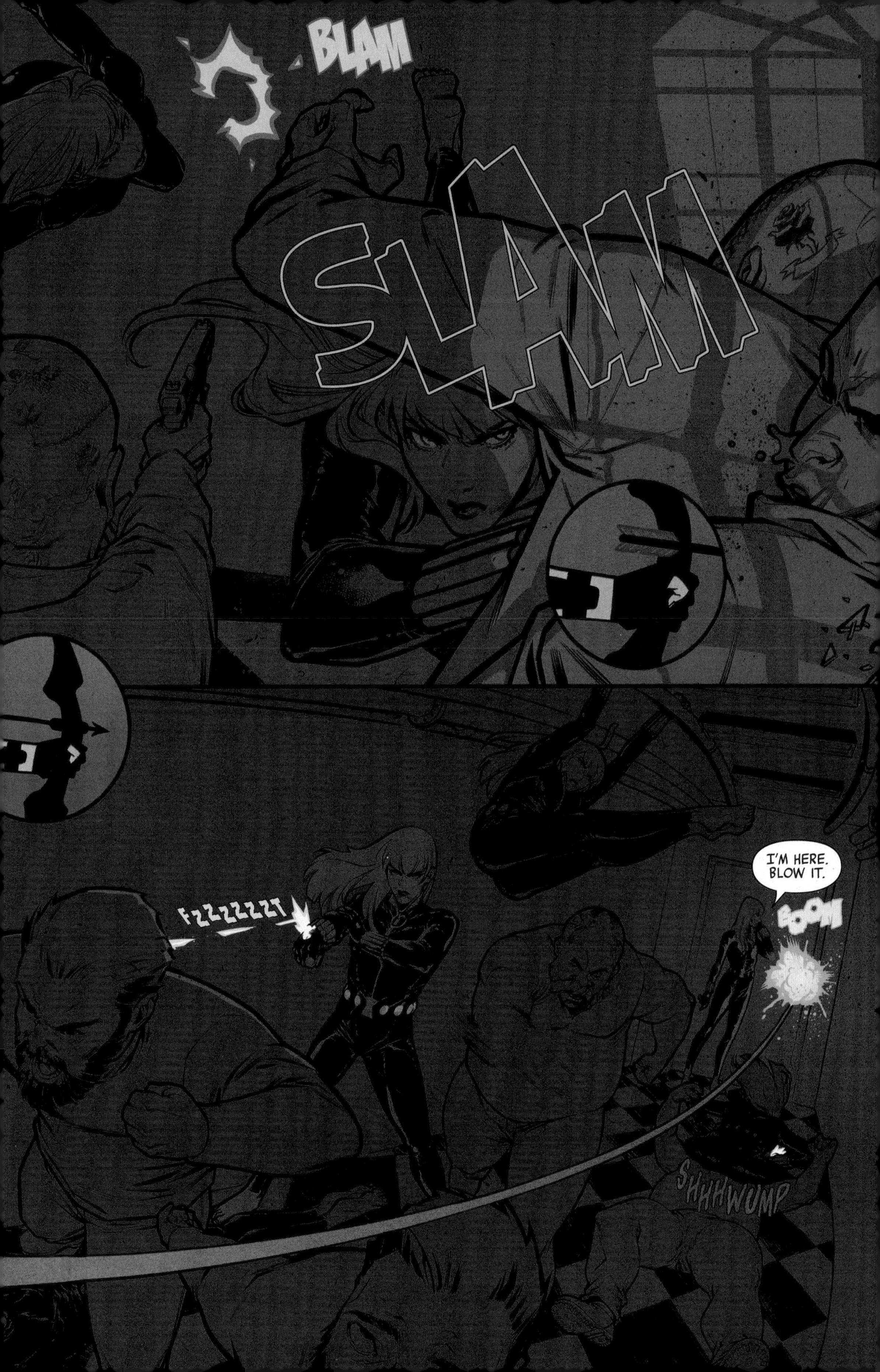
BLAM
SLAM
FZZZZZZZT
I'M HERE. BLOW IT.
BOOM
SHHHWUMP

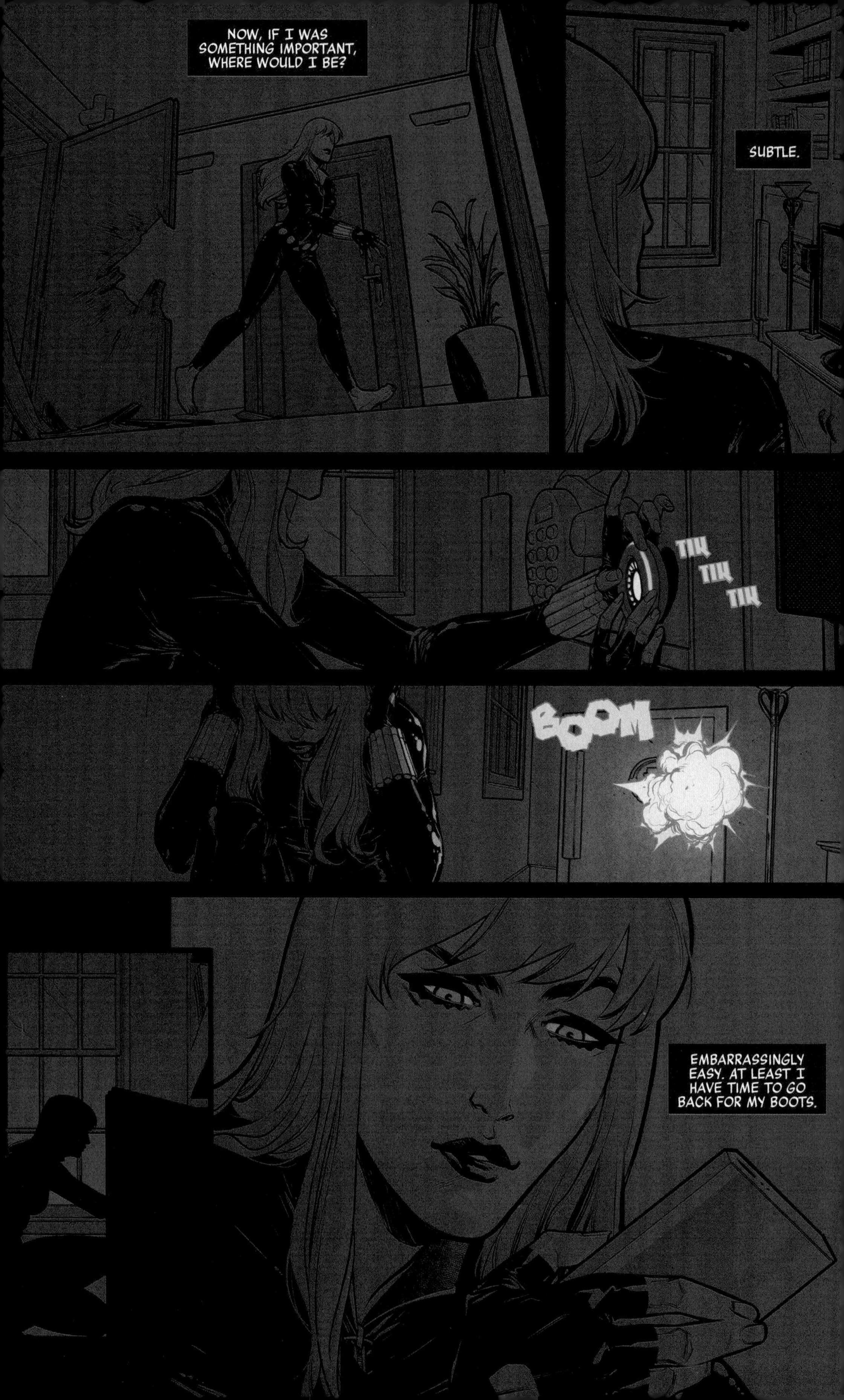
NOW, IF I WAS SOMETHING IMPORTANT, WHERE WOULD I BE?
SUBTLE.
TIK
TIK
TIK
BOOM
EMBARRASSINGLY EASY. AT LEAST I HAVE TIME TO GO BACK FOR MY BOOTS.

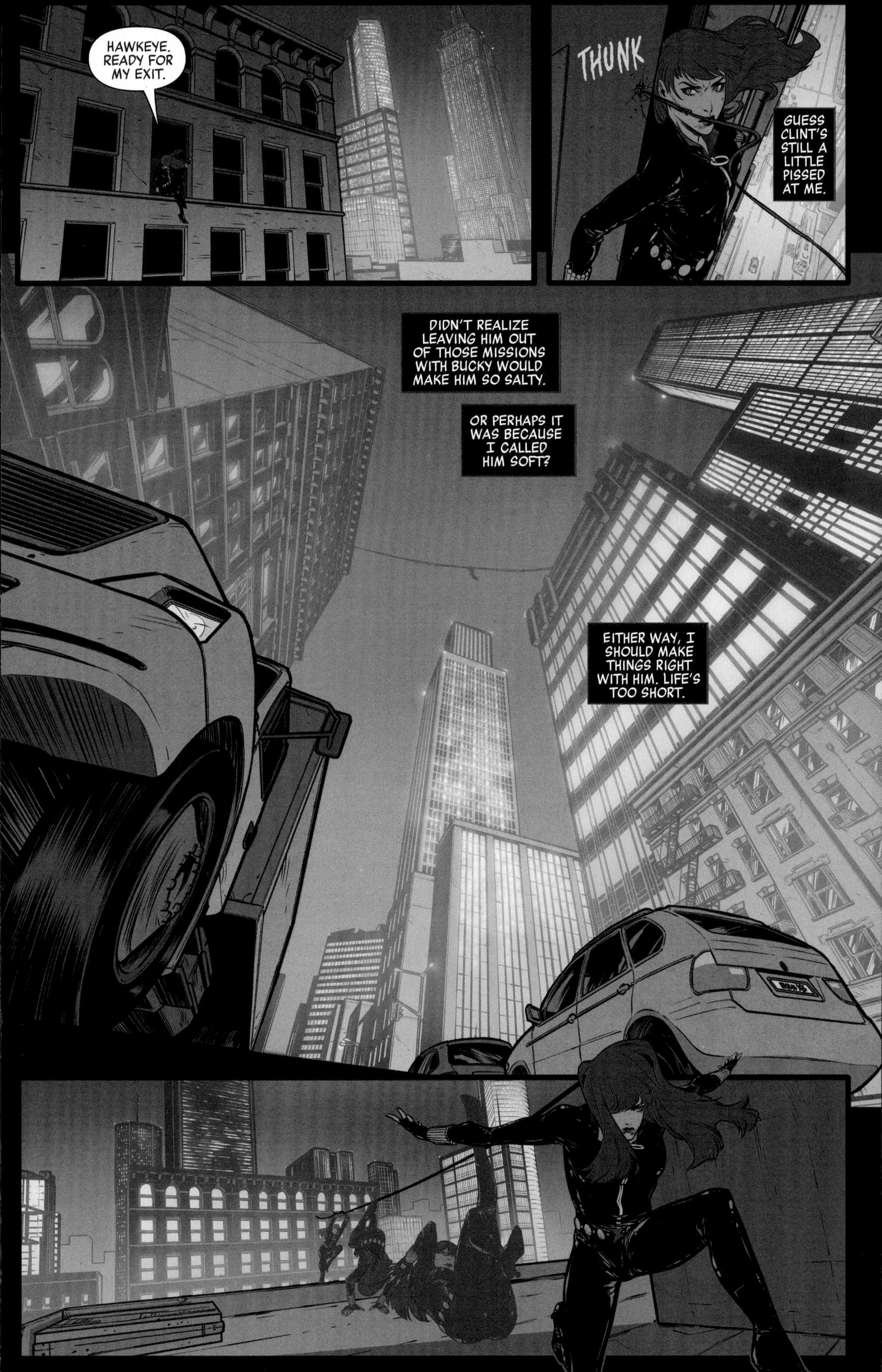
HAWKEYE. READY FOR MY EXIT.
THUNK
GUESS CLINT'S STILL A LITTLE PISSED AT ME.
DIDN'T REALIZE LEAVING HIM OUT OF THOSE MISSIONS WITH BUCKY WOULD MAKE HIM SO SALTY.
OR PERHAPS IT WAS BECAUSE I CALLED HIM SOFT?
EITHER WAY, I SHOULD MAKE THINGS RIGHT WITH HIM. LIFE'S TOO SHORT.

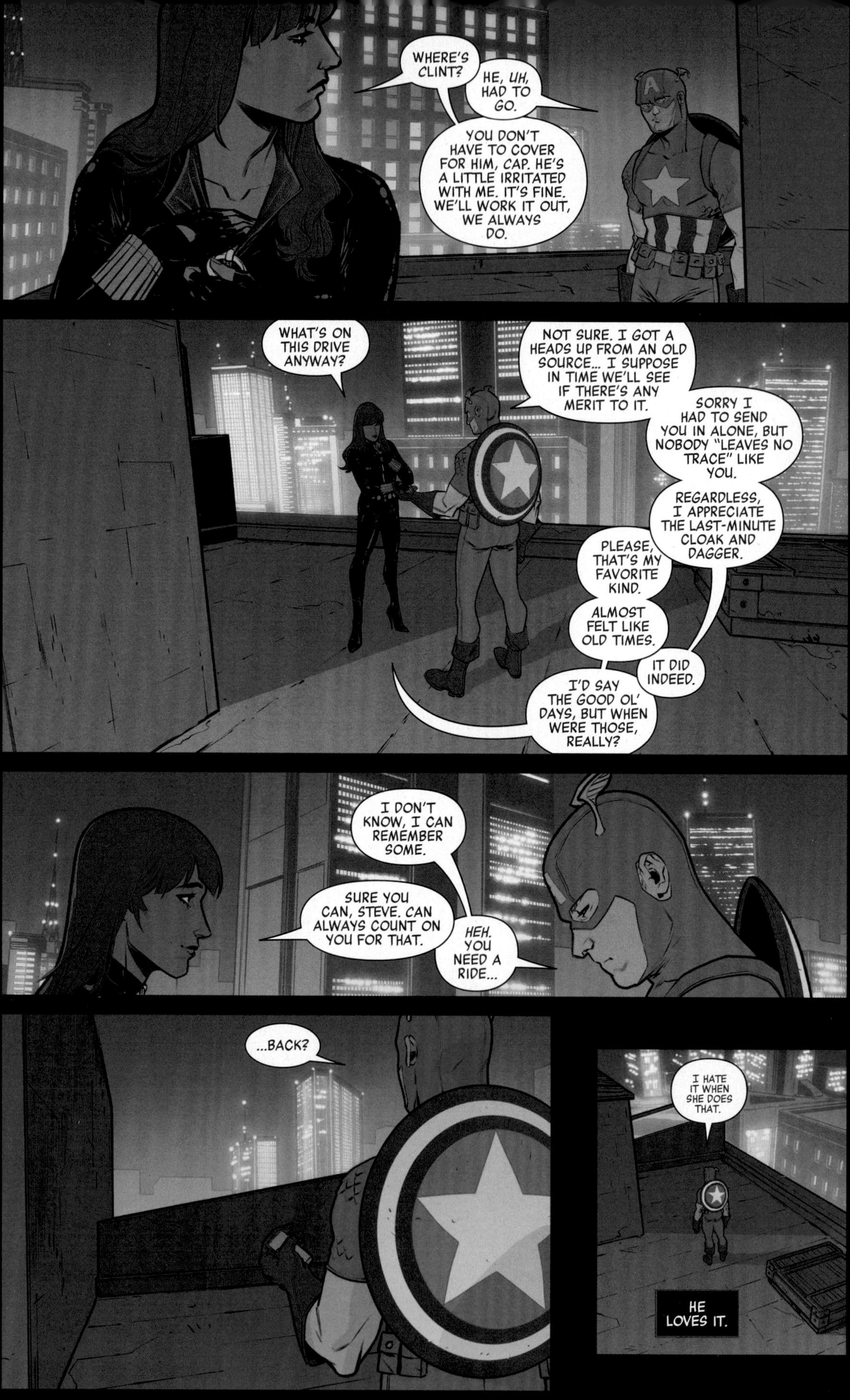
WHERE'S CLINT?
HE, UH, HAD TO GO.
YOU DON'T HAVE TO COVER FOR HIM, CAP. HE'S A LITTLE IRRITATED WITH ME. IT'S FINE. WE'LL WORK IT OUT, WE ALWAYS DO.
WHAT'S ON THIS DRIVE ANYWAY?
NOT SURE. I GOT A HEADS UP FROM AN OLD SOURCE... I SUPPOSE IN TIME WE'LL SEE IF THERE'S ANY MERIT TO IT.
SORRY I HAD TO SEND YOU IN ALONE, BUT NOBODY "LEAVES NO TRACE" LIKE YOU.
REGARDLESS, I APPRECIATE THE LAST-MINUTE CLOAK AND DAGGER.
PLEASE, THAT'S MY FAVORITE KIND.
ALMOST FELT LIKE OLD TIMES.
IT DID INDEED.
I'D SAY THE GOOD OL' DAYS, BUT WHEN WERE THOSE, REALLY?
I DON'T KNOW, I CAN REMEMBER SOME.
SURE YOU CAN, STEVE. CAN ALWAYS COUNT ON YOU FOR THAT.
HEH. YOU NEED A RIDE...
...BACK?
I HATE IT WHEN SHE DOES THAT.
HE LOVES IT.

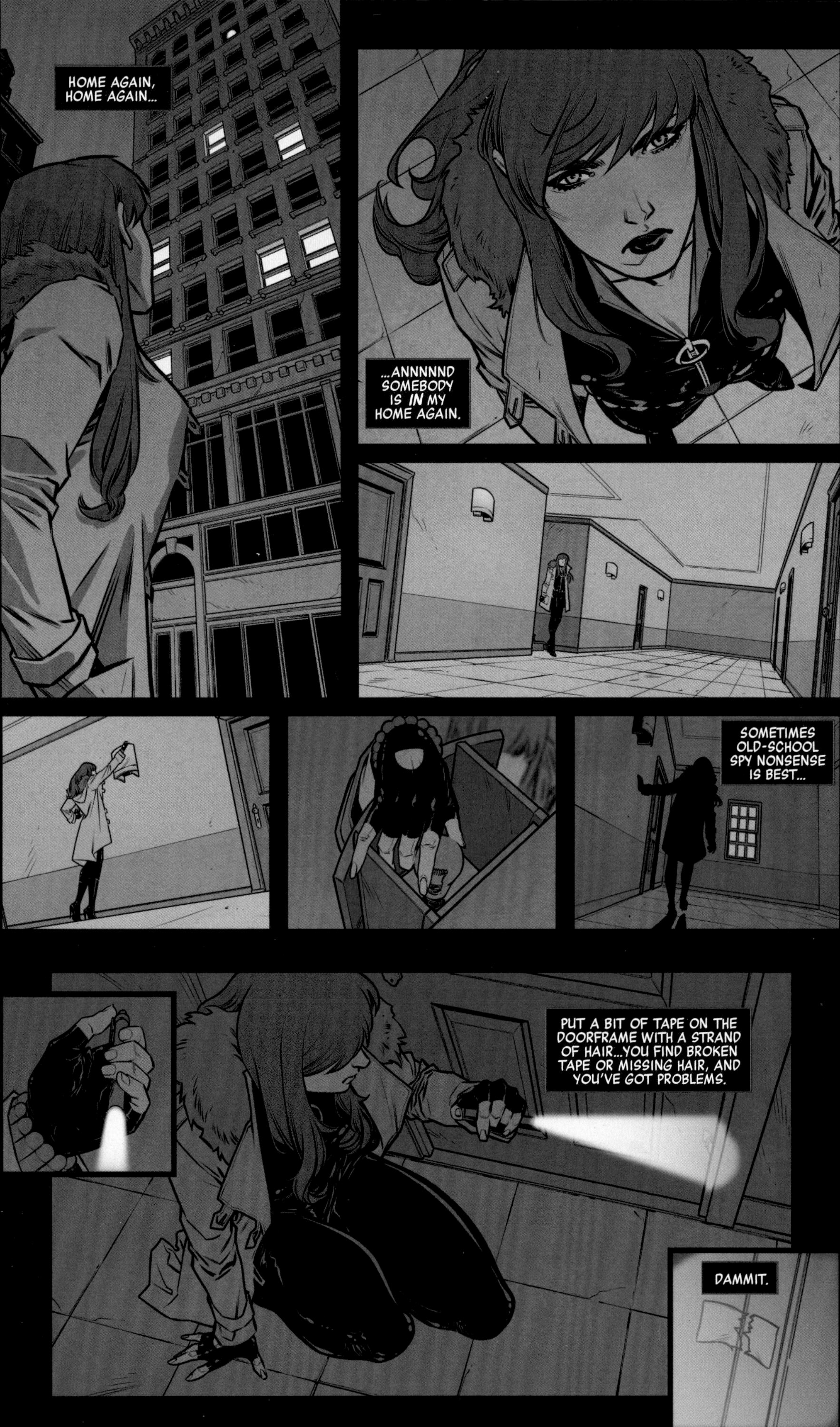
HOME AGAIN, HOME AGAIN...
...ANNNNND SOMEBODY IS IN MY HOME AGAIN.
SOMETIMES OLD-SCHOOL SPY NONSENSE IS BEST...
PUT A BIT OF TAPE ON THE DOORFRAME WITH A STRAND OF HAIR...YOU FIND BROKEN TAPE OR MISSING HAIR, AND YOU'VE GOT PROBLEMS.
DAMMIT.

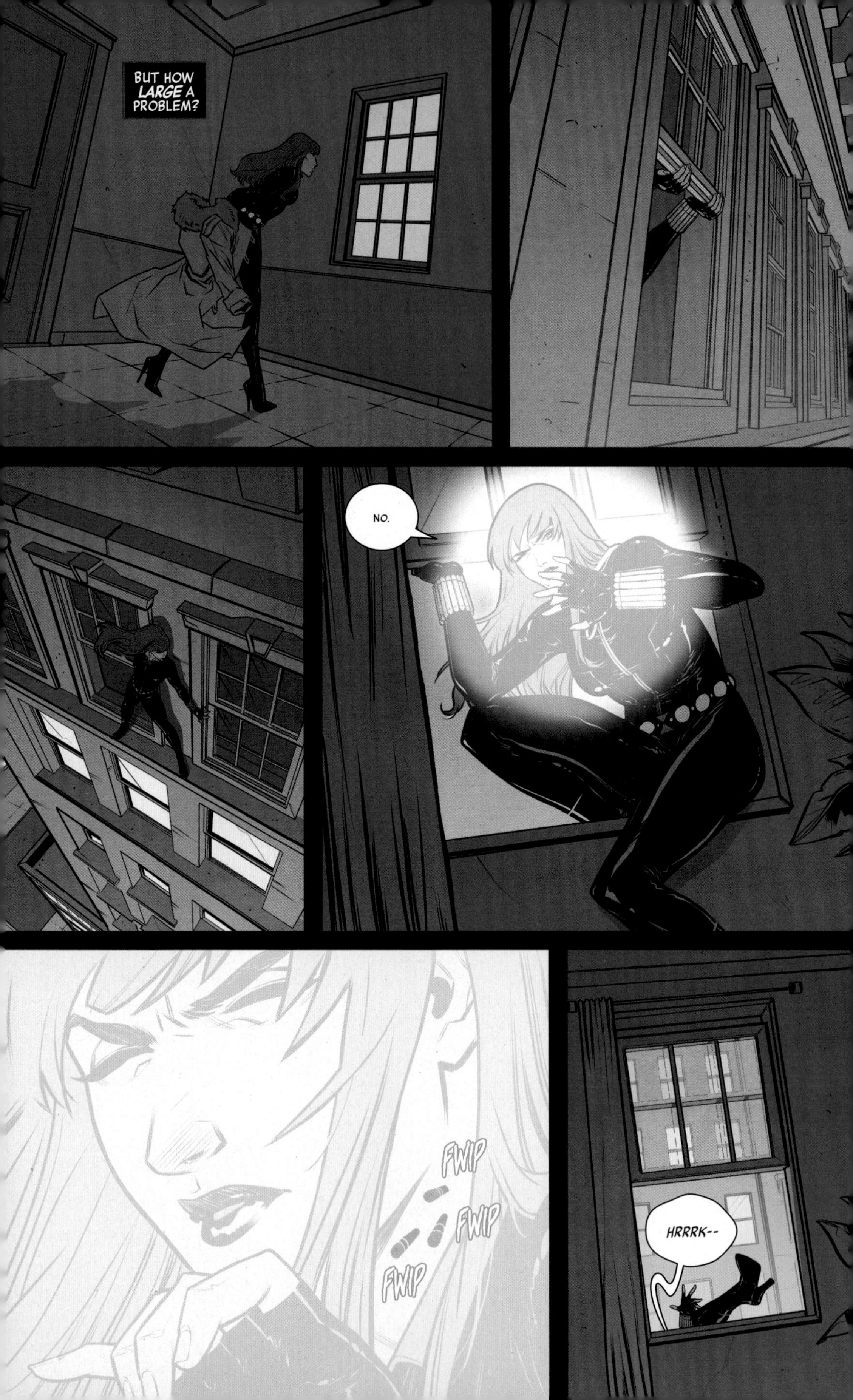
BUT HOW *LARGE* A PROBLEM?
NO.
FWIP
FWIP
FWIP
HRRRK--

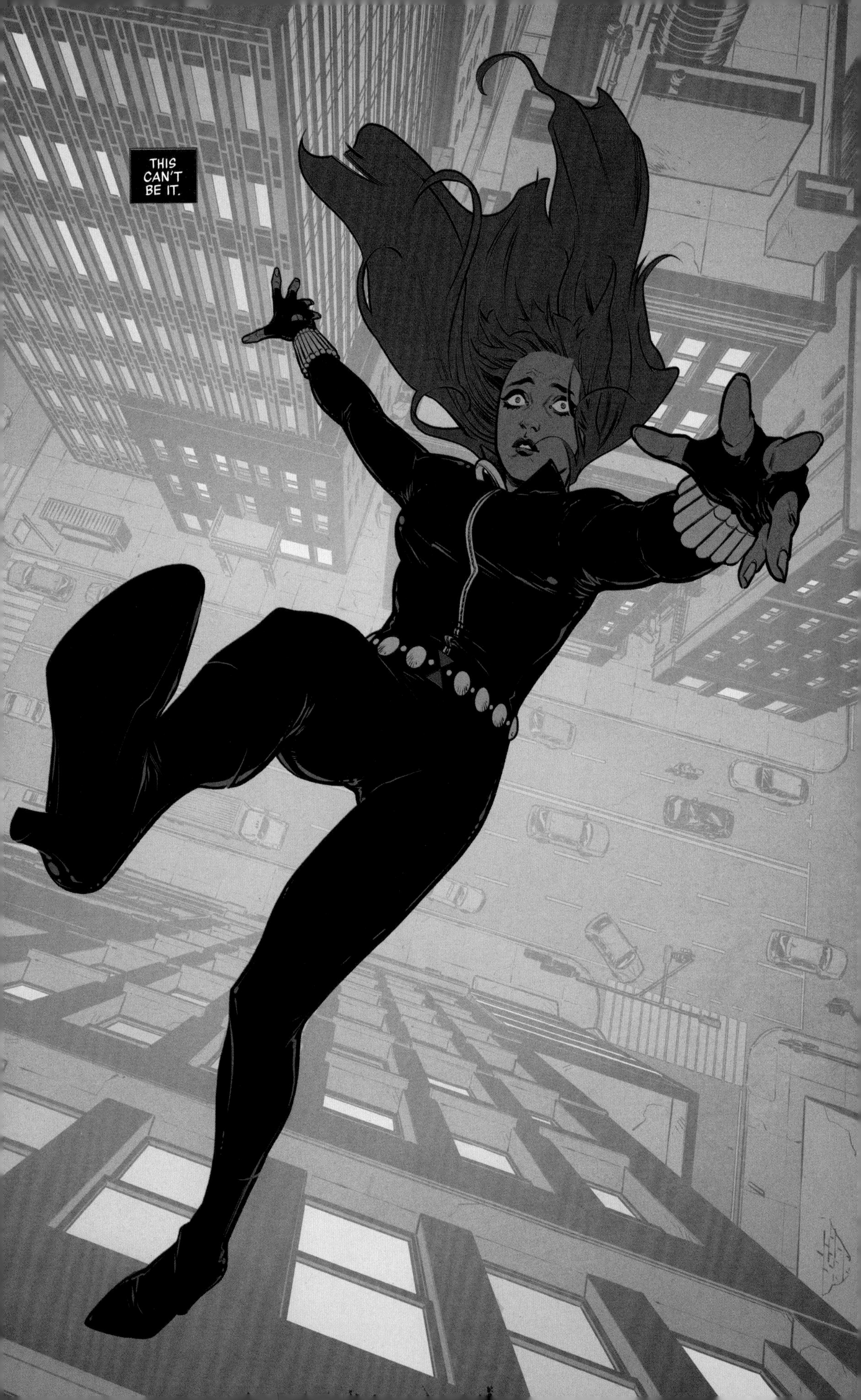
THIS CAN'T BE IT.

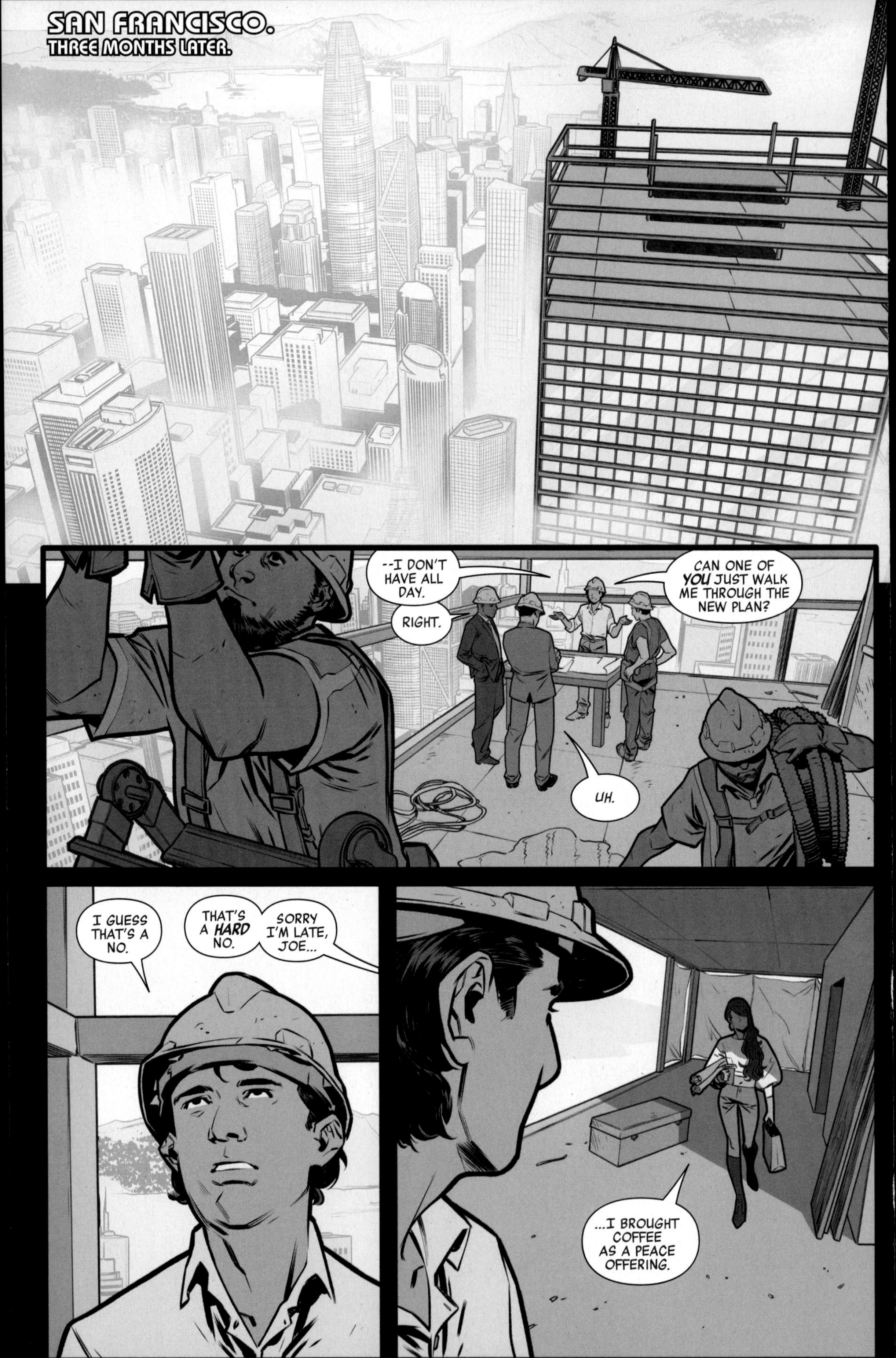
SAN FRANCISCO.
THREE MONTHS LATER.
--I DON'T HAVE ALL DAY.
RIGHT.
CAN ONE OF YOU JUST WALK ME THROUGH THE NEW PLAN?
UH.
I GUESS THAT'S A NO.
THAT'S A HARD NO.
SORRY I'M LATE, JOE...
...I BROUGHT COFFEE AS A PEACE OFFERING.

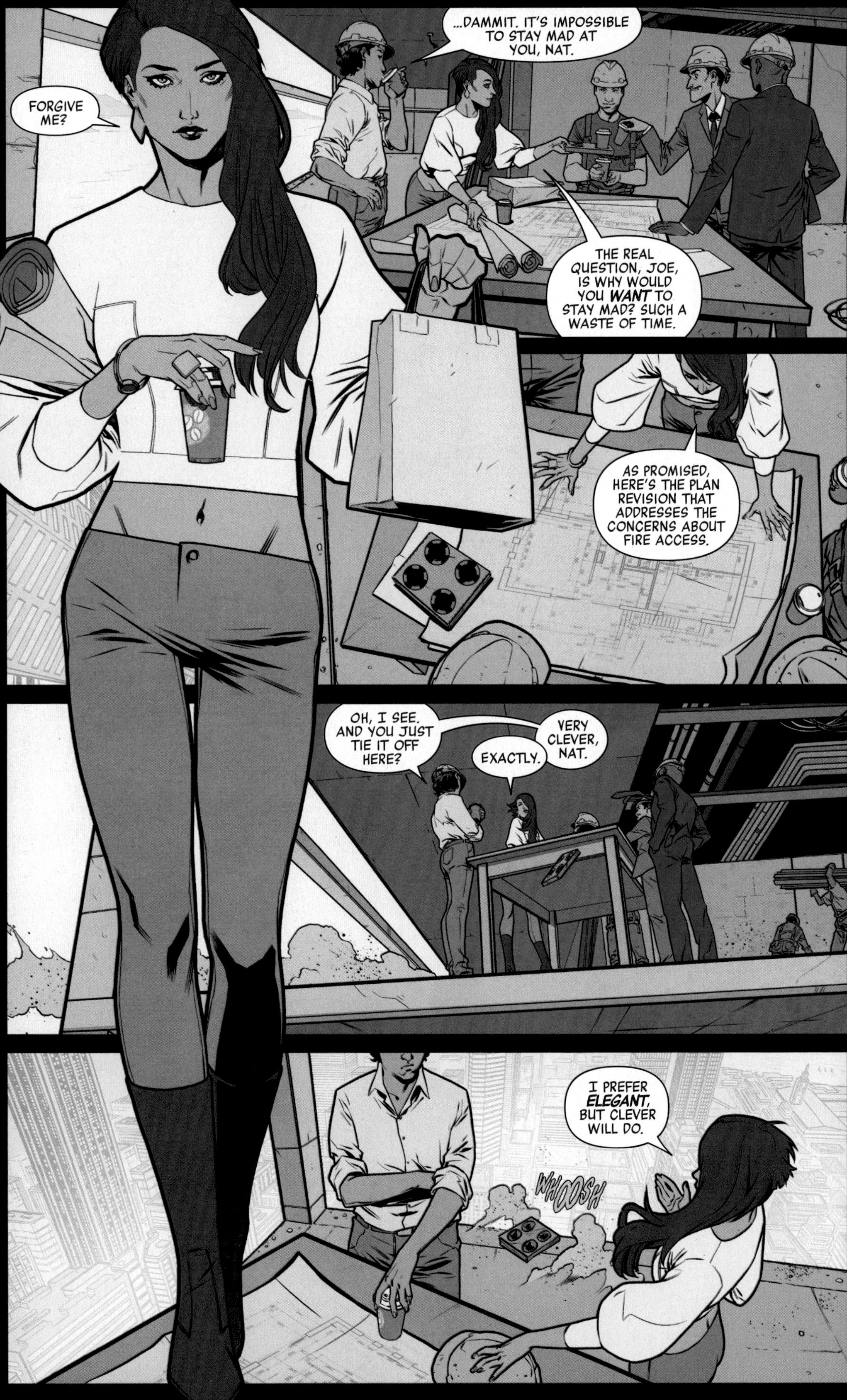
FORGIVE ME?
...DAMMIT. IT'S IMPOSSIBLE TO STAY MAD AT YOU, NAT.
THE REAL QUESTION, JOE, IS WHY WOULD YOU WANT TO STAY MAD? SUCH A WASTE OF TIME.
AS PROMISED, HERE'S THE PLAN REVISION THAT ADDRESSES THE CONCERNS ABOUT FIRE ACCESS.
OH, I SEE. AND YOU JUST TIE IT OFF HERE?
EXACTLY.
VERY CLEVER, NAT.
I PREFER ELEGANT, BUT CLEVER WILL DO.
WHOOSH

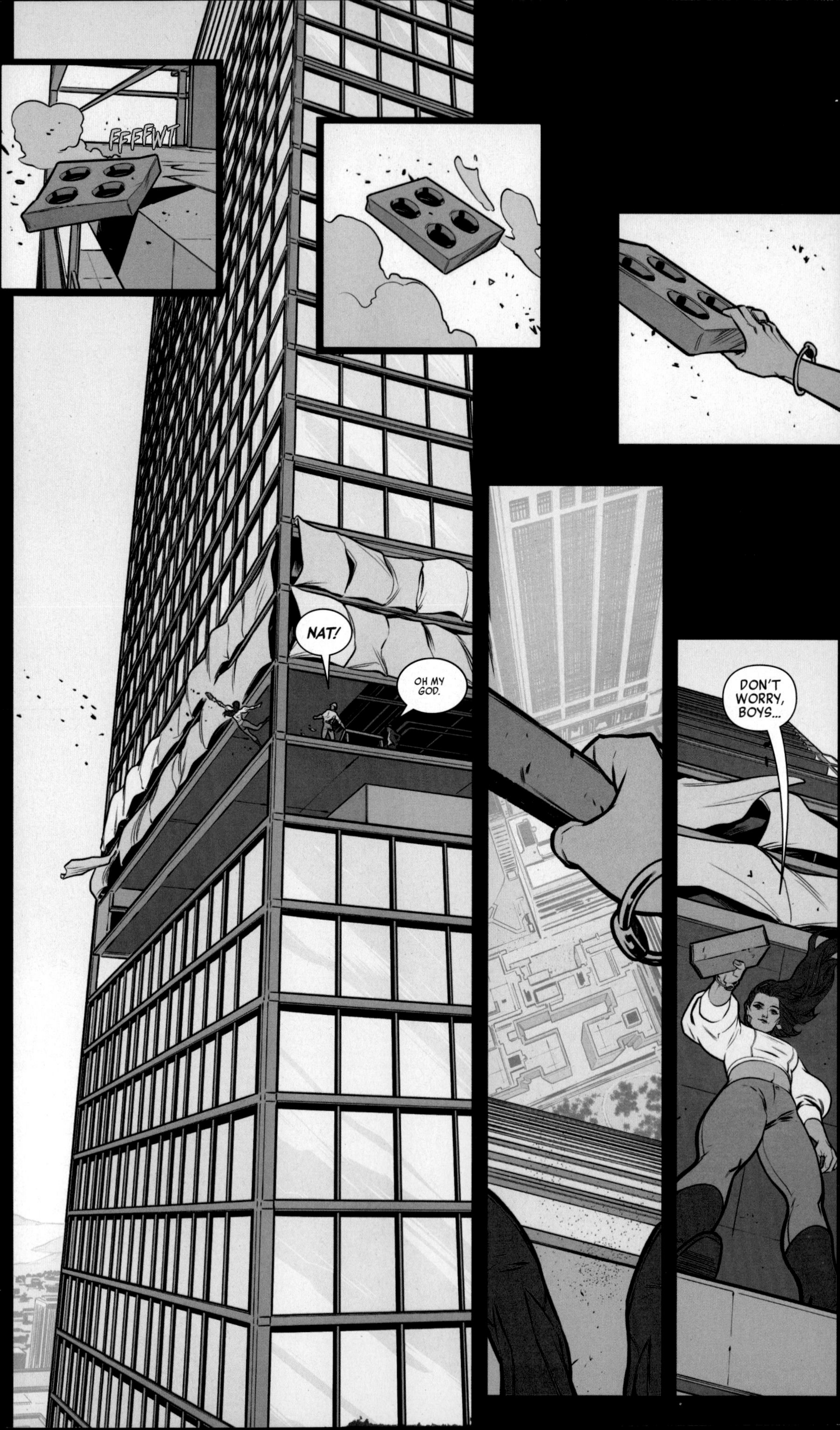
FFFFWT
NAT!
OH MY GOD.
DON'T WORRY, BOYS...

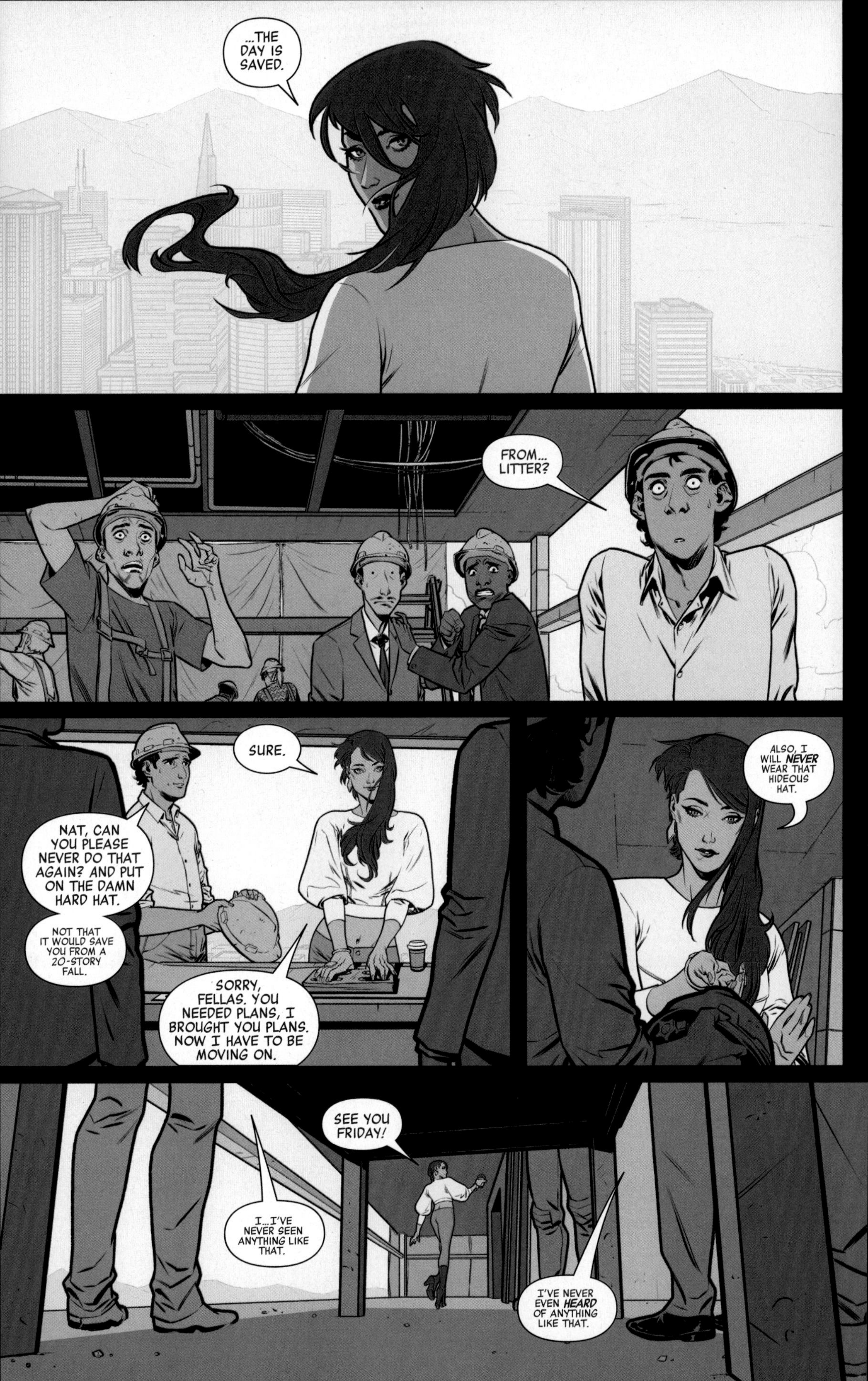
...THE DAY IS SAVED.
FROM... LITTER?
SURE.
NAT, CAN YOU PLEASE NEVER DO THAT AGAIN? AND PUT ON THE DAMN HARD HAT.
NOT THAT IT WOULD SAVE YOU FROM A 20-STORY FALL.
SORRY, FELLAS. YOU NEEDED PLANS, I BROUGHT YOU PLANS. NOW I HAVE TO BE MOVING ON.
ALSO, I WILL NEVER WEAR THAT HIDEOUS HAT.
SEE YOU FRIDAY!
I...I'VE NEVER SEEN ANYTHING LIKE THAT.
I'VE NEVER EVEN HEARD OF ANYTHING LIKE THAT.

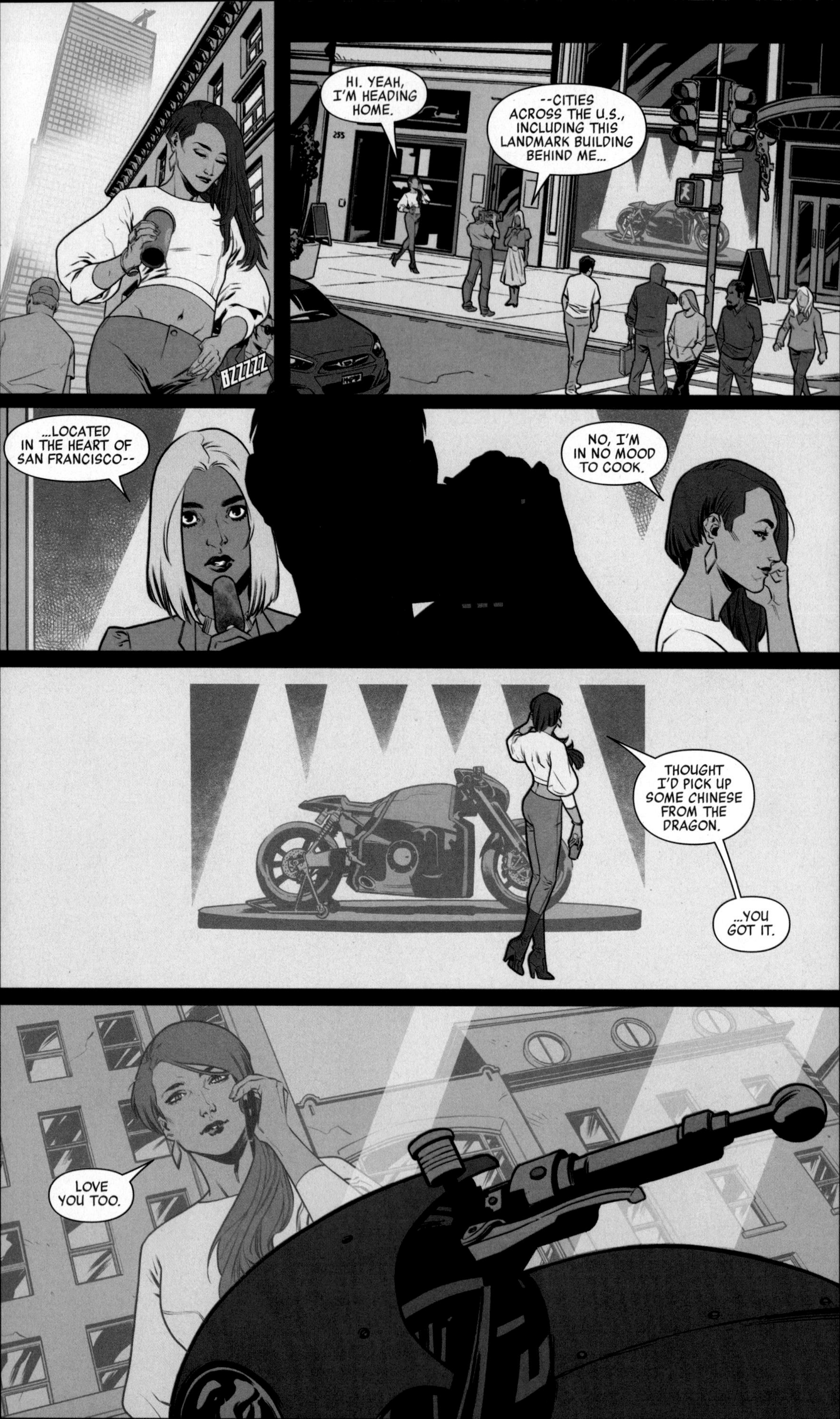
BZZZZZ
HI. YEAH, I'M HEADING HOME.
--CITIES ACROSS THE U.S., INCLUDING THIS LANDMARK BUILDING BEHIND ME...
255
...LOCATED IN THE HEART OF SAN FRANCISCO--
NO, I'M IN NO MOOD TO COOK.
THOUGHT I'D PICK UP SOME CHINESE FROM THE DRAGON.
...YOU GOT IT.
LOVE YOU TOO.

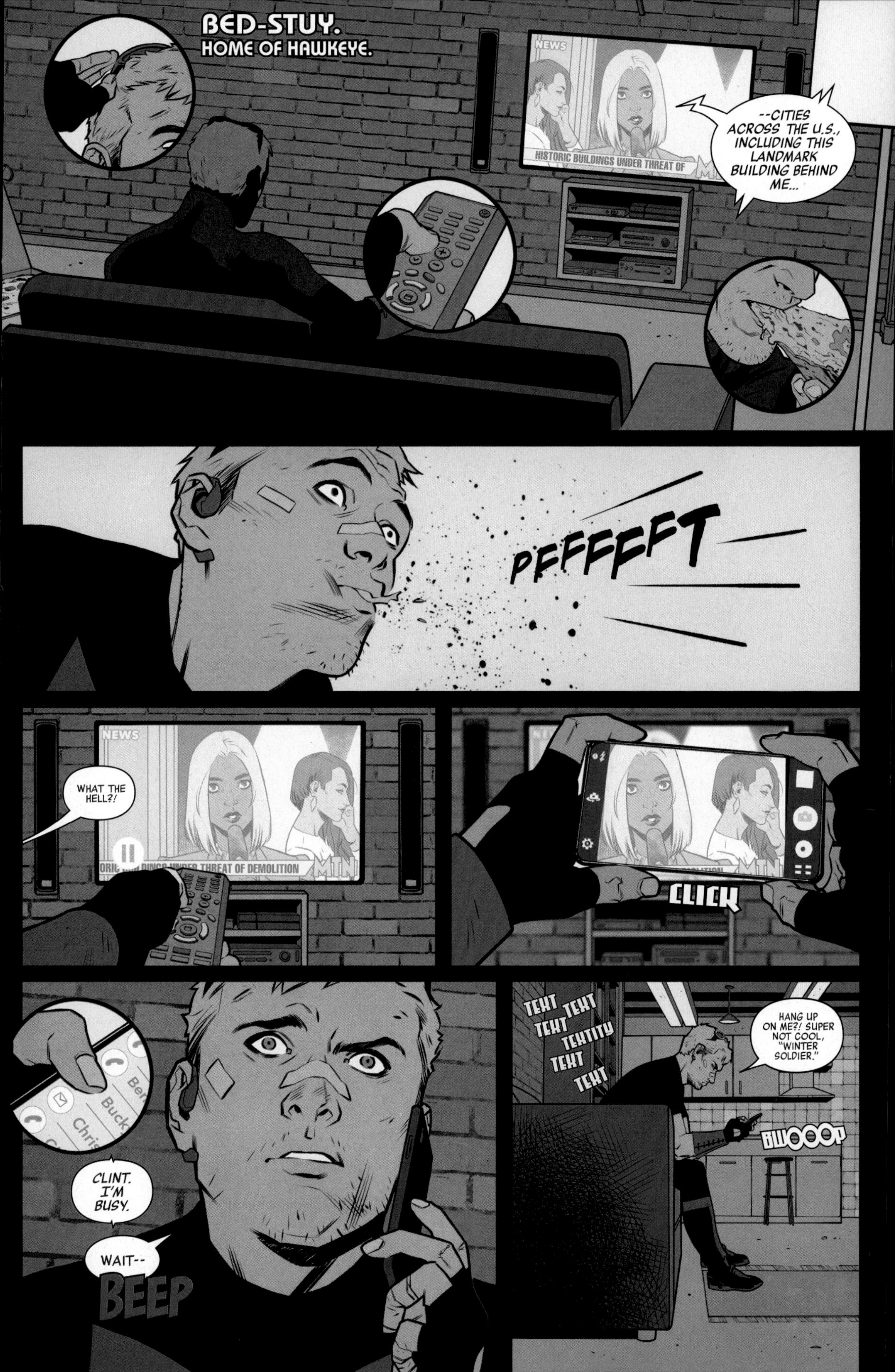
BED-STUY.
HOME OF HAWKEYE.
NEWS
HISTORIC BUILDINGS UNDER THREAT OF
--CITIES ACROSS THE U.S., INCLUDING THIS LANDMARK BUILDING BEHIND ME...
PFFFFFT
NEWS
WHAT THE HELL?!
UNDER THREAT OF DEMOLITION
CLICK
Bucky
CLINT. I'M BUSY.
WAIT--
BEEP
TEXT TEXT TEXT TEXTITY TEXT TEXT
HANG UP ON ME?! SUPER NOT COOL, "WINTER SOLDIER."
BWOOOP

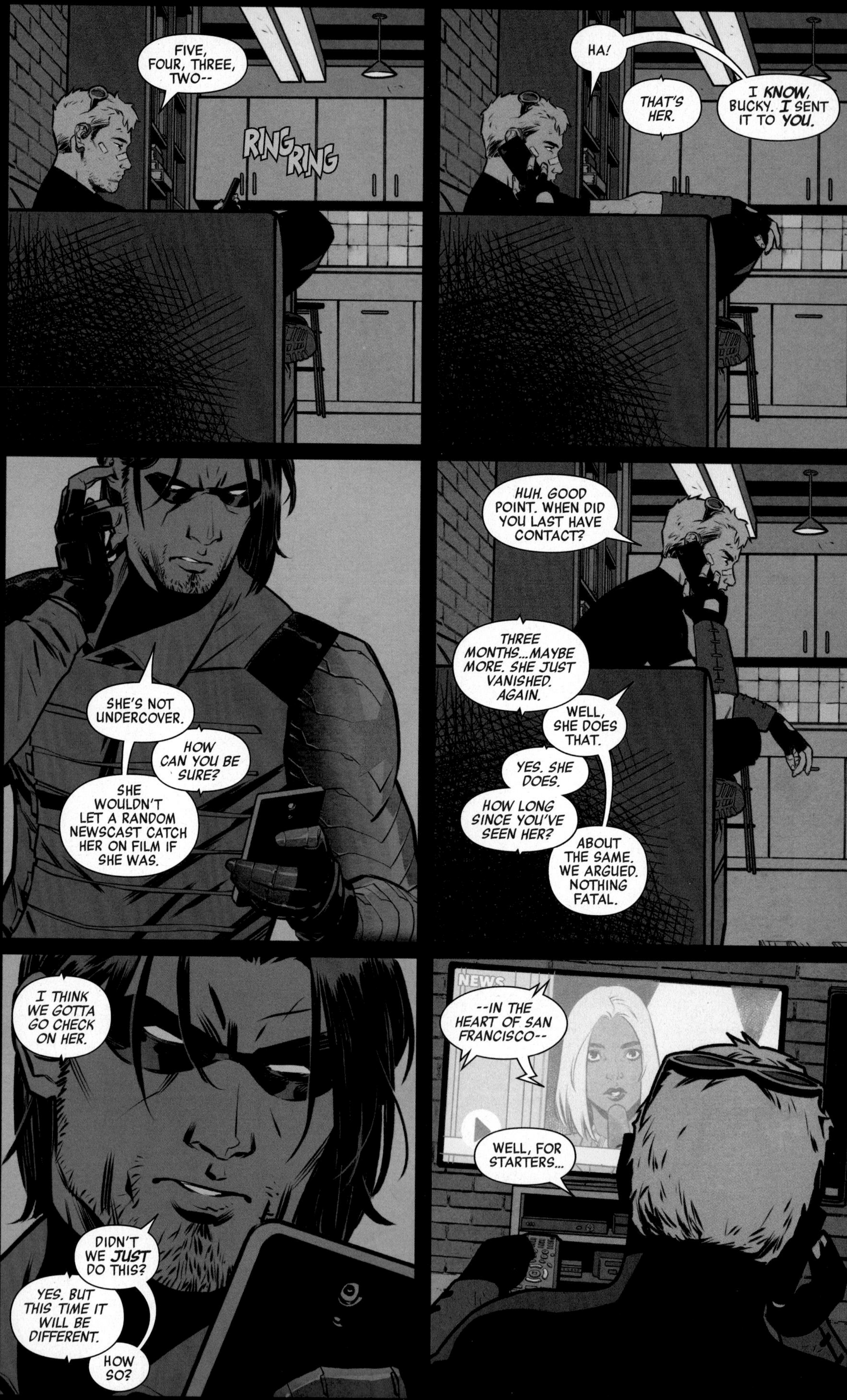
FIVE, FOUR, THREE, TWO--
RING RING
HA!
THAT'S HER.
I KNOW, BUCKY. I SENT IT TO YOU.
SHE'S NOT UNDERCOVER.
HOW CAN YOU BE SURE?
SHE WOULDN'T LET A RANDOM NEWSCAST CATCH HER ON FILM IF SHE WAS.
HUH. GOOD POINT. WHEN DID YOU LAST HAVE CONTACT?
THREE MONTHS...MAYBE MORE. SHE JUST VANISHED. AGAIN.
WELL, SHE DOES THAT.
YES. SHE DOES.
HOW LONG SINCE YOU'VE SEEN HER?
ABOUT THE SAME. WE ARGUED. NOTHING FATAL.
I THINK WE GOTTA GO CHECK ON HER.
DIDN'T WE JUST DO THIS?
YES. BUT THIS TIME IT WILL BE DIFFERENT.
HOW SO?
NEWS
--IN THE HEART OF SAN FRANCISCO--
WELL, FOR STARTERS...

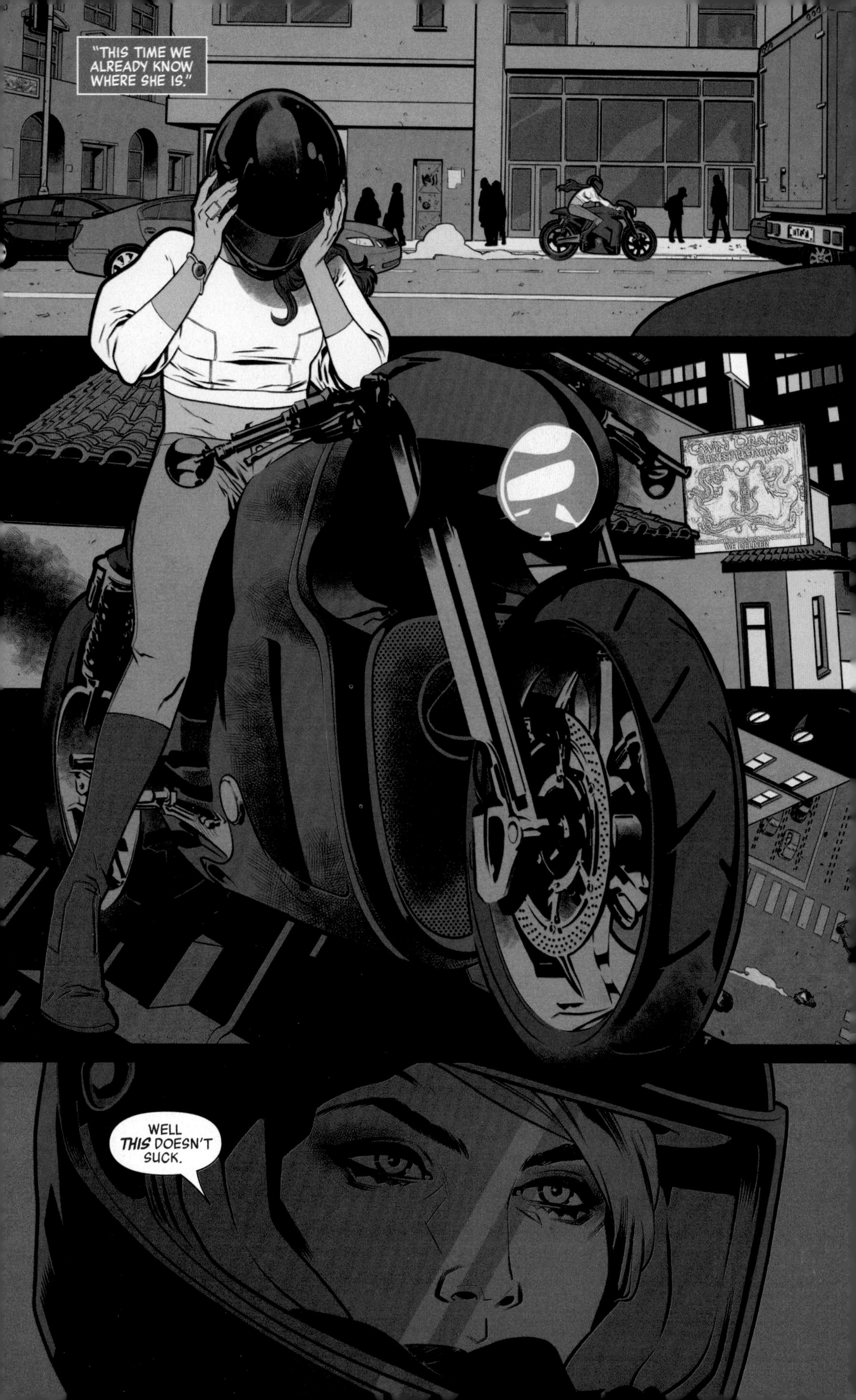
"THIS TIME WE ALREADY KNOW WHERE SHE IS."
WE DELIVER
WELL *THIS* DOESN'T SUCK.

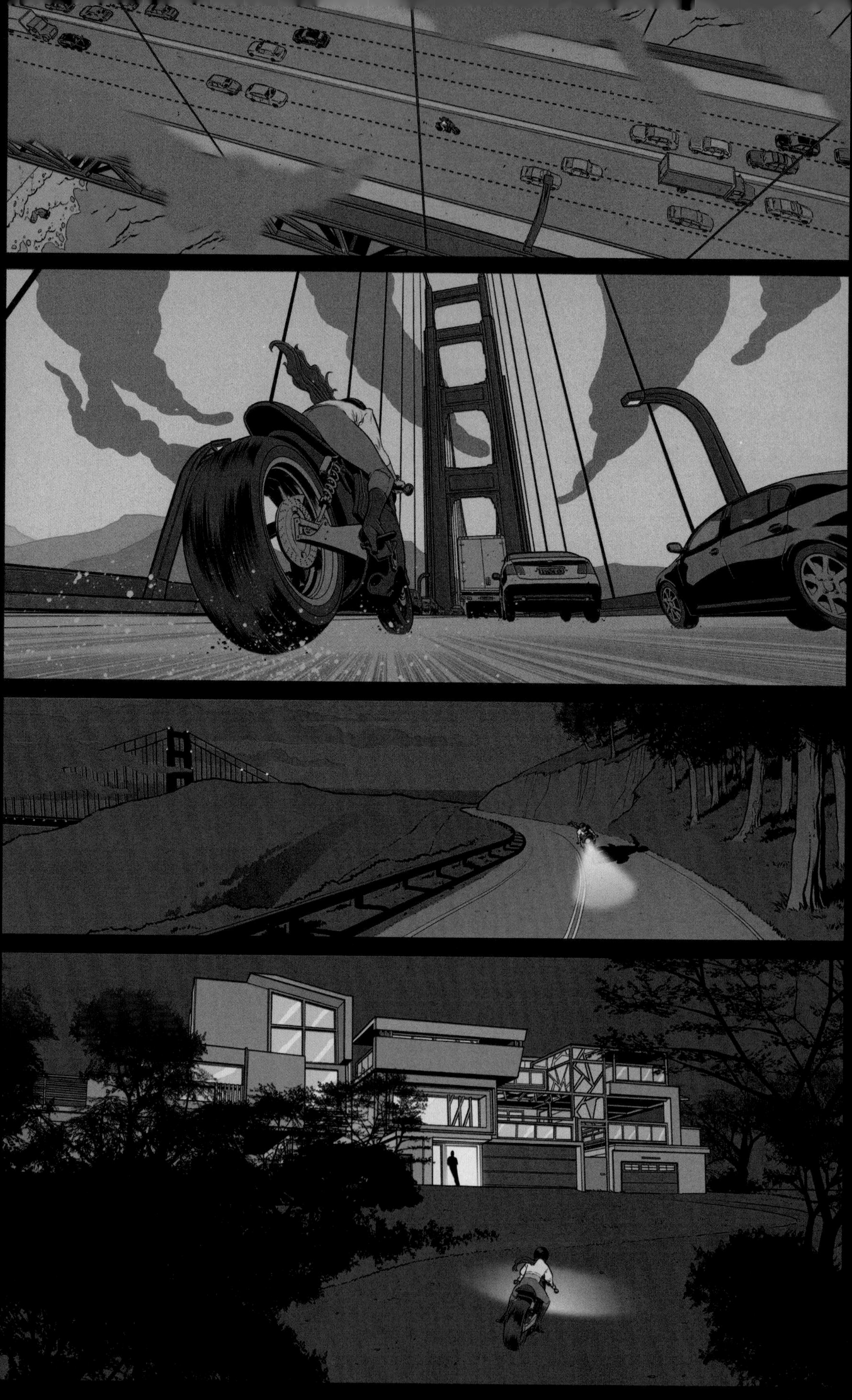

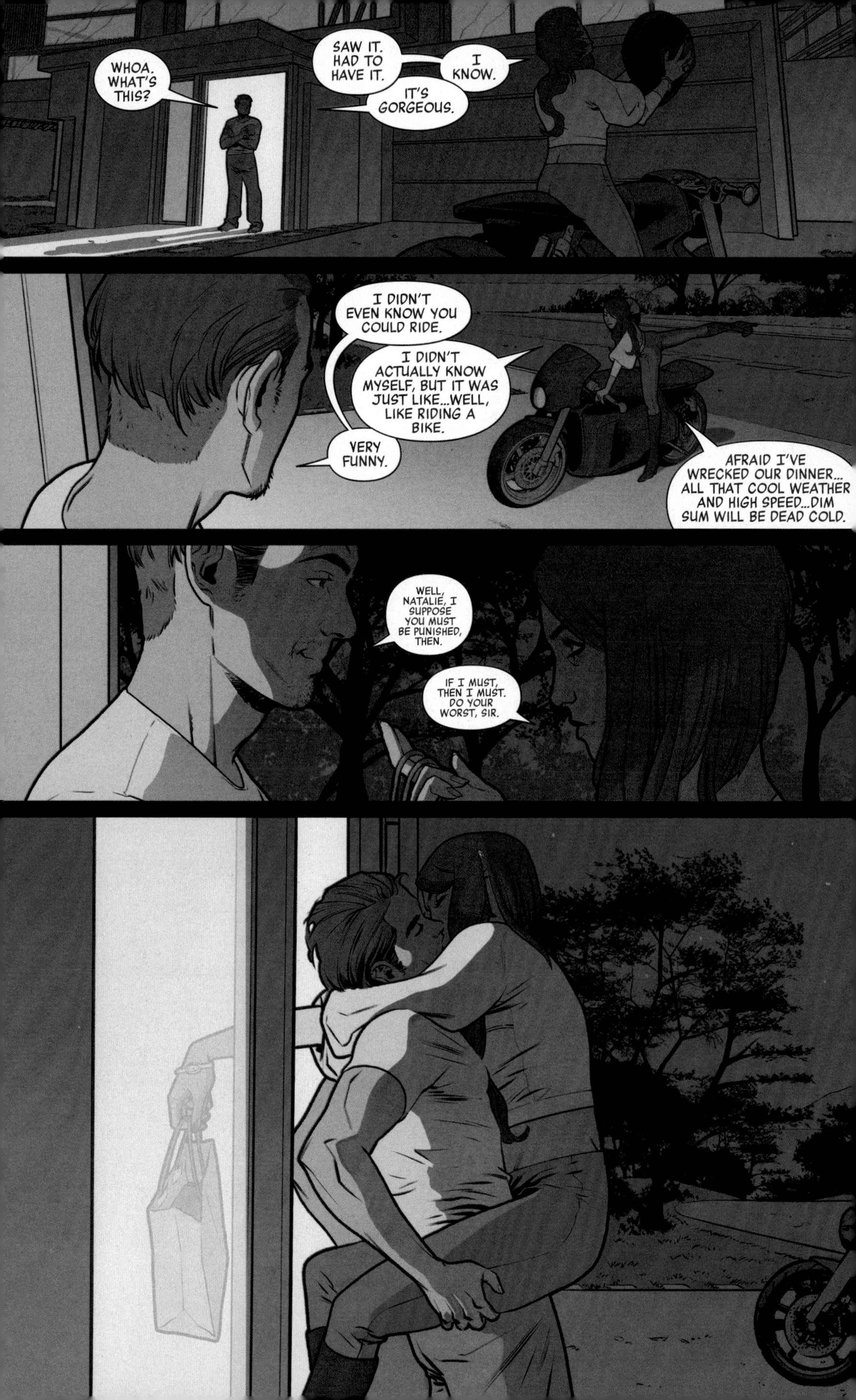
WHOA. WHAT'S THIS?
SAW IT. HAD TO HAVE IT.
I KNOW.
IT'S GORGEOUS.
I DIDN'T EVEN KNOW YOU COULD RIDE.
I DIDN'T ACTUALLY KNOW MYSELF, BUT IT WAS JUST LIKE...WELL, LIKE RIDING A BIKE.
VERY FUNNY.
AFRAID I'VE WRECKED OUR DINNER... ALL THAT COOL WEATHER AND HIGH SPEED...DIM SUM WILL BE DEAD COLD.
WELL, NATALIE, I SUPPOSE YOU MUST BE PUNISHED, THEN.
IF I MUST, THEN I MUST. DO YOUR WORST, SIR.

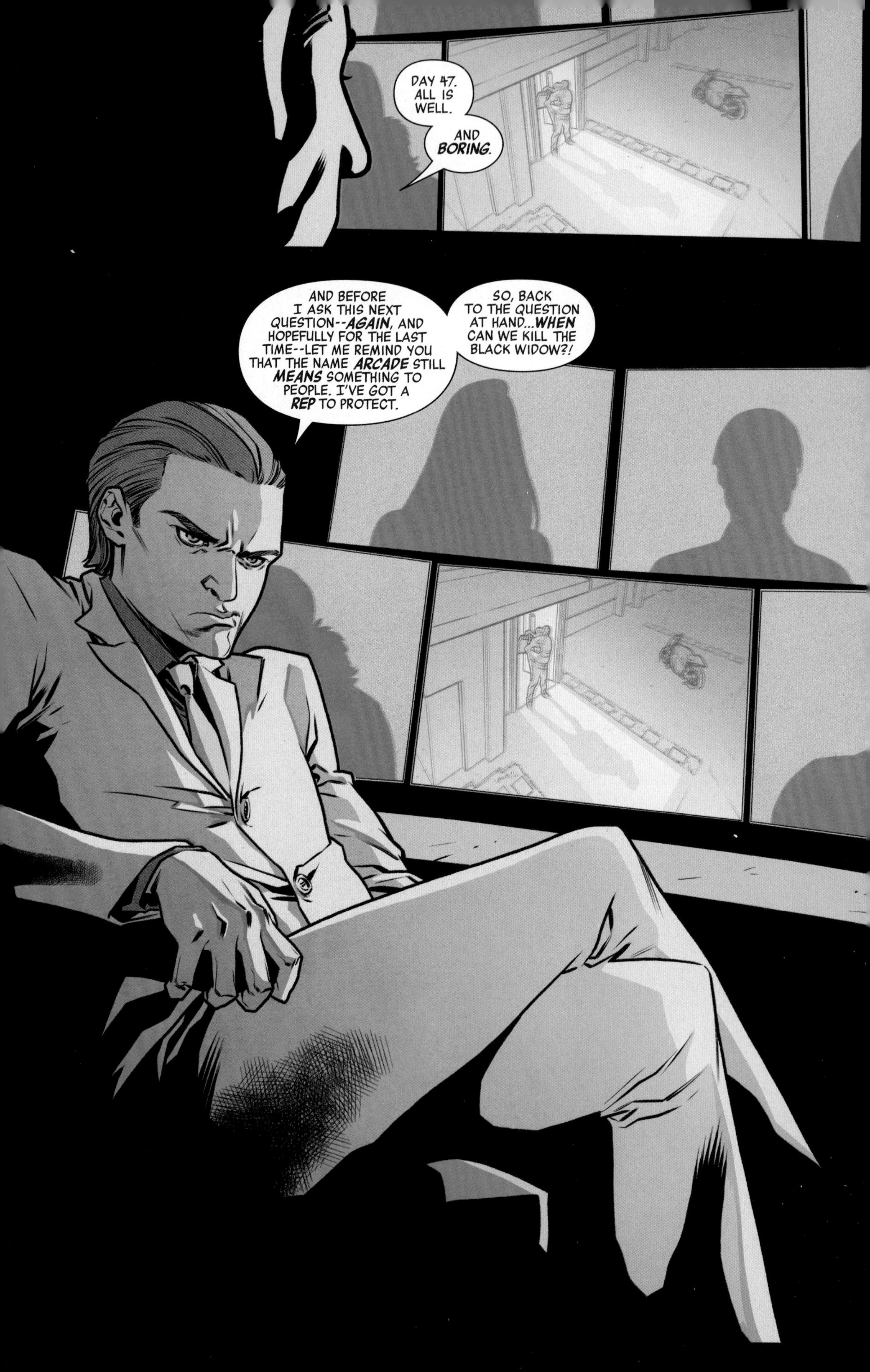
DAY 47. ALL IS WELL.
AND BORING.
AND BEFORE I ASK THIS NEXT QUESTION--AGAIN, AND HOPEFULLY FOR THE LAST TIME--LET ME REMIND YOU THAT THE NAME ARCADE STILL MEANS SOMETHING TO PEOPLE. I'VE GOT A REP TO PROTECT.
SO, BACK TO THE QUESTION AT HAND...WHEN CAN WE KILL THE BLACK WIDOW?!

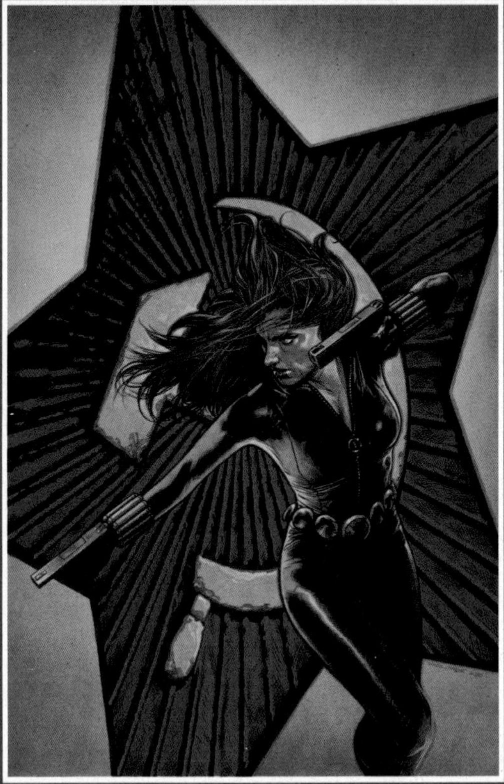

#1 VARIANT BY TRAVIS CHAREST

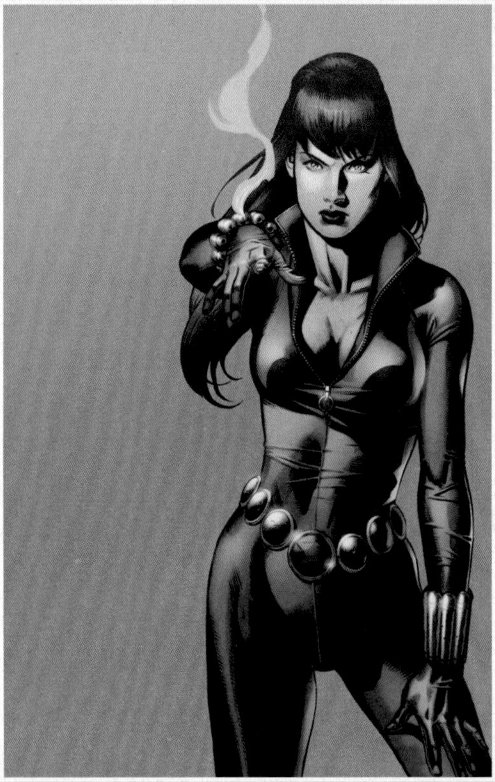

#1 VARIANT BY J.G. JONES & DAVE McCAIG

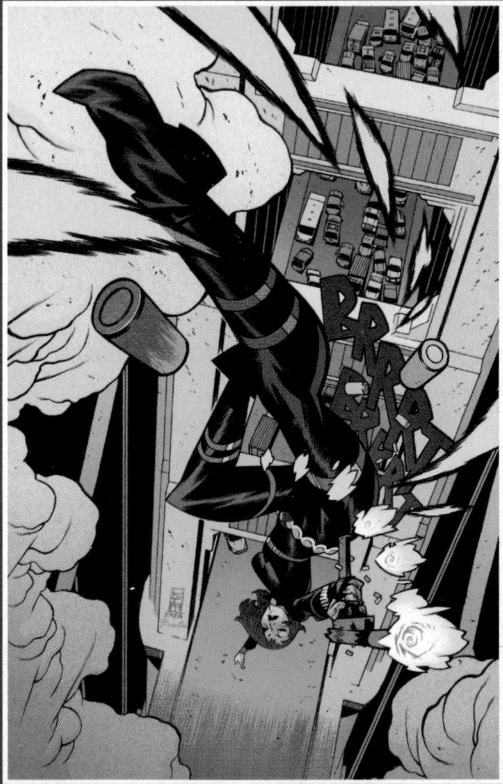

#1 VARIANT BY KIM JACINTO & TAMRA BONVILLAIN

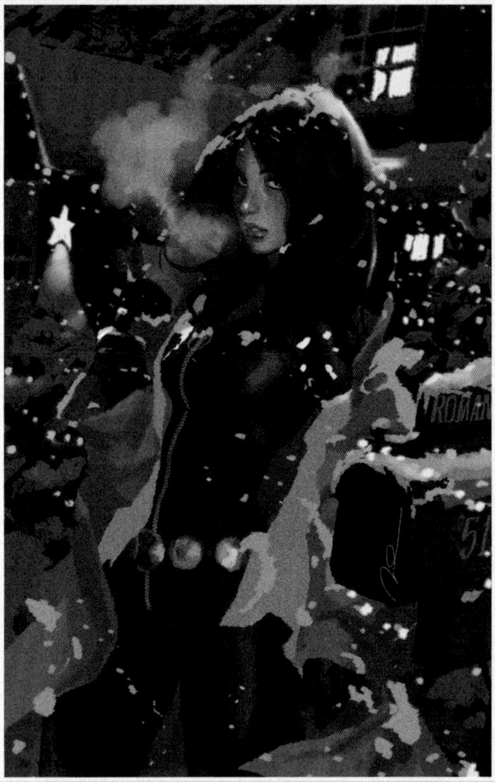

#1 VARIANT BY GERALD PAREL

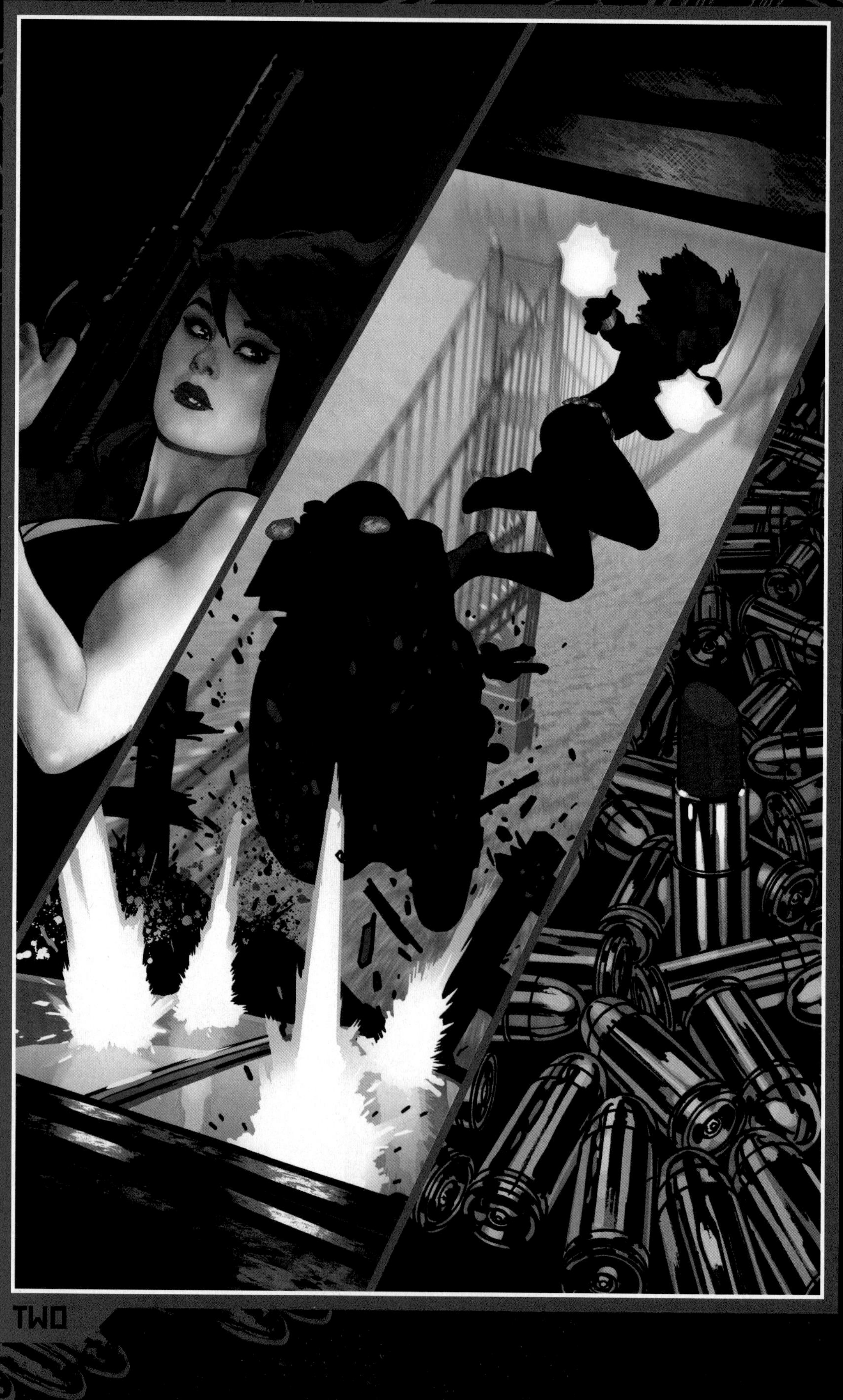
TWO

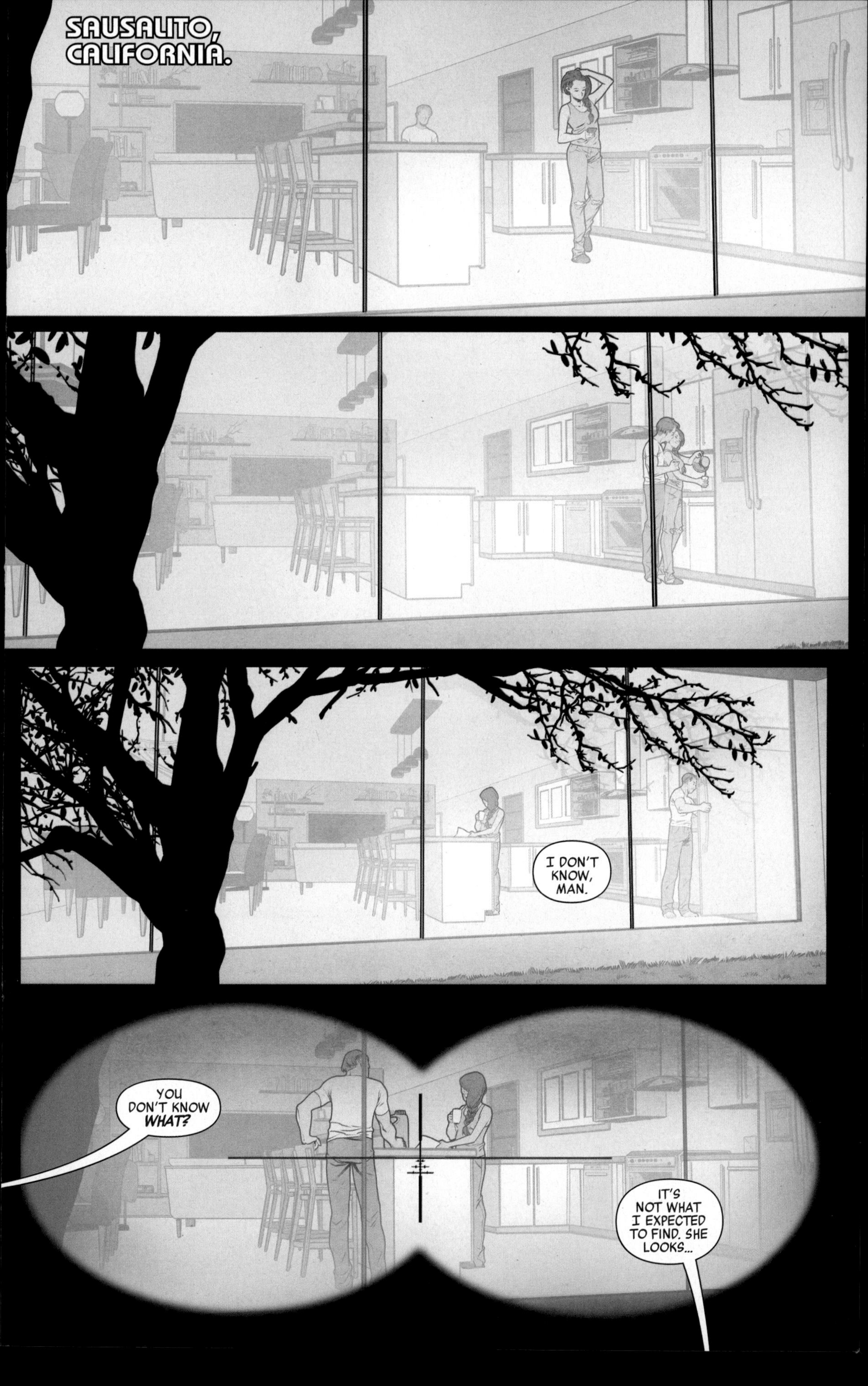
SAUSALITO, CALIFORNIA.
I DON'T KNOW, MAN.
YOU DON'T KNOW *WHAT?*
IT'S NOT WHAT I EXPECTED TO FIND. SHE LOOKS...

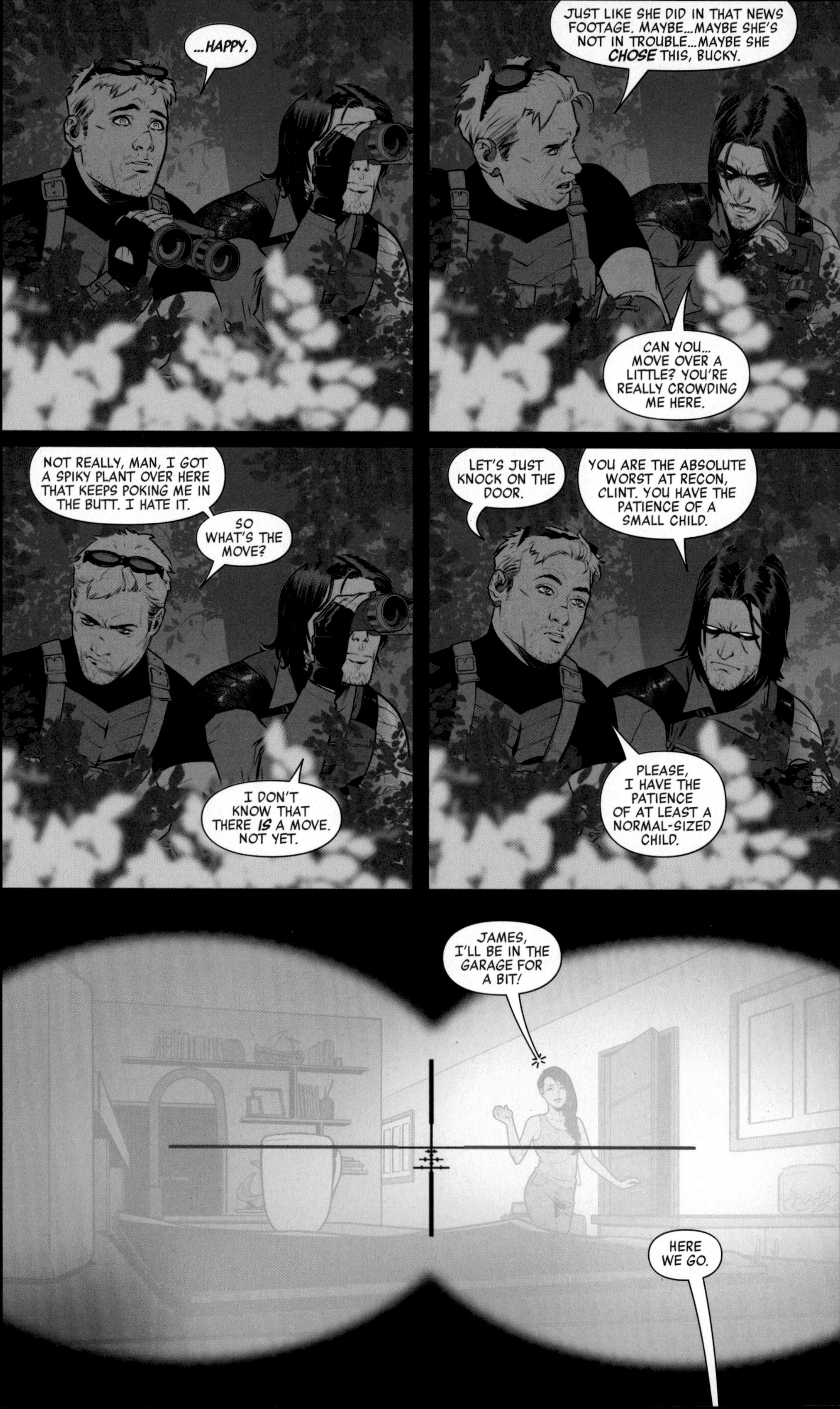

...HAPPY.
JUST LIKE SHE DID IN THAT NEWS FOOTAGE. MAYBE...MAYBE SHE'S NOT IN TROUBLE...MAYBE SHE CHOSE THIS, BUCKY.
CAN YOU... MOVE OVER A LITTLE? YOU'RE REALLY CROWDING ME HERE.
NOT REALLY, MAN, I GOT A SPIKY PLANT OVER HERE THAT KEEPS POKING ME IN THE BUTT. I HATE IT.
SO WHAT'S THE MOVE?
I DON'T KNOW THAT THERE IS A MOVE. NOT YET.
LET'S JUST KNOCK ON THE DOOR.
YOU ARE THE ABSOLUTE WORST AT RECON, CLINT. YOU HAVE THE PATIENCE OF A SMALL CHILD.
PLEASE, I HAVE THE PATIENCE OF AT LEAST A NORMAL-SIZED CHILD.
JAMES, I'LL BE IN THE GARAGE FOR A BIT!
HERE WE GO.

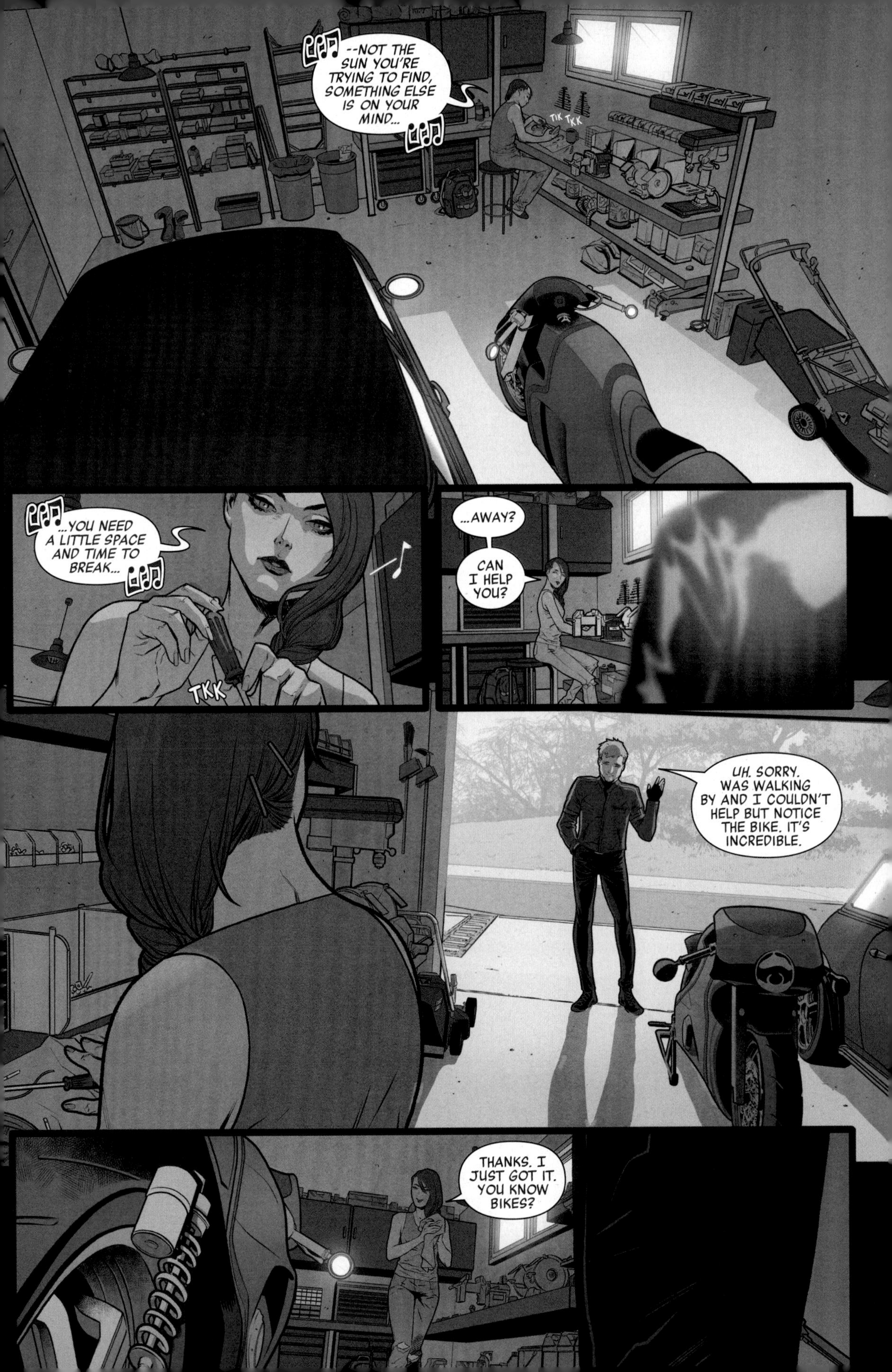
--NOT THE SUN YOU'RE TRYING TO FIND, SOMETHING ELSE IS ON YOUR MIND...
TIK TKK
...YOU NEED A LITTLE SPACE AND TIME TO BREAK...
TKK
...AWAY?
CAN I HELP YOU?
UH. SORRY. WAS WALKING BY AND I COULDN'T HELP BUT NOTICE THE BIKE. IT'S INCREDIBLE.
THANKS. I JUST GOT IT. YOU KNOW BIKES?

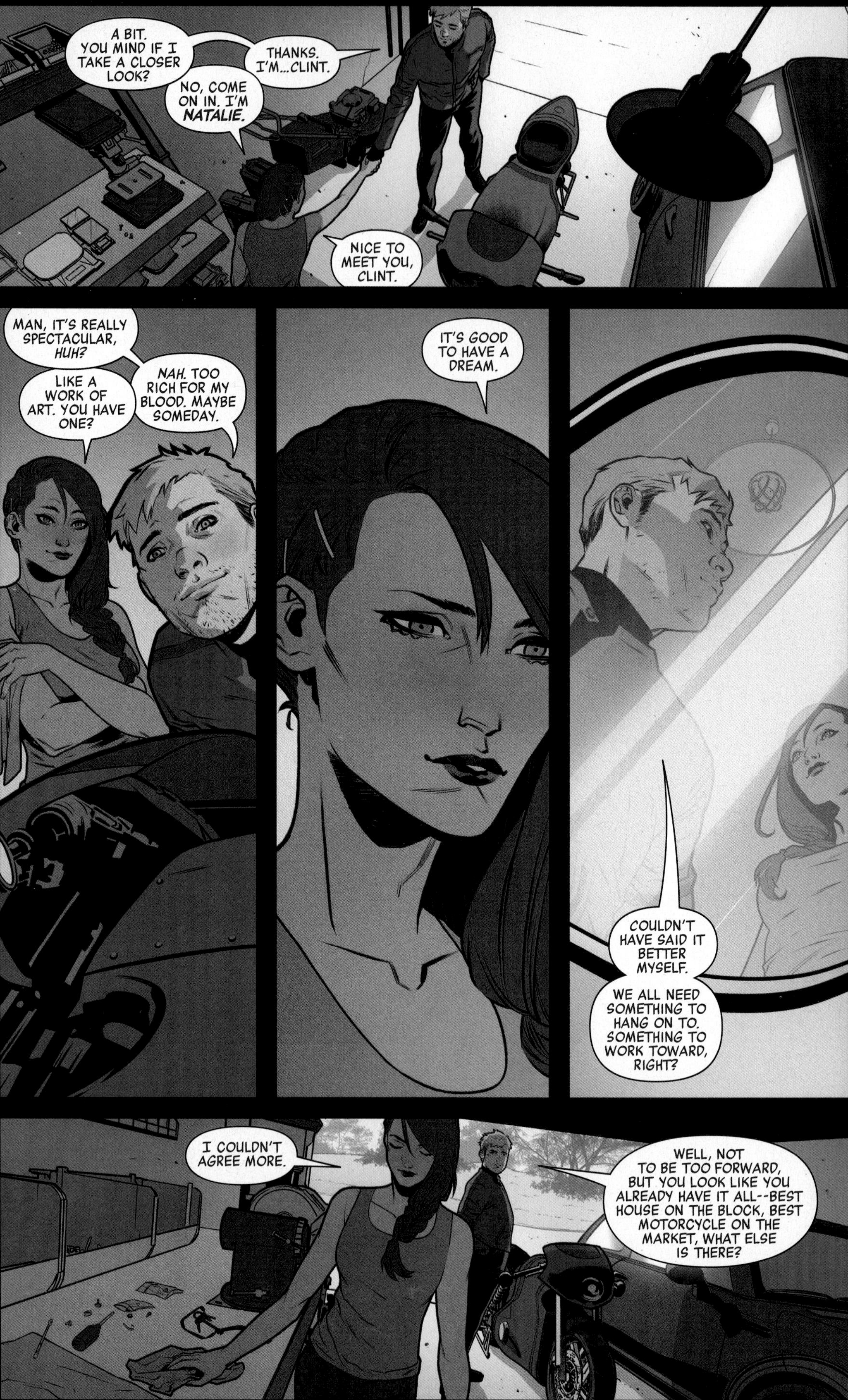
A BIT. YOU MIND IF I TAKE A CLOSER LOOK?
NO, COME ON IN. I'M **NATALIE.**
THANKS. I'M...CLINT.
NICE TO MEET YOU, CLINT.
MAN, IT'S REALLY SPECTACULAR, *HUH?*
LIKE A WORK OF ART. YOU HAVE ONE?
NAH. TOO RICH FOR MY BLOOD. MAYBE SOMEDAY.
IT'S GOOD TO HAVE A DREAM.
COULDN'T HAVE SAID IT BETTER MYSELF.
WE ALL NEED SOMETHING TO HANG ON TO. SOMETHING TO WORK TOWARD, RIGHT?
I COULDN'T AGREE MORE.
WELL, NOT TO BE TOO FORWARD, BUT YOU LOOK LIKE YOU ALREADY HAVE IT ALL--BEST HOUSE ON THE BLOCK, BEST MOTORCYCLE ON THE MARKET, WHAT ELSE IS THERE?

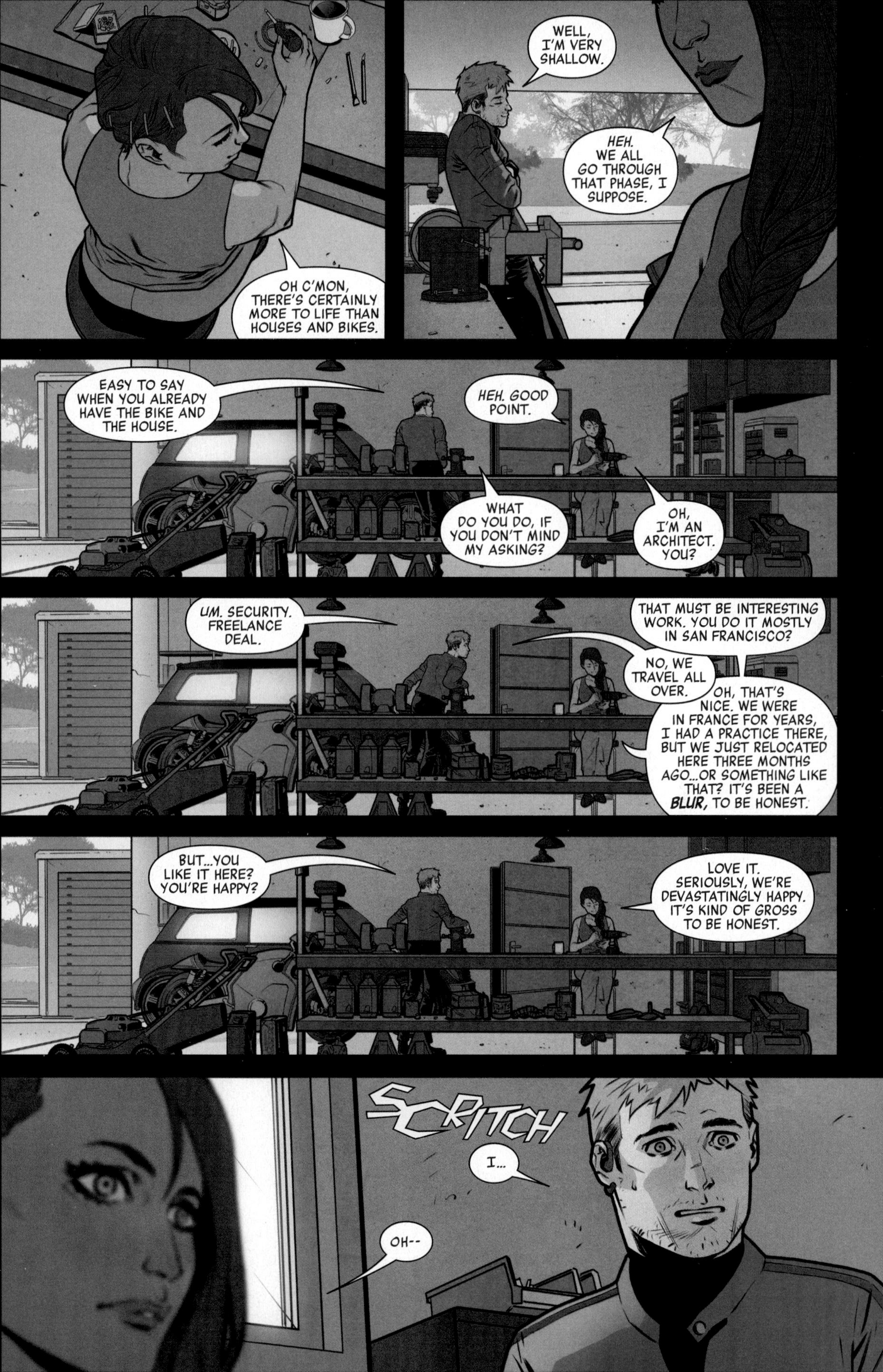

OH C'MON, THERE'S CERTAINLY MORE TO LIFE THAN HOUSES AND BIKES.
WELL, I'M VERY SHALLOW.
HEH. WE ALL GO THROUGH THAT PHASE, I SUPPOSE.
EASY TO SAY WHEN YOU ALREADY HAVE THE BIKE AND THE HOUSE.
HEH. GOOD POINT.
WHAT DO YOU DO, IF YOU DON'T MIND MY ASKING?
OH, I'M AN ARCHITECT. YOU?
UM. SECURITY. FREELANCE DEAL.
THAT MUST BE INTERESTING WORK. YOU DO IT MOSTLY IN SAN FRANCISCO?
NO, WE TRAVEL ALL OVER.
OH, THAT'S NICE. WE WERE IN FRANCE FOR YEARS, I HAD A PRACTICE THERE, BUT WE JUST RELOCATED HERE THREE MONTHS AGO...OR SOMETHING LIKE THAT? IT'S BEEN A BLUR, TO BE HONEST.
BUT...YOU LIKE IT HERE? YOU'RE HAPPY?
LOVE IT. SERIOUSLY, WE'RE DEVASTATINGLY HAPPY. IT'S KIND OF GROSS TO BE HONEST.
SCRITCH
I...
OH--

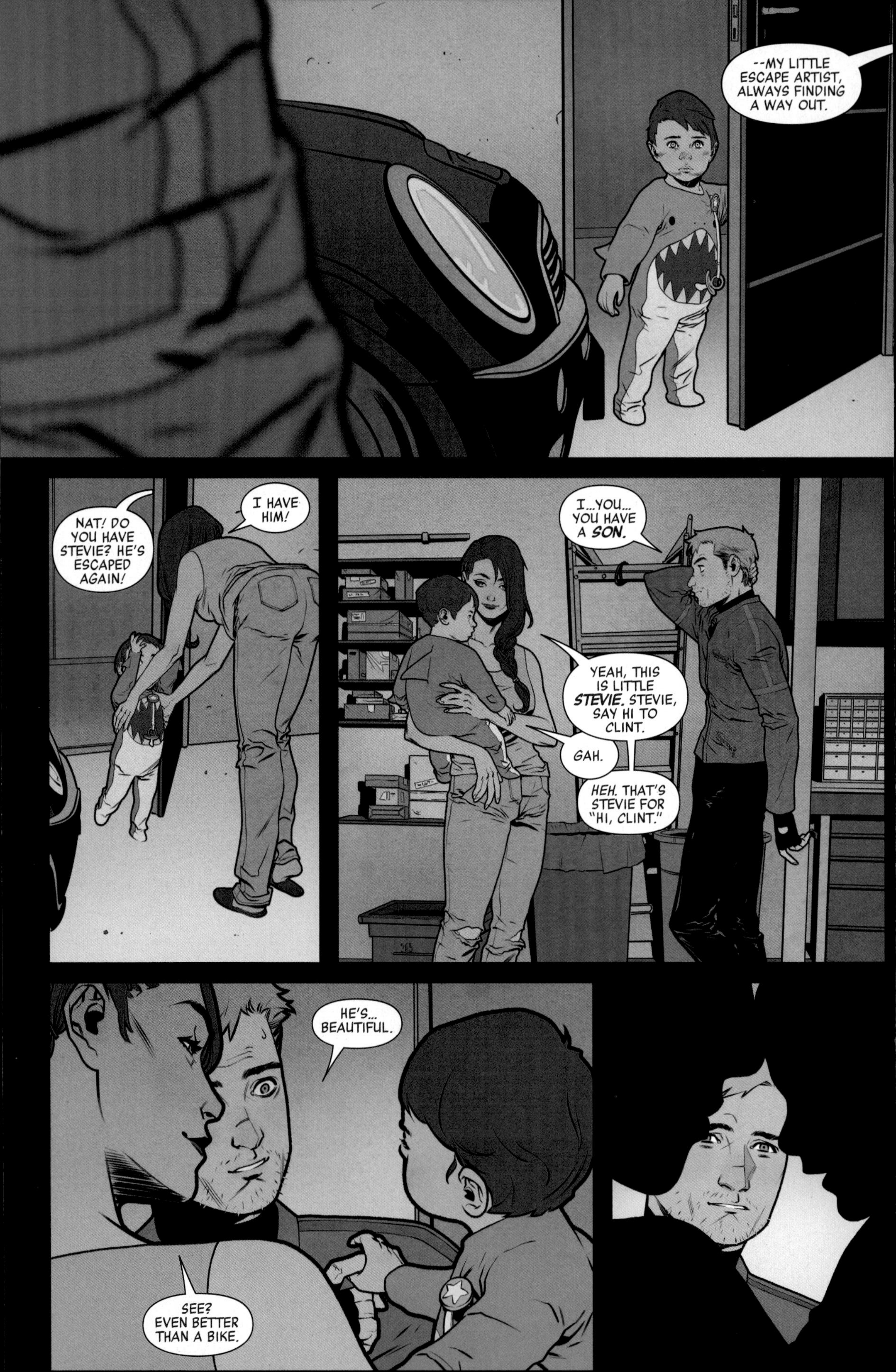
--MY LITTLE ESCAPE ARTIST, ALWAYS FINDING A WAY OUT.
NAT! DO YOU HAVE STEVIE? HE'S ESCAPED AGAIN!
I HAVE HIM!
I...YOU... YOU HAVE A SON.
YEAH, THIS IS LITTLE STEVIE. STEVIE, SAY HI TO CLINT.
GAH.
HEH. THAT'S STEVIE FOR "HI, CLINT."
HE'S... BEAUTIFUL.
SEE? EVEN BETTER THAN A BIKE.

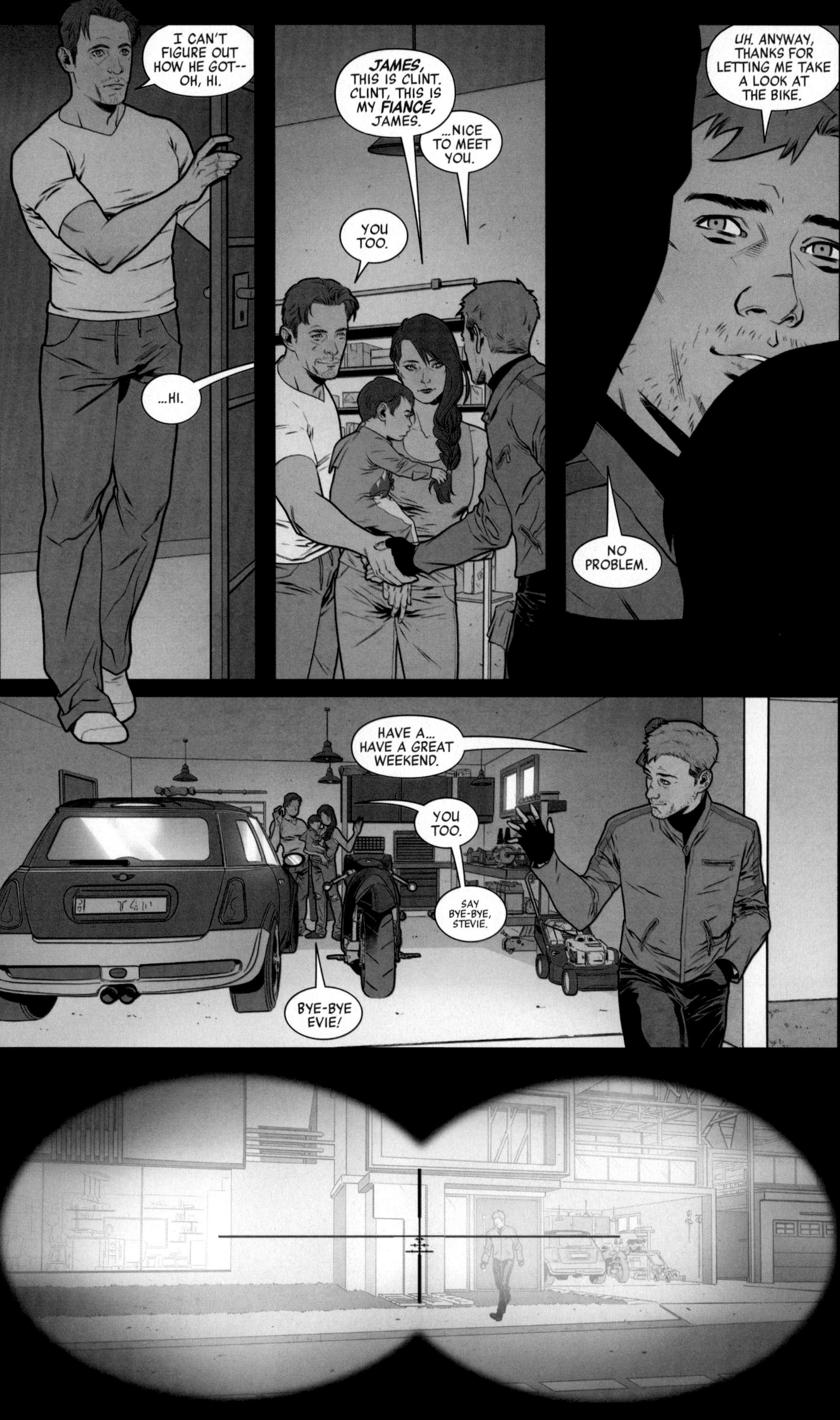
I CAN'T FIGURE OUT HOW HE GOT-- OH, HI.
...HI.
JAMES, THIS IS CLINT. CLINT, THIS IS MY FIANCÉ, JAMES.
...NICE TO MEET YOU.
YOU TOO.
UH. ANYWAY, THANKS FOR LETTING ME TAKE A LOOK AT THE BIKE.
NO PROBLEM.
HAVE A... HAVE A GREAT WEEKEND.
YOU TOO.
SAY BYE-BYE, STEVIE.
BYE-BYE EVIE!

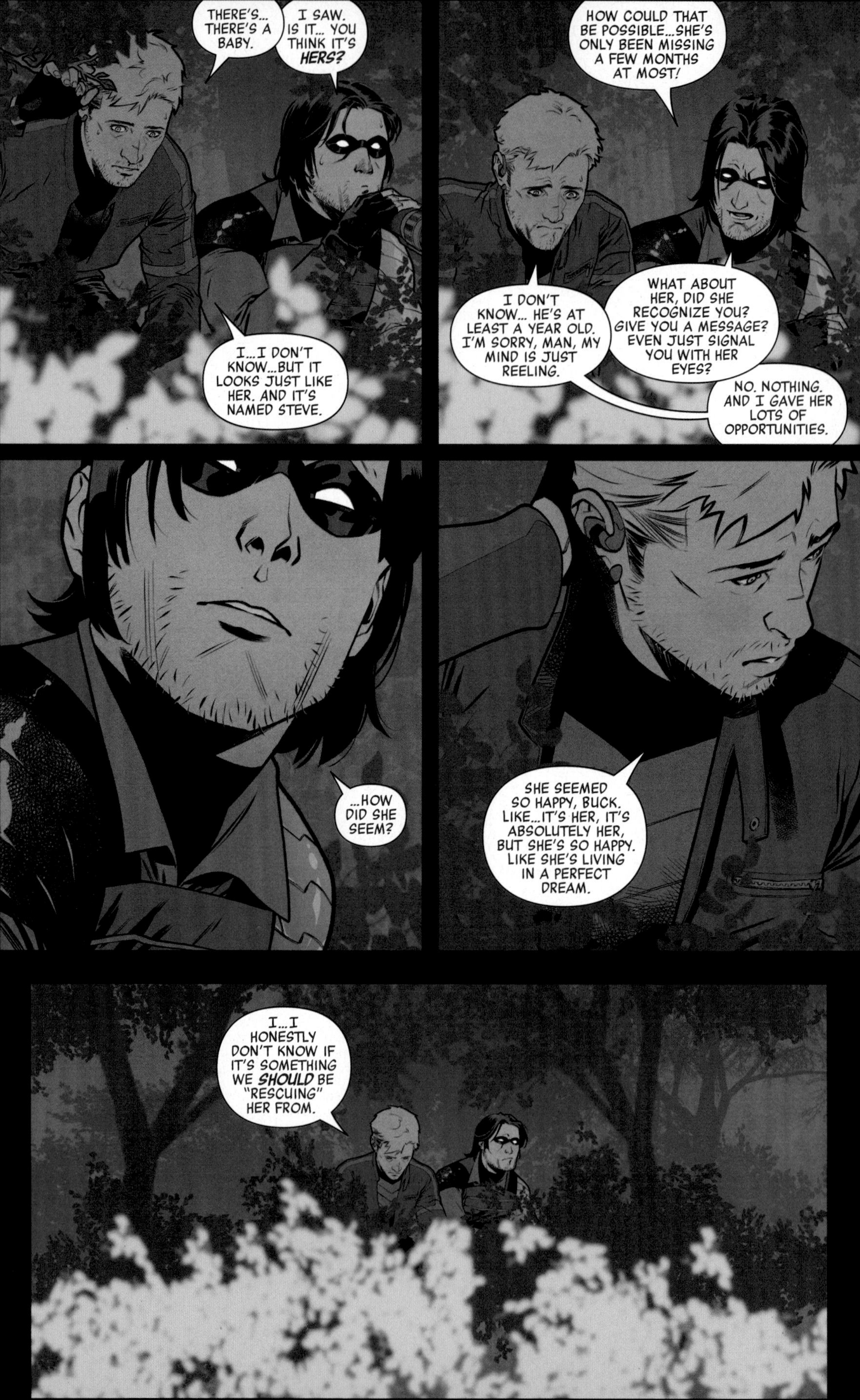
THERE'S... THERE'S A BABY.
I SAW. IS IT... YOU THINK IT'S *HERS?*
I...I DON'T KNOW...BUT IT LOOKS JUST LIKE HER. AND IT'S NAMED STEVE.
HOW COULD THAT BE POSSIBLE...SHE'S ONLY BEEN MISSING A FEW MONTHS AT MOST!
I DON'T KNOW... HE'S AT LEAST A YEAR OLD. I'M SORRY, MAN, MY MIND IS JUST REELING.
WHAT ABOUT HER, DID SHE RECOGNIZE YOU? GIVE YOU A MESSAGE? EVEN JUST SIGNAL YOU WITH HER EYES?
NO. NOTHING. AND I GAVE HER LOTS OF OPPORTUNITIES.
...HOW DID SHE SEEM?
SHE SEEMED SO HAPPY, BUCK. LIKE...IT'S HER, IT'S ABSOLUTELY HER, BUT SHE'S SO HAPPY. LIKE SHE'S LIVING IN A PERFECT DREAM.
I...I HONESTLY DON'T KNOW IF IT'S SOMETHING WE *SHOULD* BE "RESCUING" HER FROM.

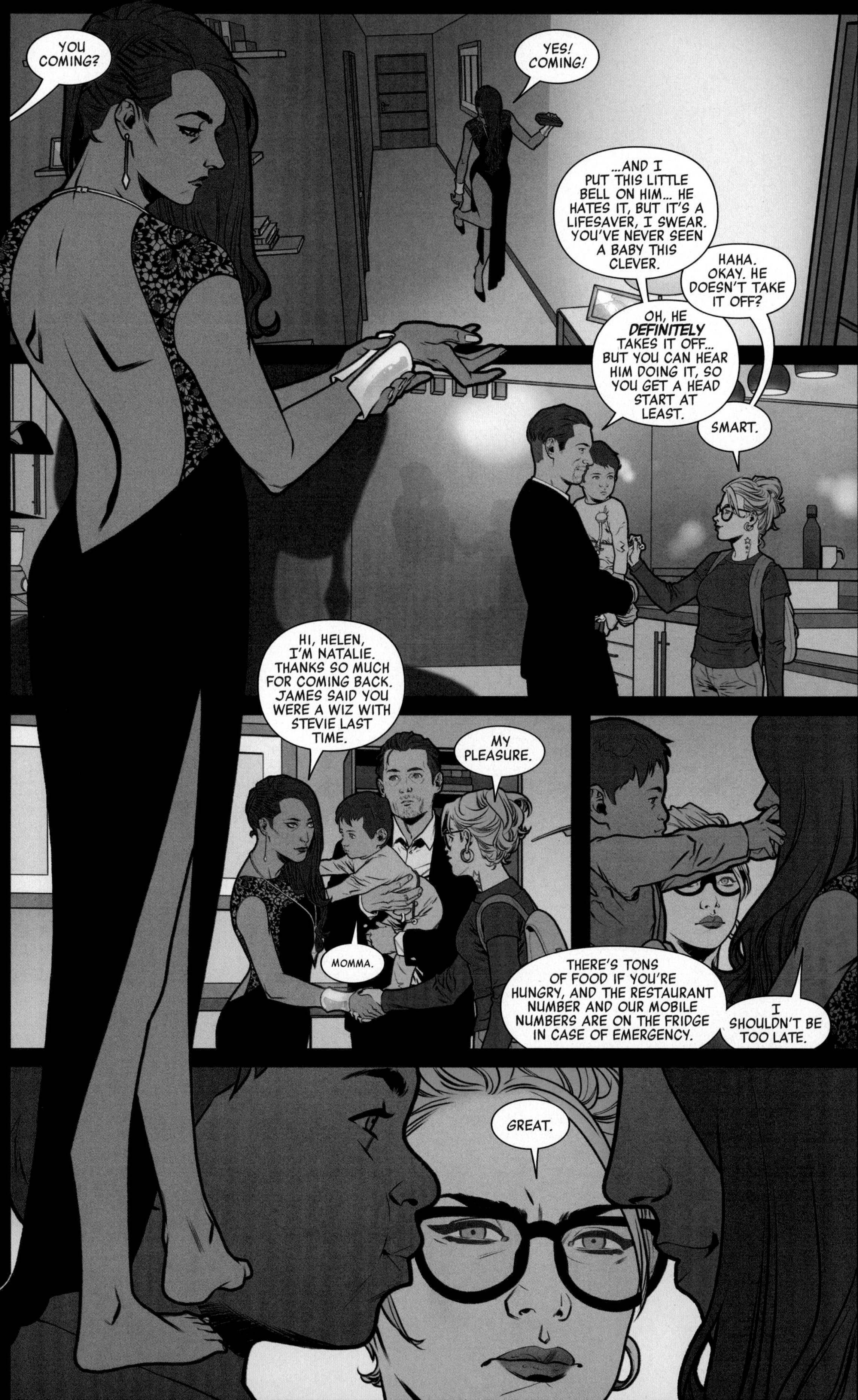
YOU COMING?
YES! COMING!
...AND I PUT THIS LITTLE BELL ON HIM... HE HATES IT, BUT IT'S A LIFESAVER, I SWEAR. YOU'VE NEVER SEEN A BABY THIS CLEVER.
HAHA. OKAY. HE DOESN'T TAKE IT OFF?
OH, HE DEFINITELY TAKES IT OFF... BUT YOU CAN HEAR HIM DOING IT, SO YOU GET A HEAD START AT LEAST.
SMART.
HI, HELEN, I'M NATALIE. THANKS SO MUCH FOR COMING BACK. JAMES SAID YOU WERE A WIZ WITH STEVIE LAST TIME.
MY PLEASURE.
MOMMA.
THERE'S TONS OF FOOD IF YOU'RE HUNGRY, AND THE RESTAURANT NUMBER AND OUR MOBILE NUMBERS ARE ON THE FRIDGE IN CASE OF EMERGENCY.
I SHOULDN'T BE TOO LATE.
GREAT.

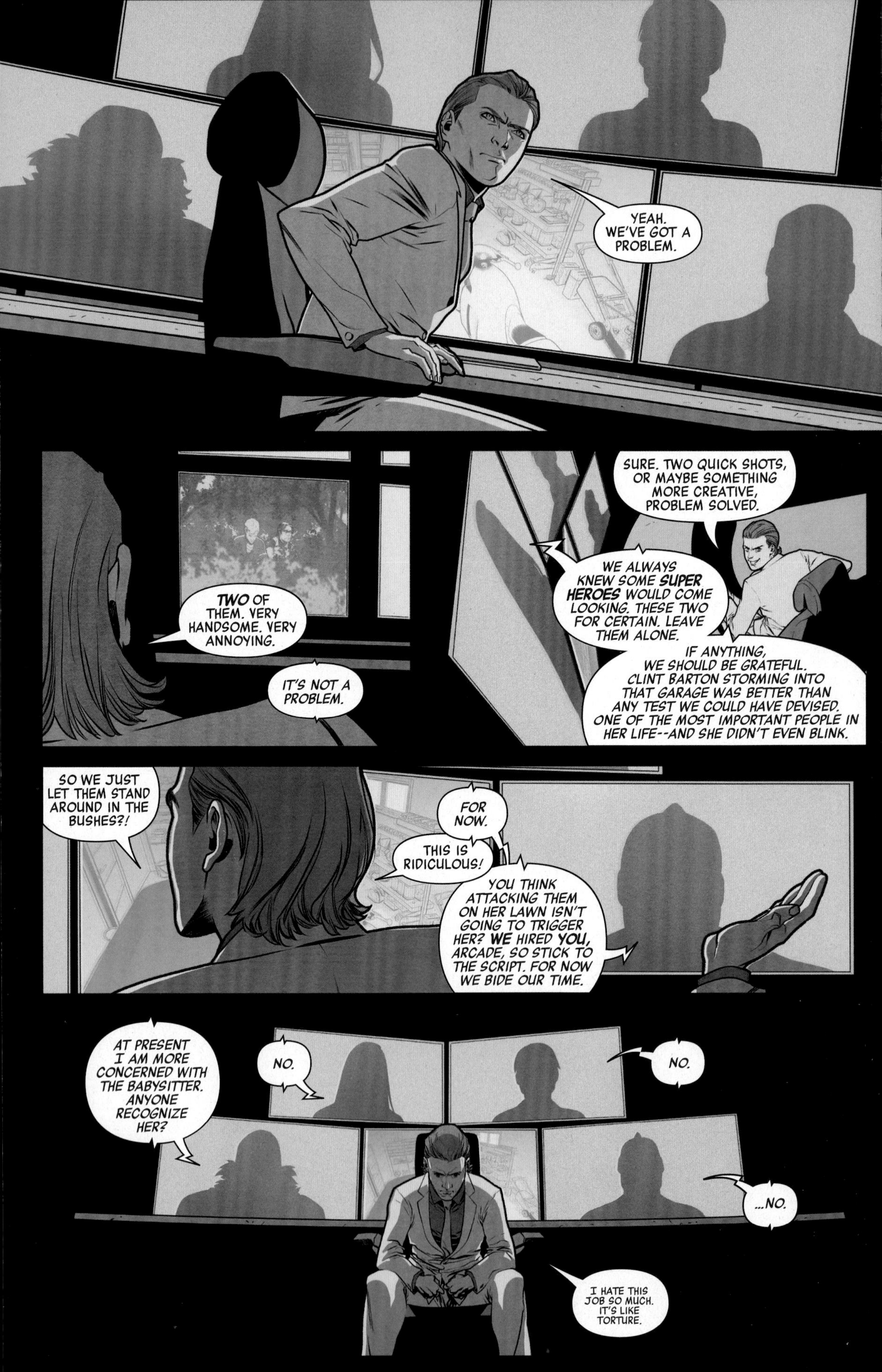
YEAH. WE'VE GOT A PROBLEM.
TWO OF THEM. VERY HANDSOME. VERY ANNOYING.
IT'S NOT A PROBLEM.
SURE. TWO QUICK SHOTS, OR MAYBE SOMETHING MORE CREATIVE, PROBLEM SOLVED.
WE ALWAYS KNEW SOME SUPER HEROES WOULD COME LOOKING. THESE TWO FOR CERTAIN. LEAVE THEM ALONE.
IF ANYTHING, WE SHOULD BE GRATEFUL. CLINT BARTON STORMING INTO THAT GARAGE WAS BETTER THAN ANY TEST WE COULD HAVE DEVISED. ONE OF THE MOST IMPORTANT PEOPLE IN HER LIFE--AND SHE DIDN'T EVEN BLINK.
SO WE JUST LET THEM STAND AROUND IN THE BUSHES?!
FOR NOW.
THIS IS RIDICULOUS!
YOU THINK ATTACKING THEM ON HER LAWN ISN'T GOING TO TRIGGER HER? WE HIRED YOU, ARCADE, SO STICK TO THE SCRIPT. FOR NOW WE BIDE OUR TIME.
AT PRESENT I AM MORE CONCERNED WITH THE BABYSITTER. ANYONE RECOGNIZE HER?
NO.
NO.
...NO.
I HATE THIS JOB SO MUCH. IT'S LIKE TORTURE.

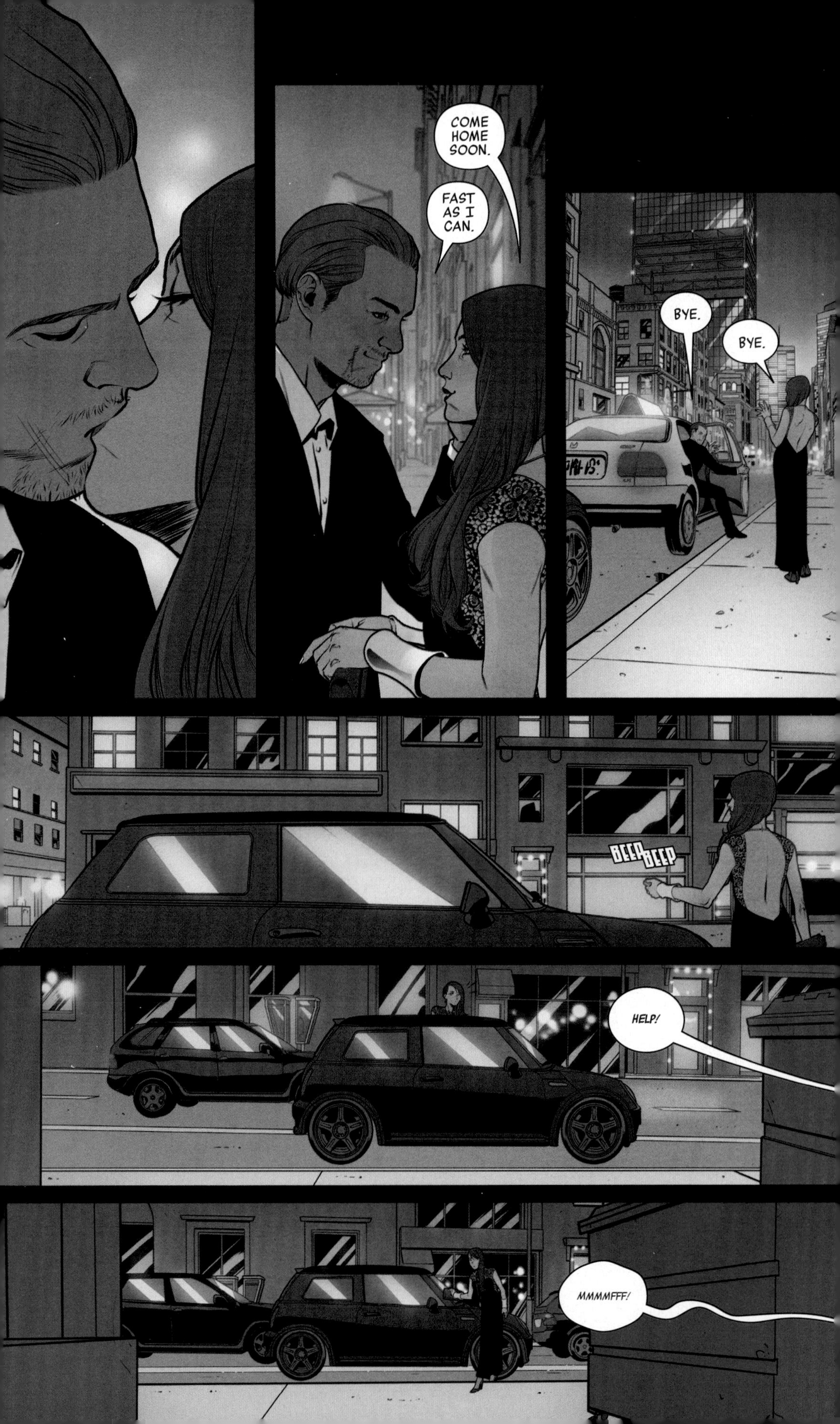
COME HOME SOON.
FAST AS I CAN.
BYE.
BYE.
BEEP BEEP
HELP!
MMMMFFF!

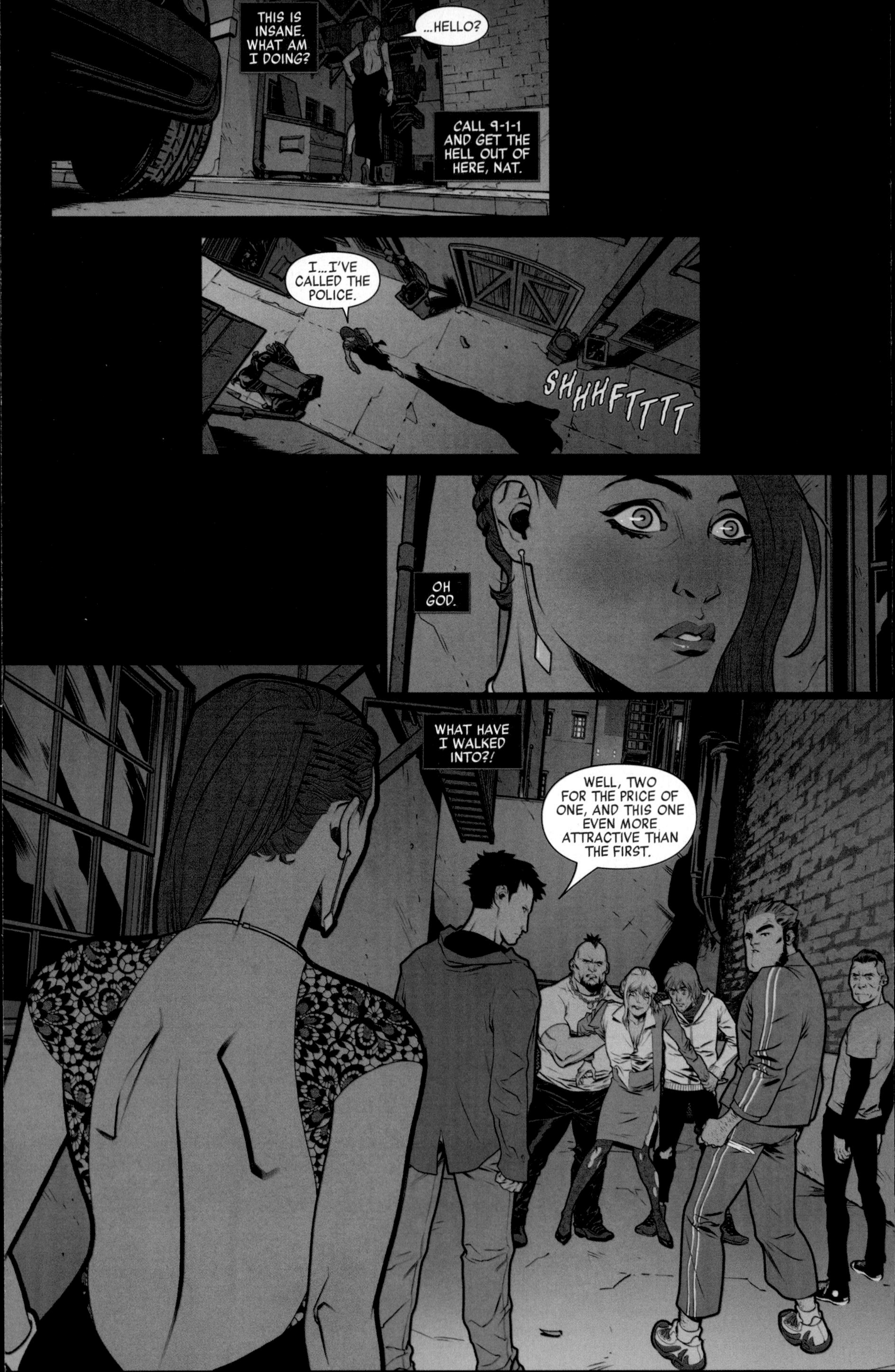
THIS IS INSANE. WHAT AM I DOING?
...HELLO?
CALL 9-1-1 AND GET THE HELL OUT OF HERE, NAT.
I...I'VE CALLED THE POLICE.
SHHHFTTTT
OH GOD.
WHAT HAVE I WALKED INTO?!
WELL, TWO FOR THE PRICE OF ONE, AND THIS ONE EVEN MORE ATTRACTIVE THAN THE FIRST.

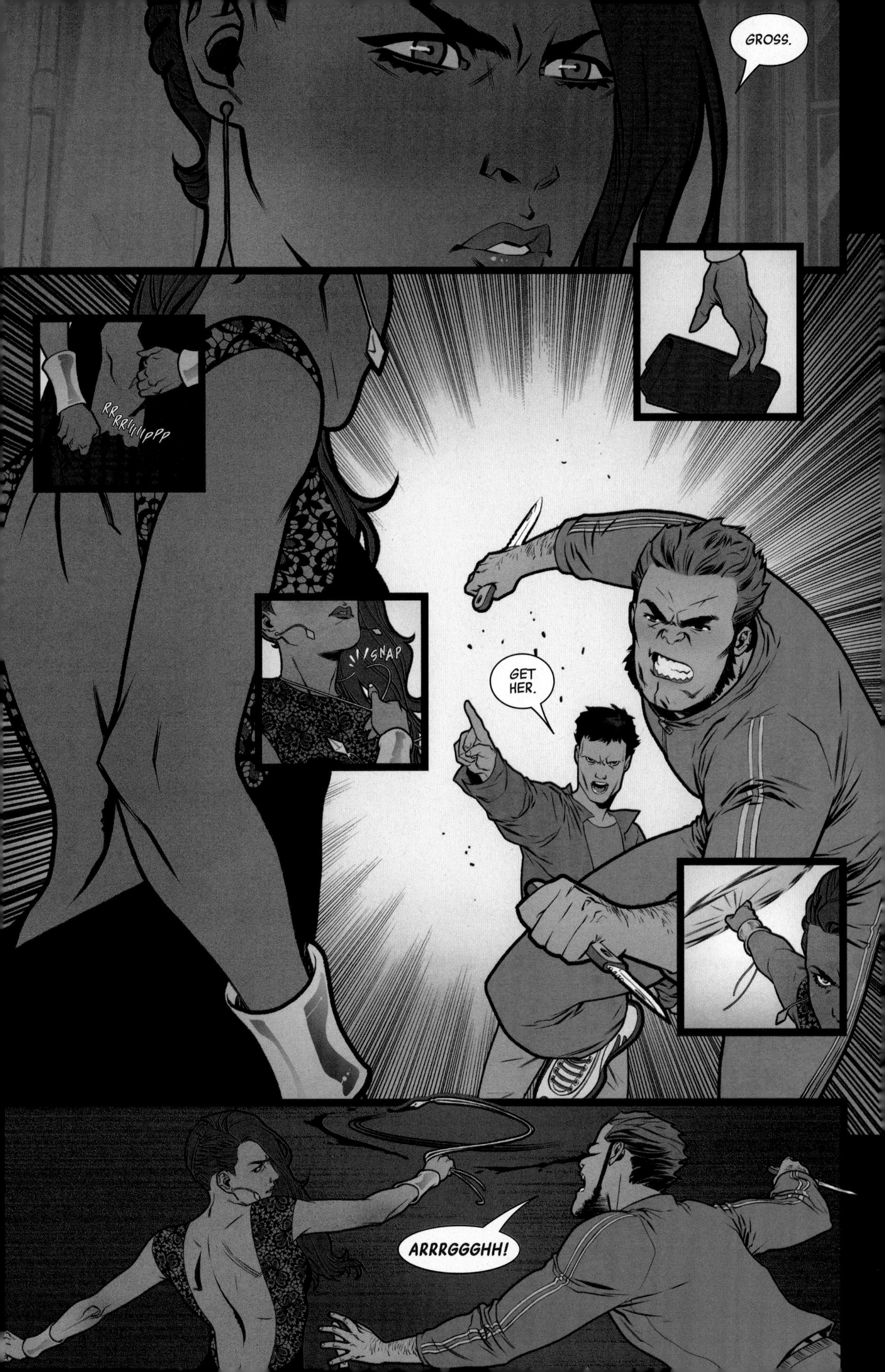
GROSS.
RRRRIIIIIPPP
SNAP
GET HER.
ARRRGGGHH!

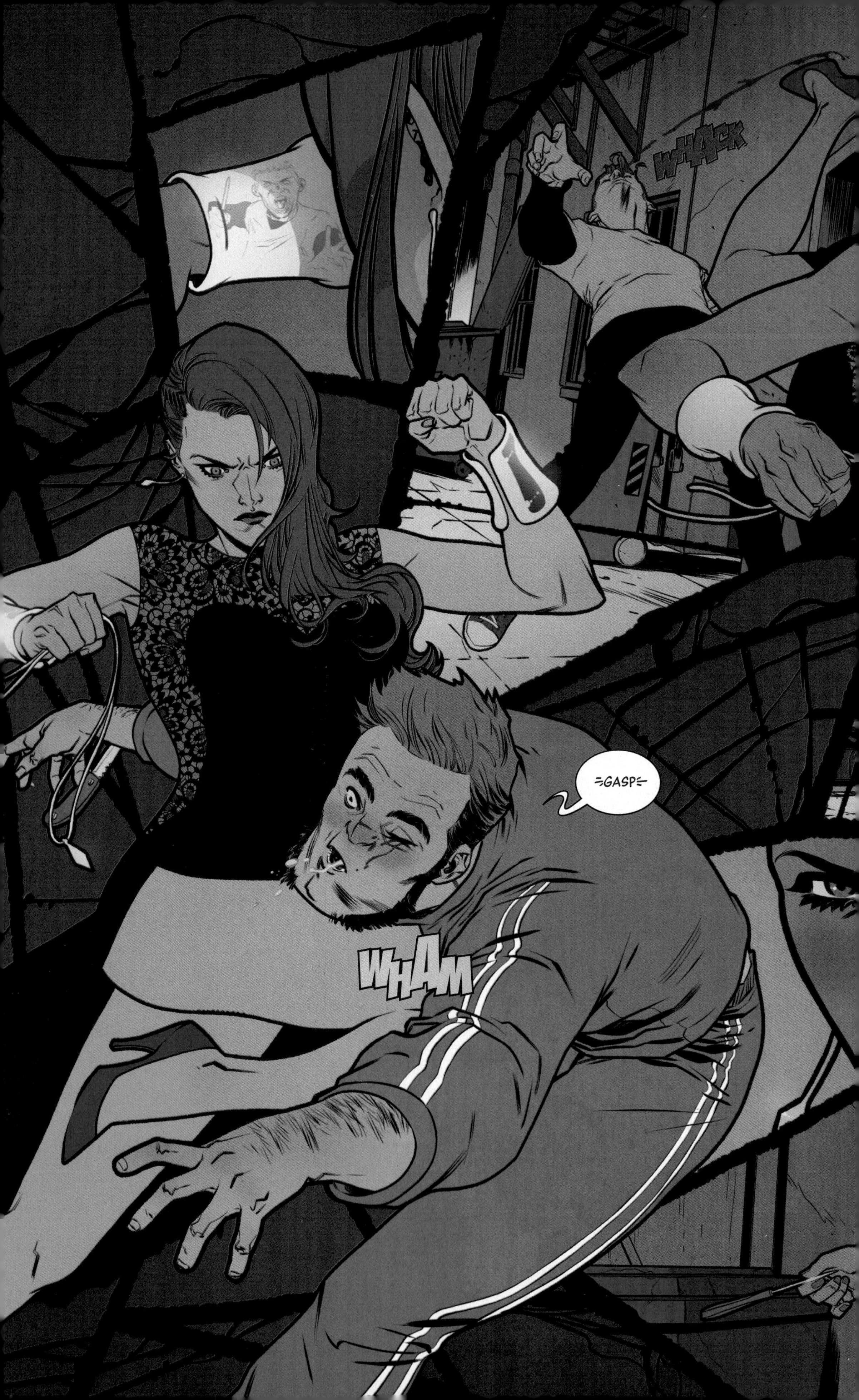
WHACK
GASP
WHAM

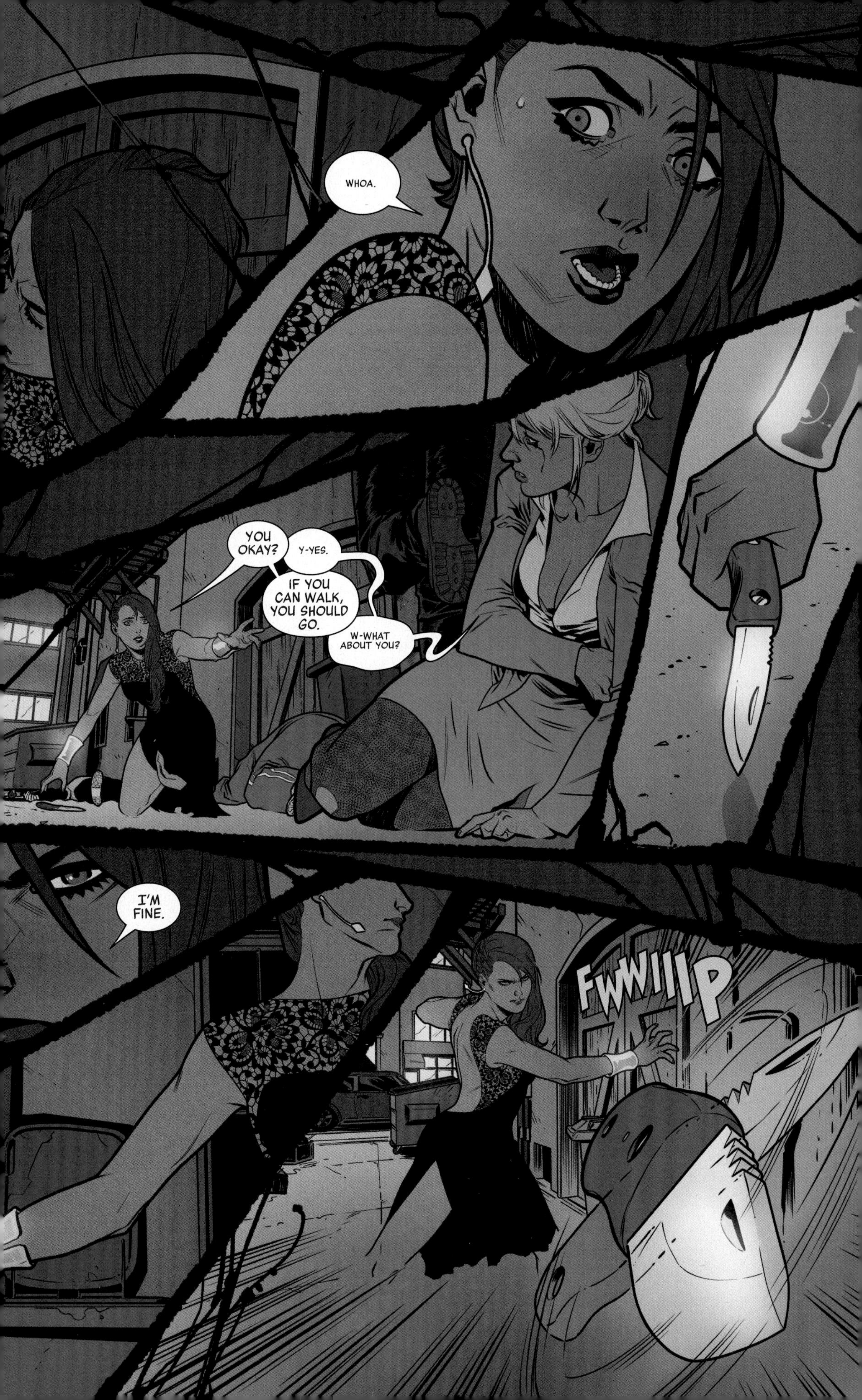
WHOA.
YOU OKAY?
Y-YES.
IF YOU CAN WALK, YOU SHOULD GO.
W-WHAT ABOUT YOU?
I'M FINE.
FWWIIIP

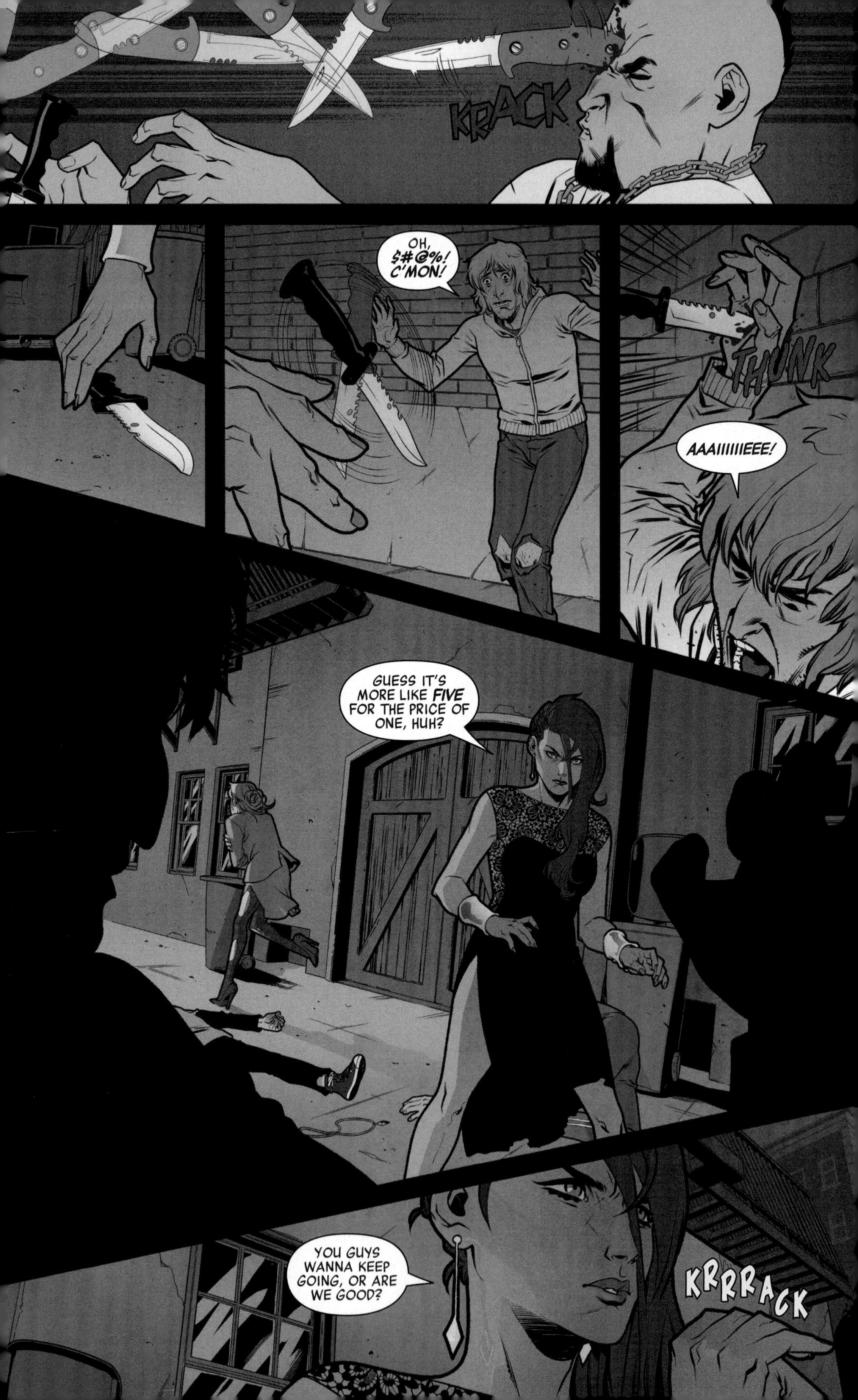
KRACK
OH, $#@%! C'MON!
THUNK
AAAIIIIIIEEE!
GUESS IT'S MORE LIKE FIVE FOR THE PRICE OF ONE, HUH?
YOU GUYS WANNA KEEP GOING, OR ARE WE GOOD?
KRRRACK

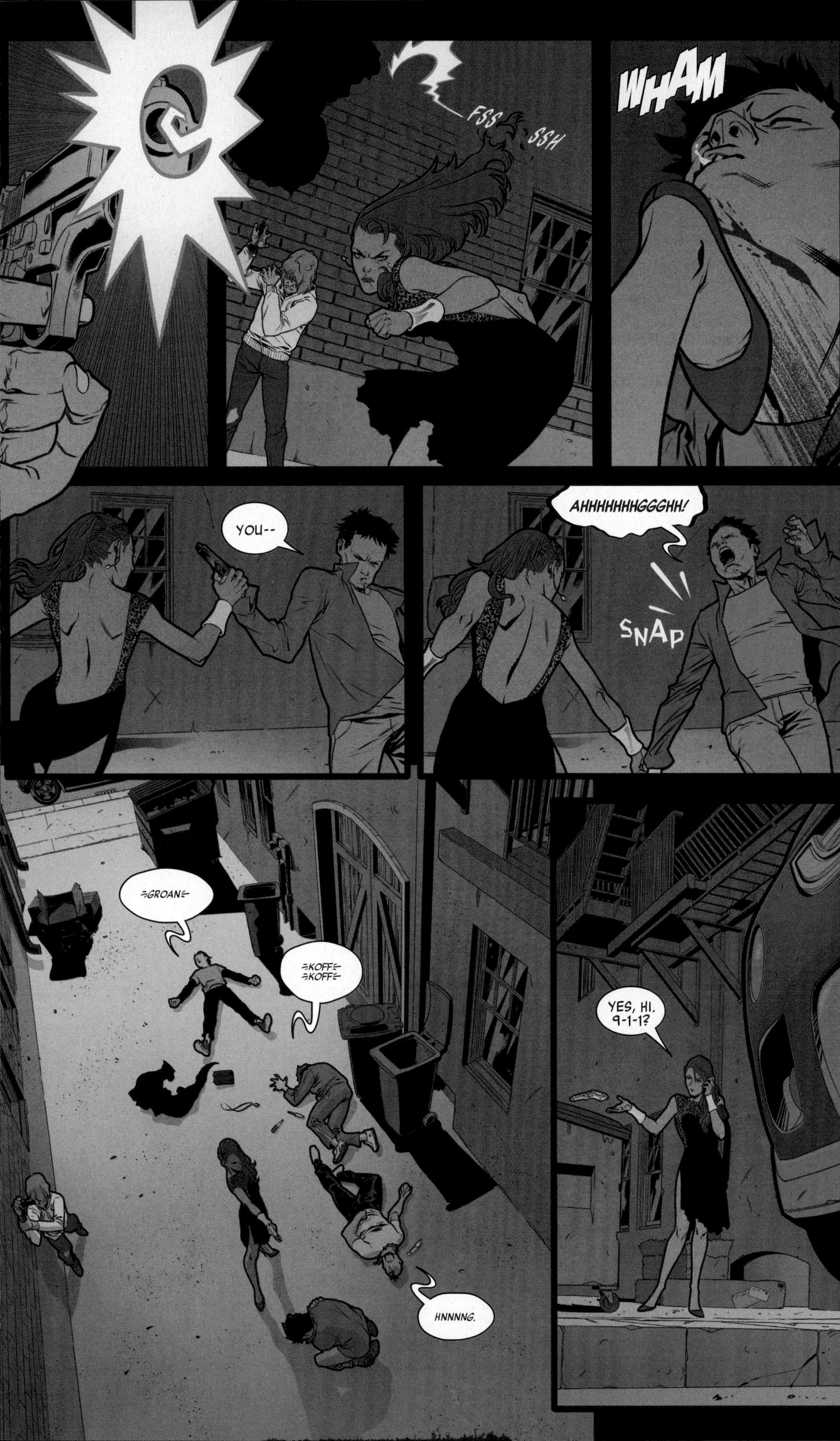
FSS
SSH
WHAM
YOU--
AHHHHHHHGGGHH!
SNAP
GROAN
KOFF KOFF
HNNNNG.
YES, HI. 9-1-1?

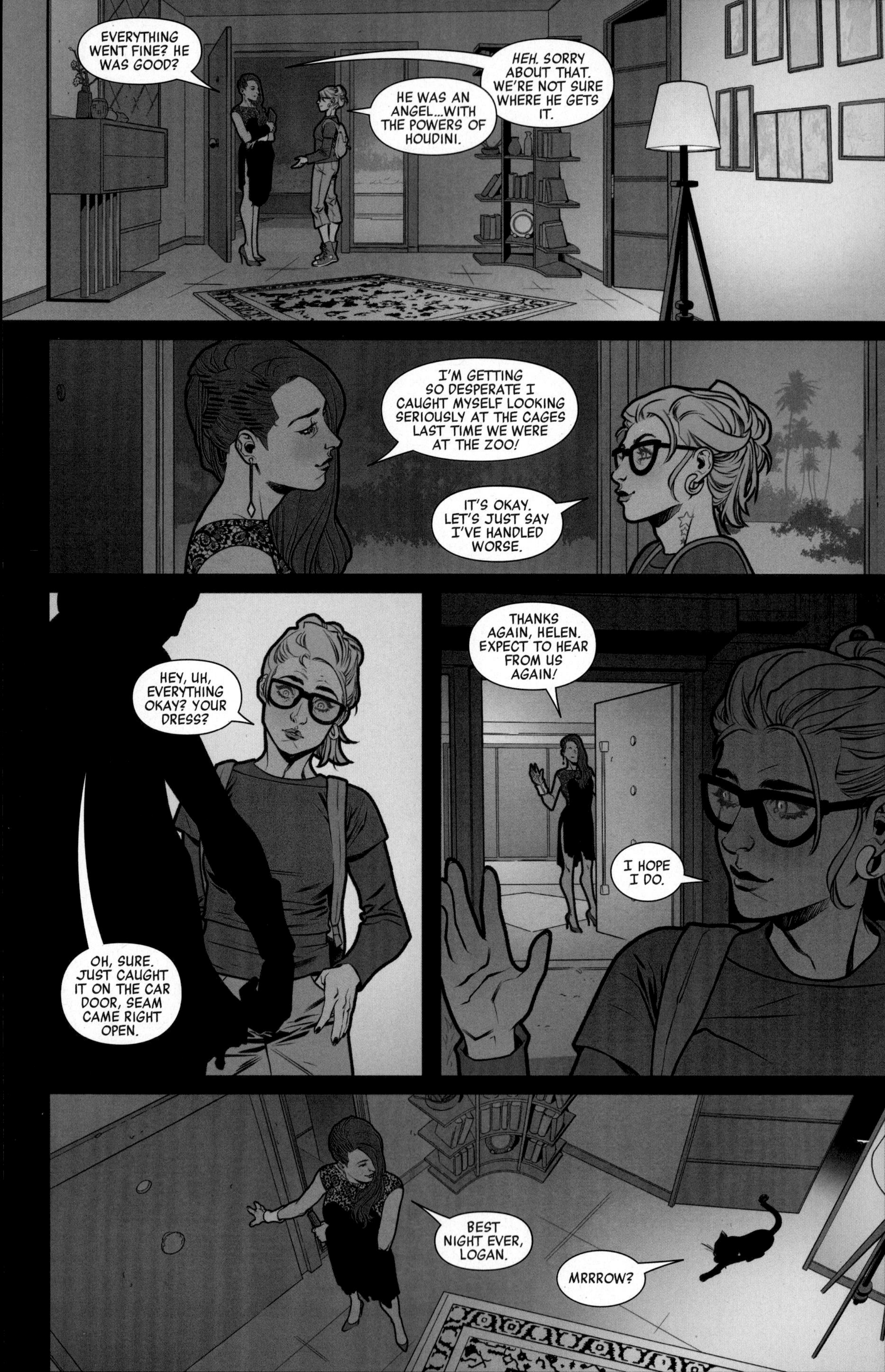
EVERYTHING WENT FINE? HE WAS GOOD?
HE WAS AN ANGEL...WITH THE POWERS OF HOUDINI.
HEH. SORRY ABOUT THAT. WE'RE NOT SURE WHERE HE GETS IT.
I'M GETTING SO DESPERATE I CAUGHT MYSELF LOOKING SERIOUSLY AT THE CAGES LAST TIME WE WERE AT THE ZOO!
IT'S OKAY. LET'S JUST SAY I'VE HANDLED WORSE.
HEY, UH, EVERYTHING OKAY? YOUR DRESS?
OH, SURE. JUST CAUGHT IT ON THE CAR DOOR, SEAM CAME RIGHT OPEN.
THANKS AGAIN, HELEN. EXPECT TO HEAR FROM US AGAIN!
I HOPE I DO.
BEST NIGHT EVER, LOGAN.
MRRROW?

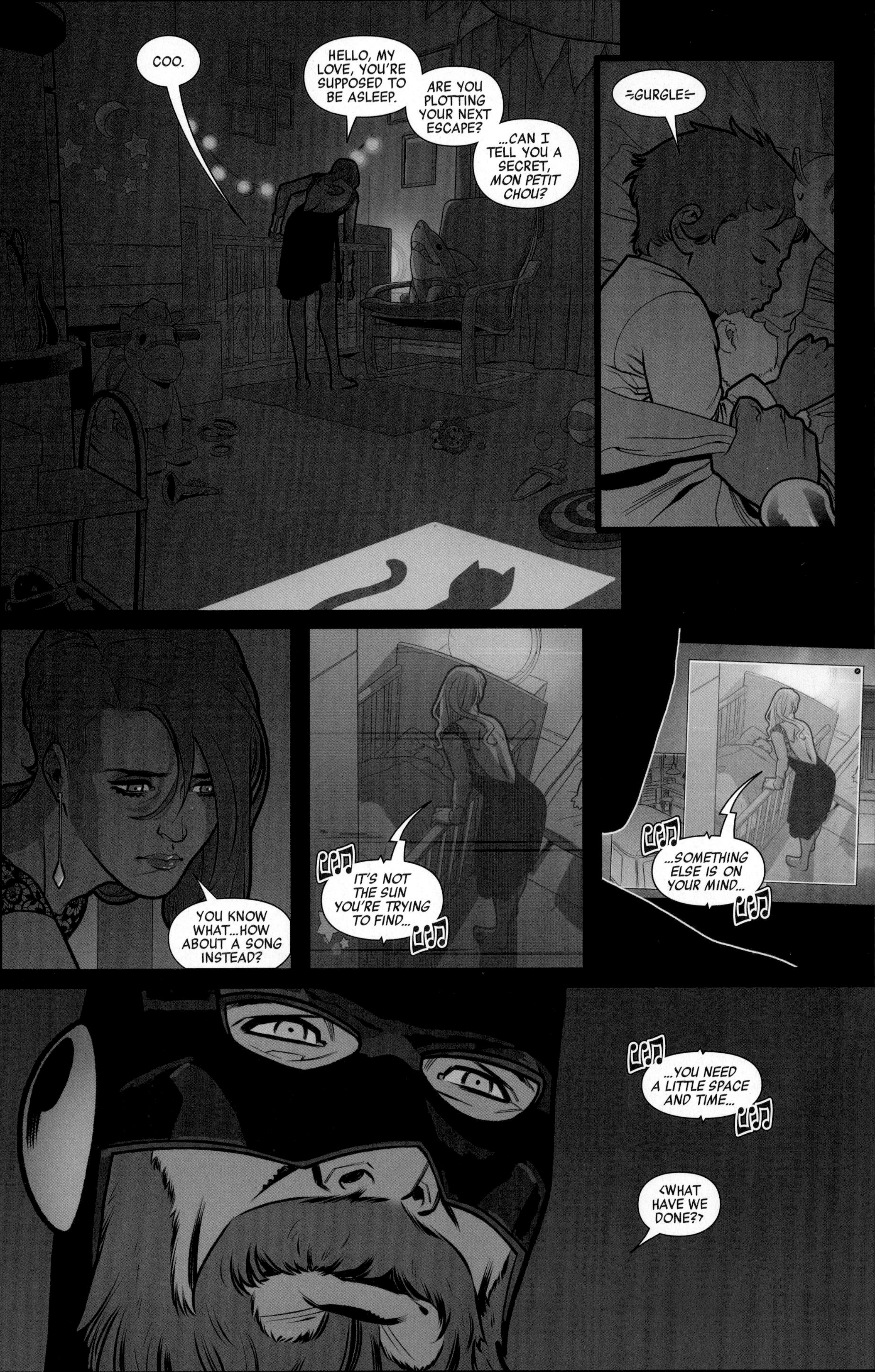
COO.
HELLO, MY LOVE, YOU'RE SUPPOSED TO BE ASLEEP.
ARE YOU PLOTTING YOUR NEXT ESCAPE?
...CAN I TELL YOU A SECRET, MON PETIT CHOU?
=GURGLE=
YOU KNOW WHAT...HOW ABOUT A SONG INSTEAD?
IT'S NOT THE SUN YOU'RE TRYING TO FIND...
...SOMETHING ELSE IS ON YOUR MIND...
...YOU NEED A LITTLE SPACE AND TIME...
<WHAT HAVE WE DONE?>

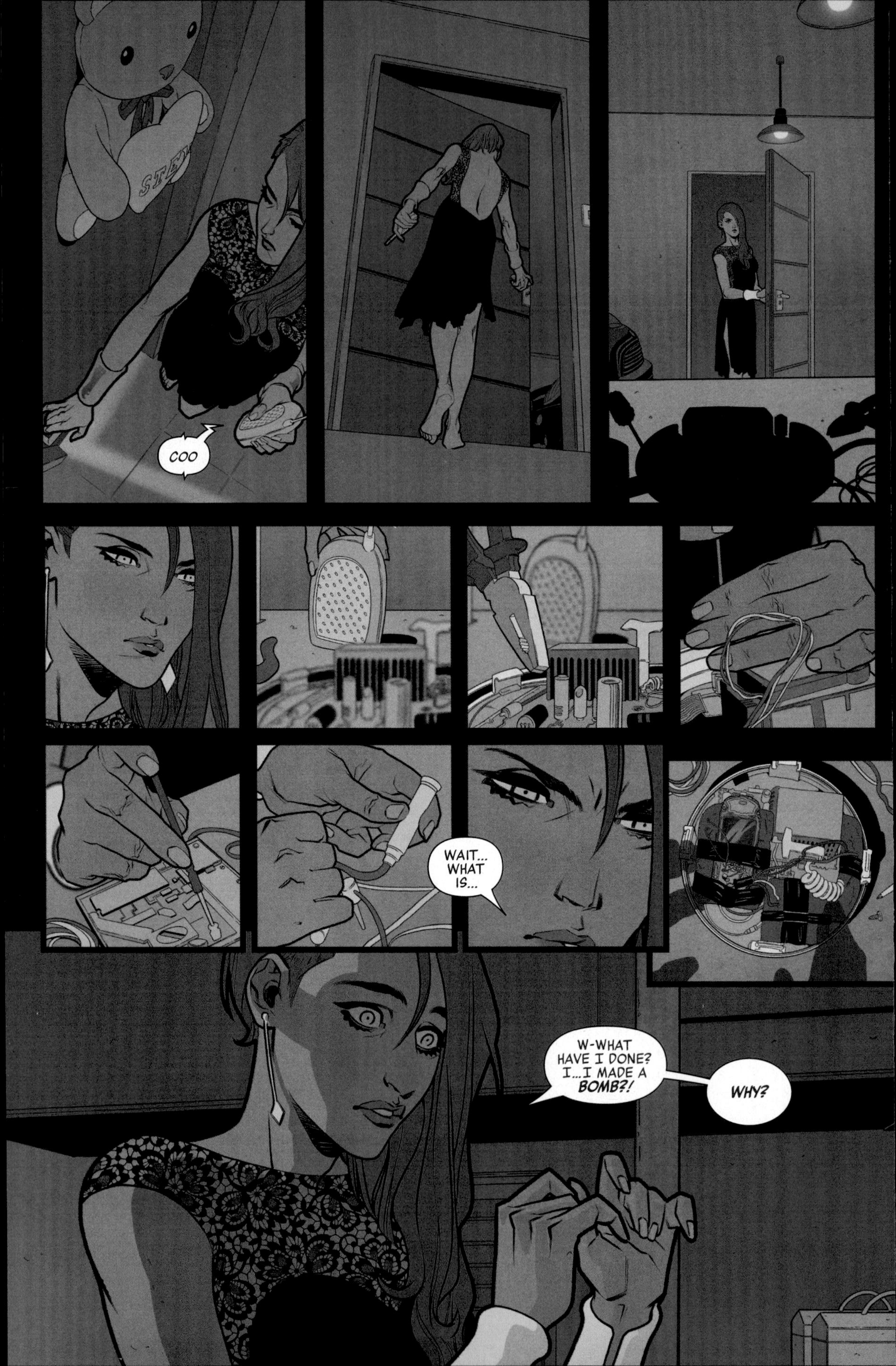
COO
WAIT... WHAT IS...
W-WHAT HAVE I DONE? I...I MADE A BOMB?!
WHY?

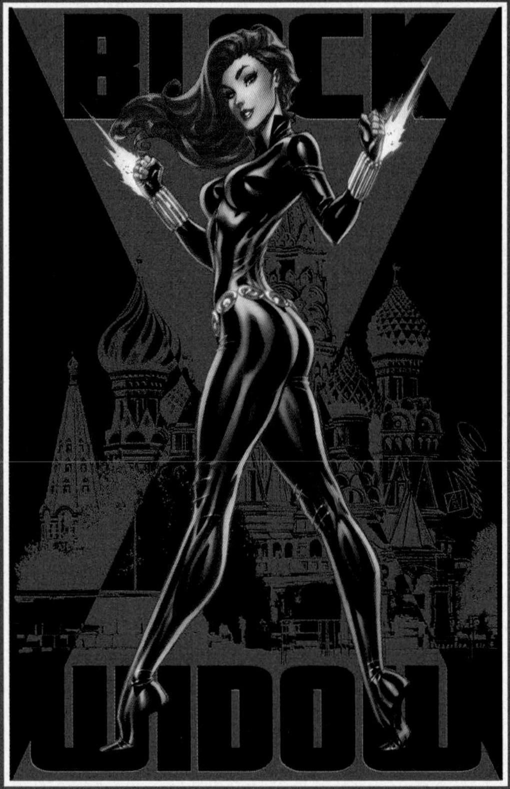
WIDOW

#1 VARIANT BY J. SCOTT CAMPBELL
& SABINE RICH

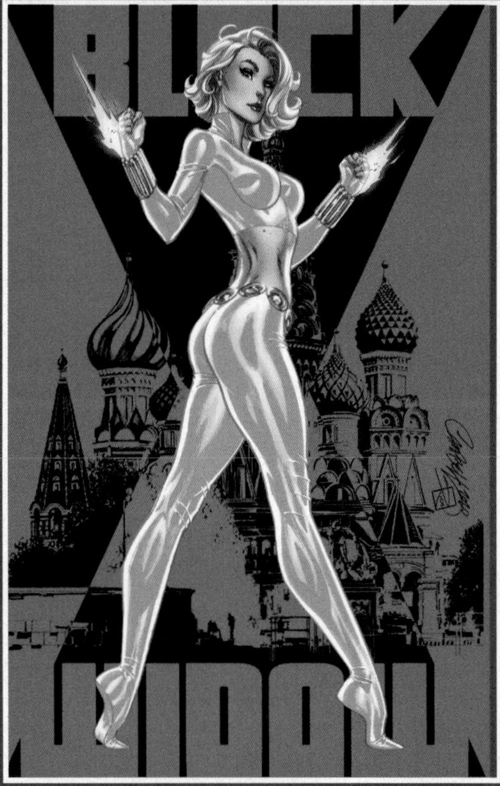
WIDOW

#2 VARIANT BY J. SCOTT CAMPBELL
& SABINE RICH

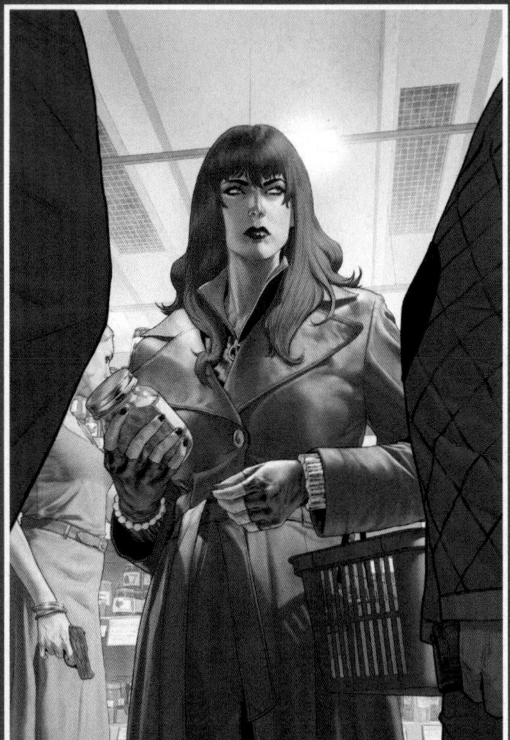

#2 VARIANT BY MATTIA DE IULIS

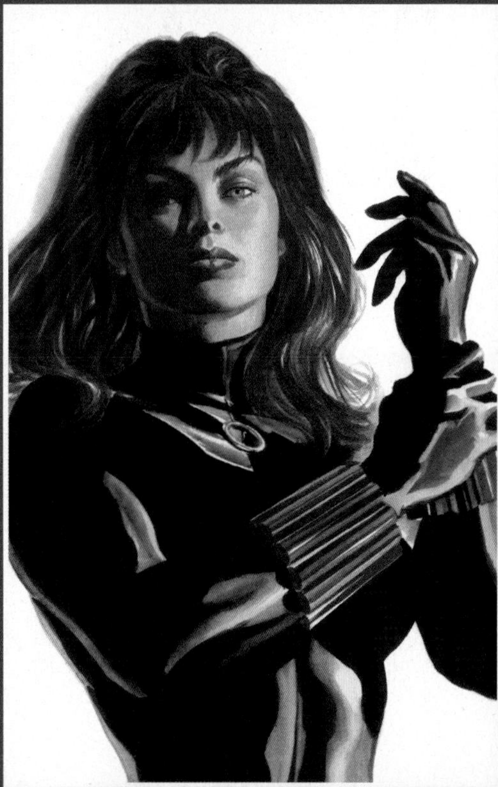

#2 VARIANT BY ALEX ROSS

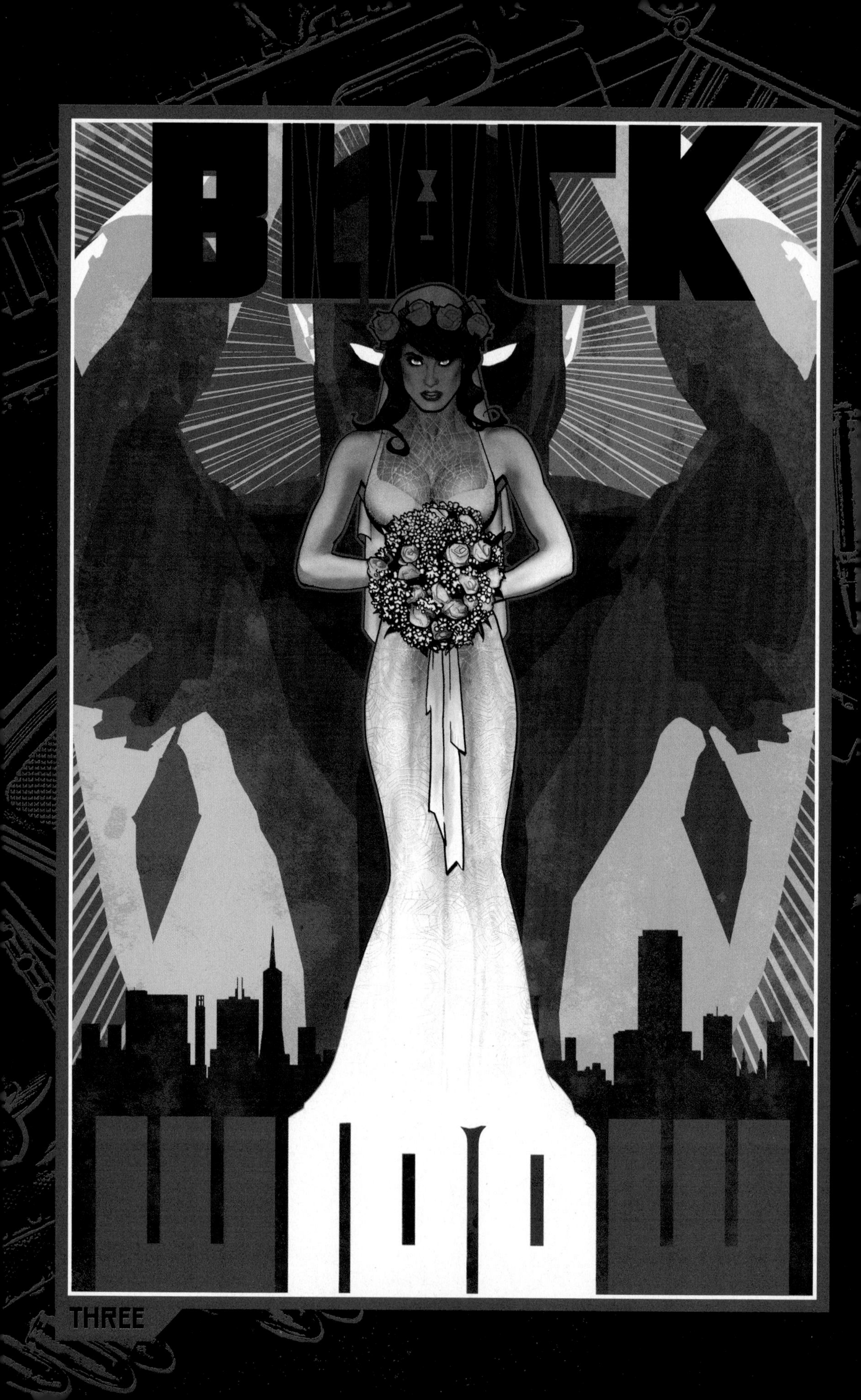
BLACK
THREE

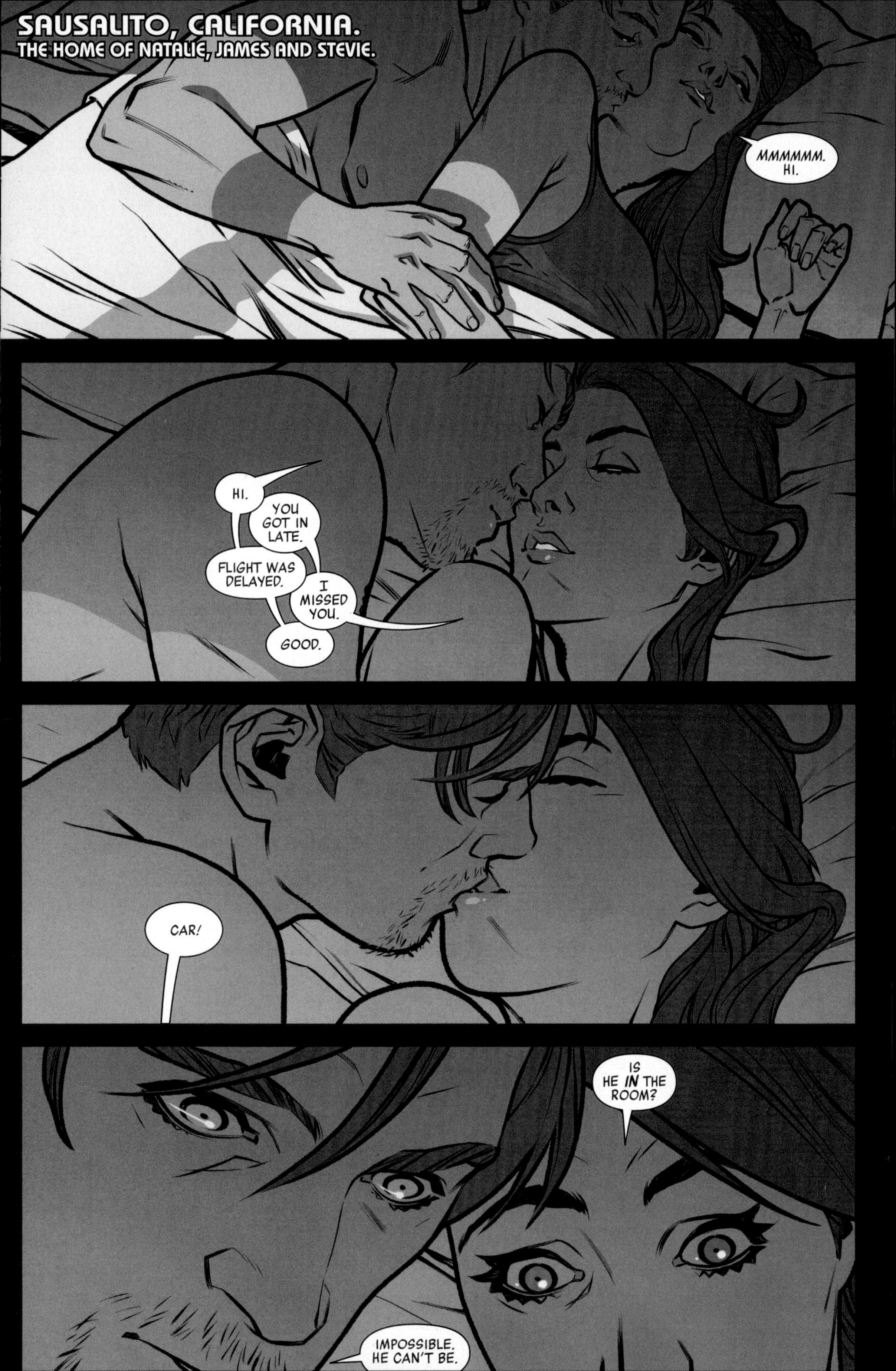
SAUSALITO, CALIFORNIA.
THE HOME OF NATALIE, JAMES AND STEVIE.
MMMMMM. HI.
HI.
YOU GOT IN LATE.
FLIGHT WAS DELAYED.
I MISSED YOU.
GOOD.
CAR!
IS HE IN THE ROOM?
IMPOSSIBLE. HE CAN'T BE.

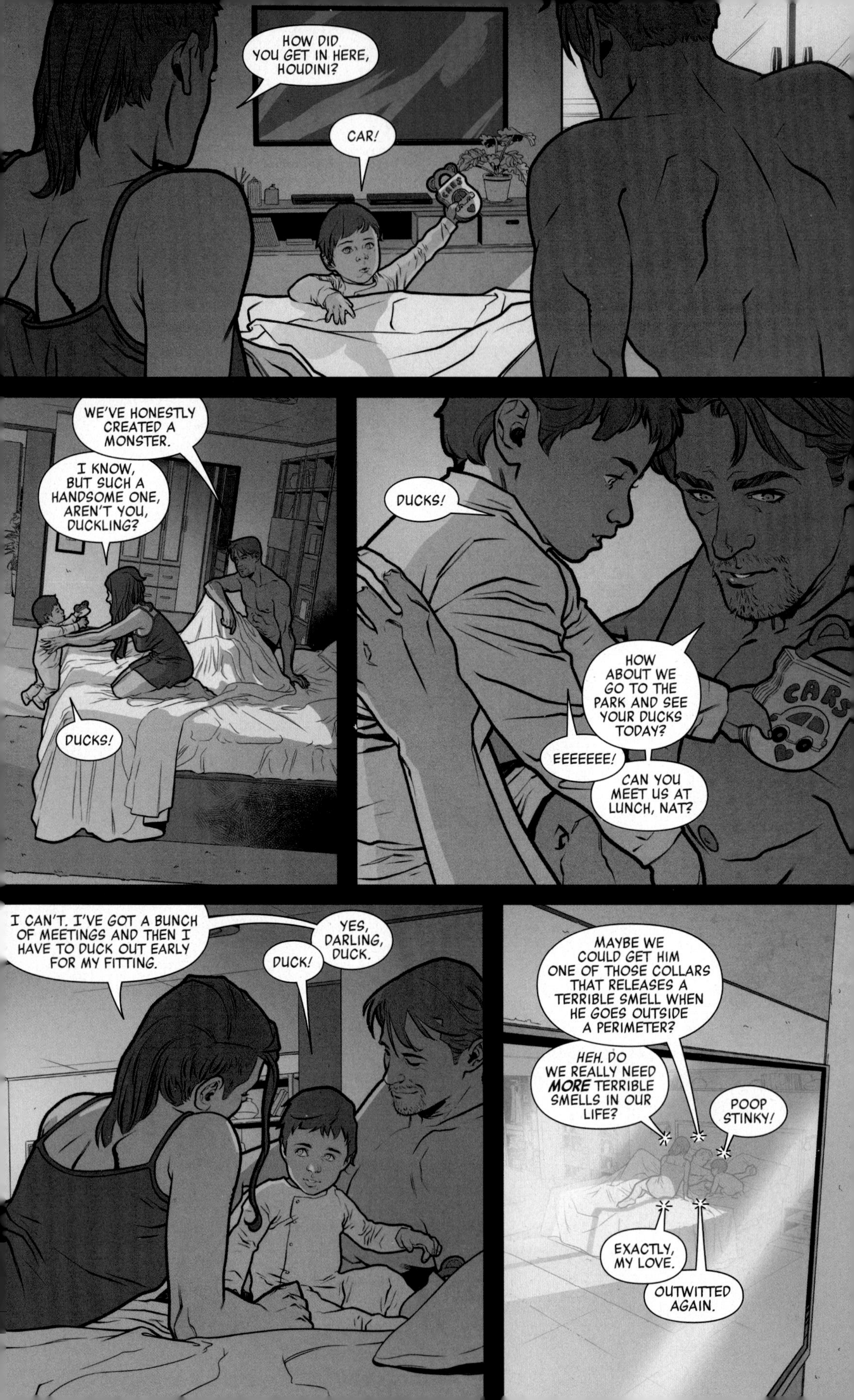
HOW DID YOU GET IN HERE, HOUDINI?
CAR!
CARS
WE'VE HONESTLY CREATED A MONSTER.
I KNOW, BUT SUCH A HANDSOME ONE, AREN'T YOU, DUCKLING?
DUCKS!
DUCKS!
HOW ABOUT WE GO TO THE PARK AND SEE YOUR DUCKS TODAY?
EEEEEEE!
CAN YOU MEET US AT LUNCH, NAT?
CARS
I CAN'T. I'VE GOT A BUNCH OF MEETINGS AND THEN I HAVE TO DUCK OUT EARLY FOR MY FITTING.
DUCK!
YES, DARLING, DUCK.
MAYBE WE COULD GET HIM ONE OF THOSE COLLARS THAT RELEASES A TERRIBLE SMELL WHEN HE GOES OUTSIDE A PERIMETER?
HEH. DO WE REALLY NEED MORE TERRIBLE SMELLS IN OUR LIFE?
POOP STINKY!
EXACTLY, MY LOVE.
OUTWITTED AGAIN.

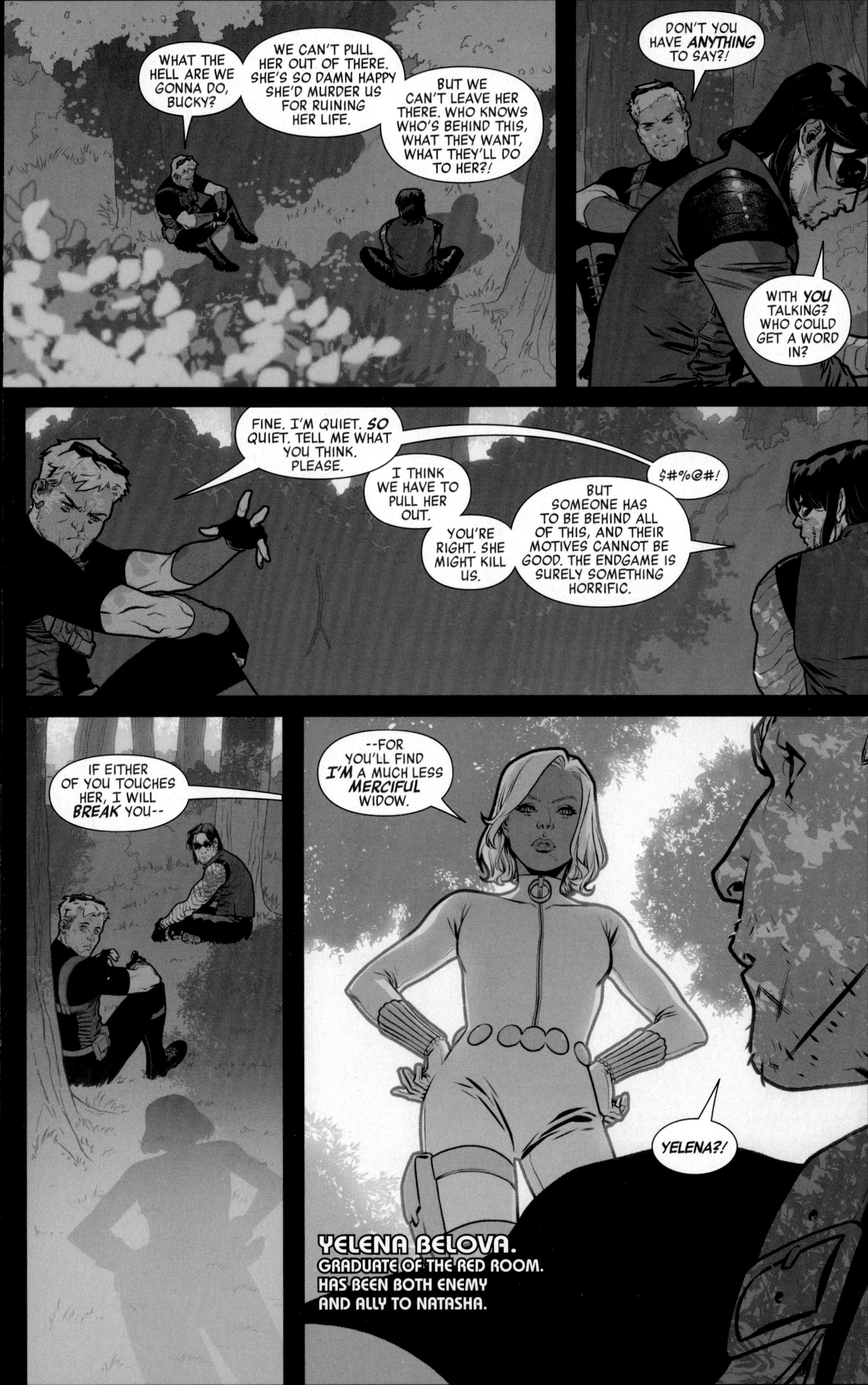

WHAT THE HELL ARE WE GONNA DO, BUCKY?
WE CAN'T PULL HER OUT OF THERE. SHE'S SO DAMN HAPPY SHE'D MURDER US FOR RUINING HER LIFE.
BUT WE CAN'T LEAVE HER THERE. WHO KNOWS WHO'S BEHIND THIS, WHAT THEY WANT, WHAT THEY'LL DO TO HER?!
DON'T YOU HAVE ANYTHING TO SAY?!
WITH YOU TALKING? WHO COULD GET A WORD IN?
FINE. I'M QUIET. SO QUIET. TELL ME WHAT YOU THINK. PLEASE.
$#%@#!
I THINK WE HAVE TO PULL HER OUT.
YOU'RE RIGHT. SHE MIGHT KILL US.
BUT SOMEONE HAS TO BE BEHIND ALL OF THIS, AND THEIR MOTIVES CANNOT BE GOOD. THE ENDGAME IS SURELY SOMETHING HORRIFIC.
IF EITHER OF YOU TOUCHES HER, I WILL BREAK YOU--
--FOR YOU'LL FIND I'M A MUCH LESS MERCIFUL WIDOW.
YELENA?!
YELENA BELOVA.
GRADUATE OF THE RED ROOM.
HAS BEEN BOTH ENEMY
AND ALLY TO NATASHA.

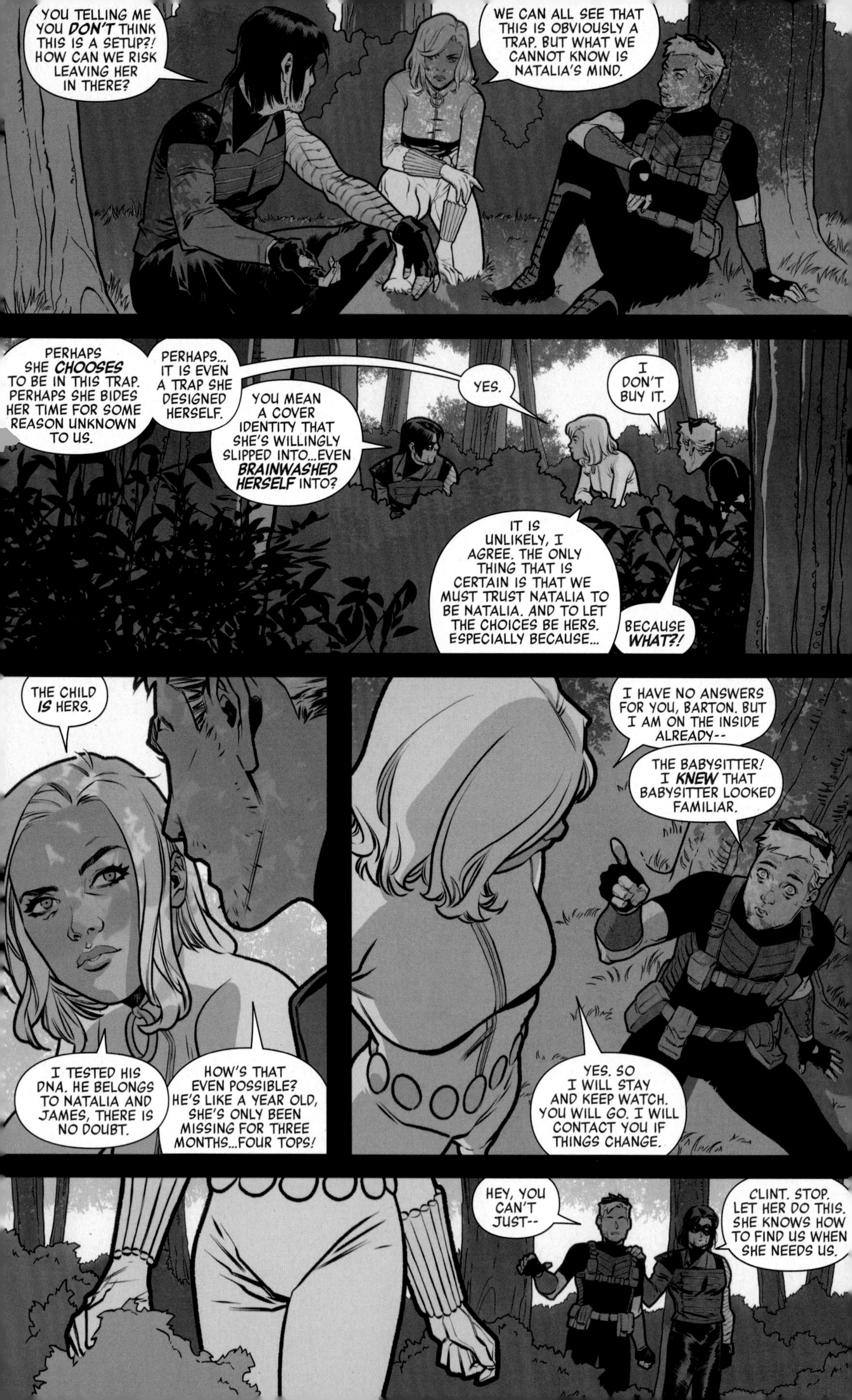
YOU TELLING ME YOU DON'T THINK THIS IS A SETUP?! HOW CAN WE RISK LEAVING HER IN THERE?
WE CAN ALL SEE THAT THIS IS OBVIOUSLY A TRAP. BUT WHAT WE CANNOT KNOW IS NATALIA'S MIND.
PERHAPS SHE CHOOSES TO BE IN THIS TRAP. PERHAPS SHE BIDES HER TIME FOR SOME REASON UNKNOWN TO US.
PERHAPS... IT IS EVEN A TRAP SHE DESIGNED HERSELF.
YOU MEAN A COVER IDENTITY THAT SHE'S WILLINGLY SLIPPED INTO...EVEN BRAINWASHED HERSELF INTO?
YES.
I DON'T BUY IT.
IT IS UNLIKELY, I AGREE. THE ONLY THING THAT IS CERTAIN IS THAT WE MUST TRUST NATALIA TO BE NATALIA. AND TO LET THE CHOICES BE HERS. ESPECIALLY BECAUSE...
BECAUSE WHAT?!
THE CHILD IS HERS.
I TESTED HIS DNA. HE BELONGS TO NATALIA AND JAMES, THERE IS NO DOUBT.
HOW'S THAT EVEN POSSIBLE? HE'S LIKE A YEAR OLD, SHE'S ONLY BEEN MISSING FOR THREE MONTHS...FOUR TOPS!
I HAVE NO ANSWERS FOR YOU, BARTON. BUT I AM ON THE INSIDE ALREADY--
THE BABYSITTER! I KNEW THAT BABYSITTER LOOKED FAMILIAR.
YES. SO I WILL STAY AND KEEP WATCH. YOU WILL GO. I WILL CONTACT YOU IF THINGS CHANGE.
HEY, YOU CAN'T JUST--
CLINT. STOP. LET HER DO THIS. SHE KNOWS HOW TO FIND US WHEN SHE NEEDS US.

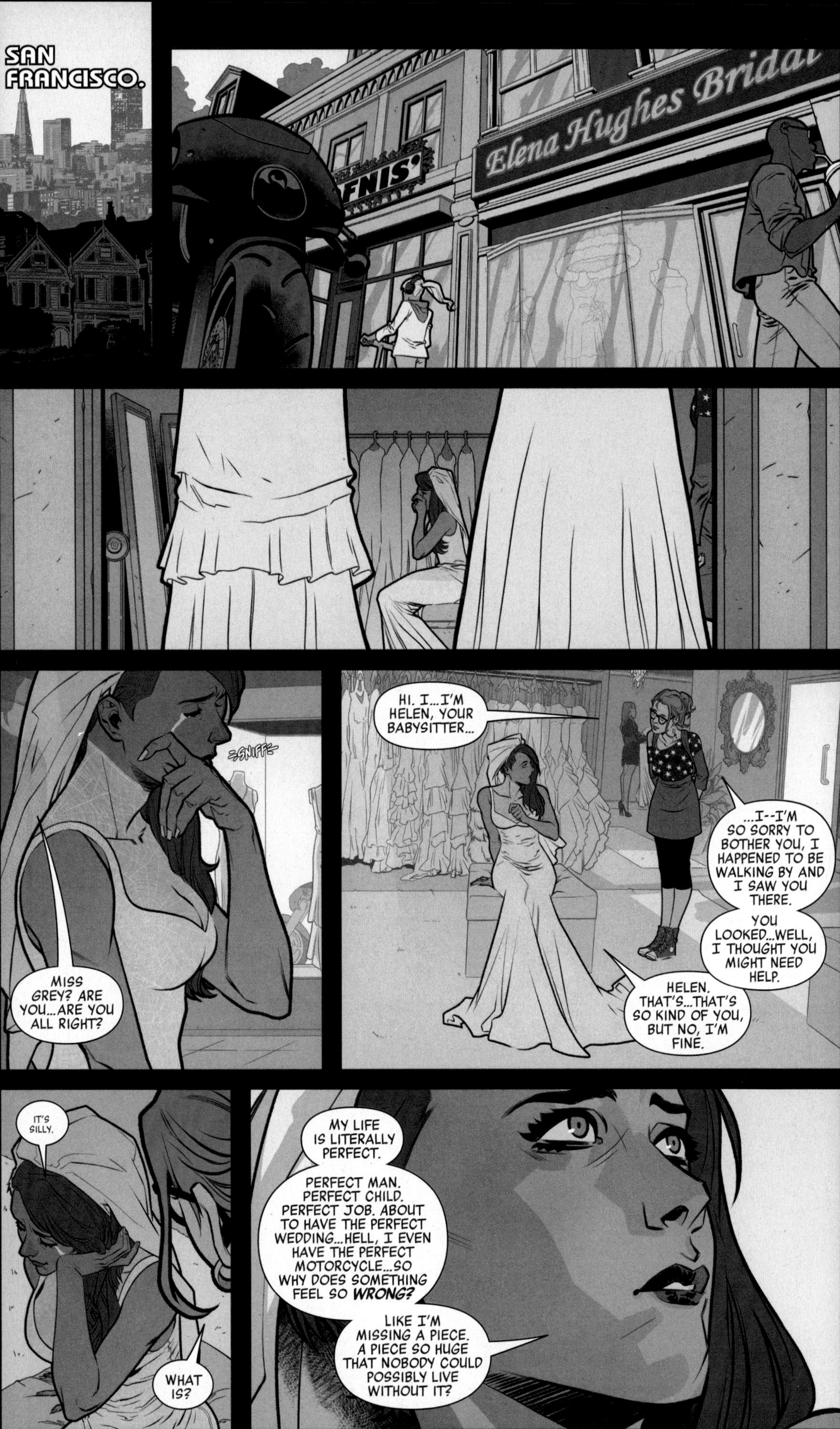
SAN FRANCISCO.
Elena Hughes Bridal
HI. I...I'M HELEN, YOUR BABYSITTER...
...I--I'M SO SORRY TO BOTHER YOU, I HAPPENED TO BE WALKING BY AND I SAW YOU THERE.
YOU LOOKED...WELL, I THOUGHT YOU MIGHT NEED HELP.
SNIFF
MISS GREY? ARE YOU...ARE YOU ALL RIGHT?
HELEN. THAT'S...THAT'S SO KIND OF YOU, BUT NO, I'M FINE.
IT'S SILLY.
WHAT IS?
MY LIFE IS LITERALLY PERFECT.
PERFECT MAN. PERFECT CHILD. PERFECT JOB. ABOUT TO HAVE THE PERFECT WEDDING...HELL, I EVEN HAVE THE PERFECT MOTORCYCLE...SO WHY DOES SOMETHING FEEL SO WRONG?
LIKE I'M MISSING A PIECE. A PIECE SO HUGE THAT NOBODY COULD POSSIBLY LIVE WITHOUT IT?

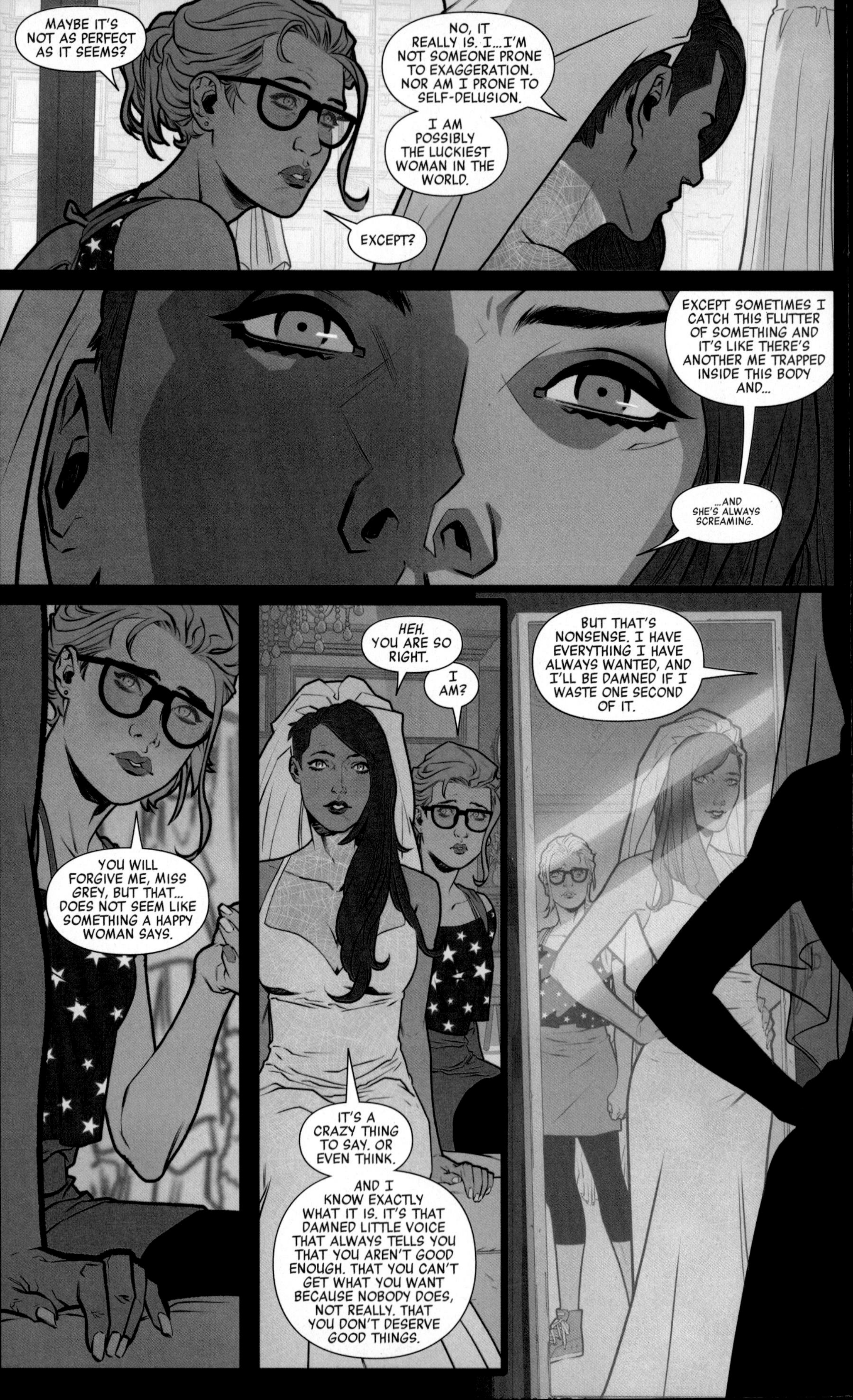
MAYBE IT'S NOT AS PERFECT AS IT SEEMS?
NO, IT REALLY IS. I...I'M NOT SOMEONE PRONE TO EXAGGERATION. NOR AM I PRONE TO SELF-DELUSION.
I AM POSSIBLY THE LUCKIEST WOMAN IN THE WORLD.
EXCEPT?
EXCEPT SOMETIMES I CATCH THIS FLUTTER OF SOMETHING AND IT'S LIKE THERE'S ANOTHER ME TRAPPED INSIDE THIS BODY AND...
...AND SHE'S ALWAYS SCREAMING.
YOU WILL FORGIVE ME, MISS GREY, BUT THAT... DOES NOT SEEM LIKE SOMETHING A HAPPY WOMAN SAYS.
HEH. YOU ARE SO RIGHT.
I AM?
IT'S A CRAZY THING TO SAY. OR EVEN THINK.
AND I KNOW EXACTLY WHAT IT IS. IT'S THAT DAMNED LITTLE VOICE THAT ALWAYS TELLS YOU THAT YOU AREN'T GOOD ENOUGH. THAT YOU CAN'T GET WHAT YOU WANT BECAUSE NOBODY DOES, NOT REALLY. THAT YOU DON'T DESERVE GOOD THINGS.
BUT THAT'S NONSENSE. I HAVE EVERYTHING I HAVE ALWAYS WANTED, AND I'LL BE DAMNED IF I WASTE ONE SECOND OF IT.

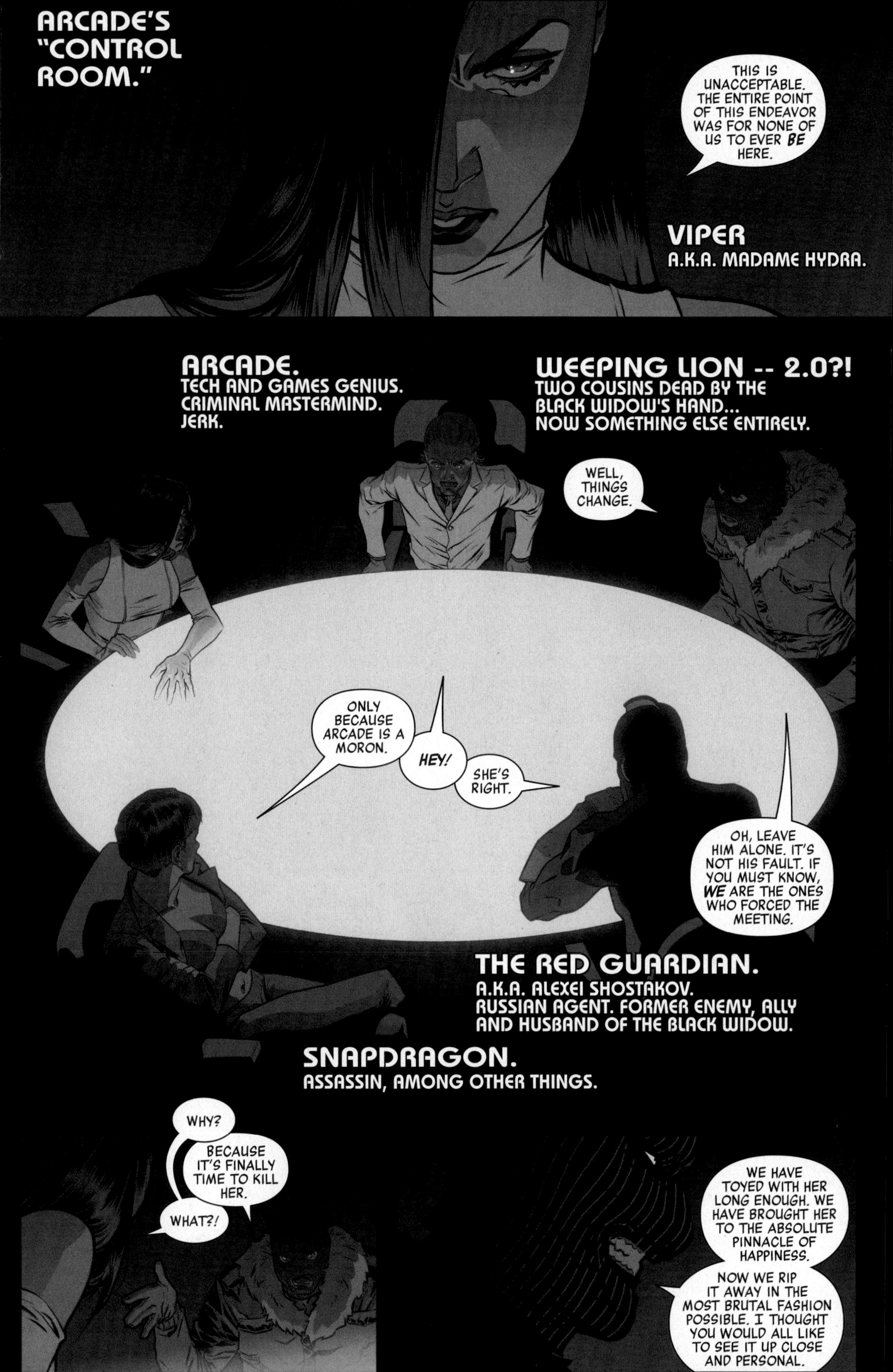

ARCADE'S "CONTROL ROOM."
THIS IS UNACCEPTABLE. THE ENTIRE POINT OF THIS ENDEAVOR WAS FOR NONE OF US TO EVER BE HERE.
VIPER
A.K.A. MADAME HYDRA.
ARCADE.
TECH AND GAMES GENIUS. CRIMINAL MASTERMIND. JERK.
WEEPING LION -- 2.0?!
TWO COUSINS DEAD BY THE BLACK WIDOW'S HAND... NOW SOMETHING ELSE ENTIRELY.
WELL, THINGS CHANGE.
ONLY BECAUSE ARCADE IS A MORON.
HEY!
SHE'S RIGHT.
OH, LEAVE HIM ALONE. IT'S NOT HIS FAULT. IF YOU MUST KNOW, WE ARE THE ONES WHO FORCED THE MEETING.
THE RED GUARDIAN.
A.K.A. ALEXEI SHOSTAKOV.
RUSSIAN AGENT. FORMER ENEMY, ALLY AND HUSBAND OF THE BLACK WIDOW.
SNAPDRAGON.
ASSASSIN, AMONG OTHER THINGS.
WHY?
BECAUSE IT'S FINALLY TIME TO KILL HER.
WHAT?!
WE HAVE TOYED WITH HER LONG ENOUGH. WE HAVE BROUGHT HER TO THE ABSOLUTE PINNACLE OF HAPPINESS.
NOW WE RIP IT AWAY IN THE MOST BRUTAL FASHION POSSIBLE. I THOUGHT YOU WOULD ALL LIKE TO SEE IT UP CLOSE AND PERSONAL.

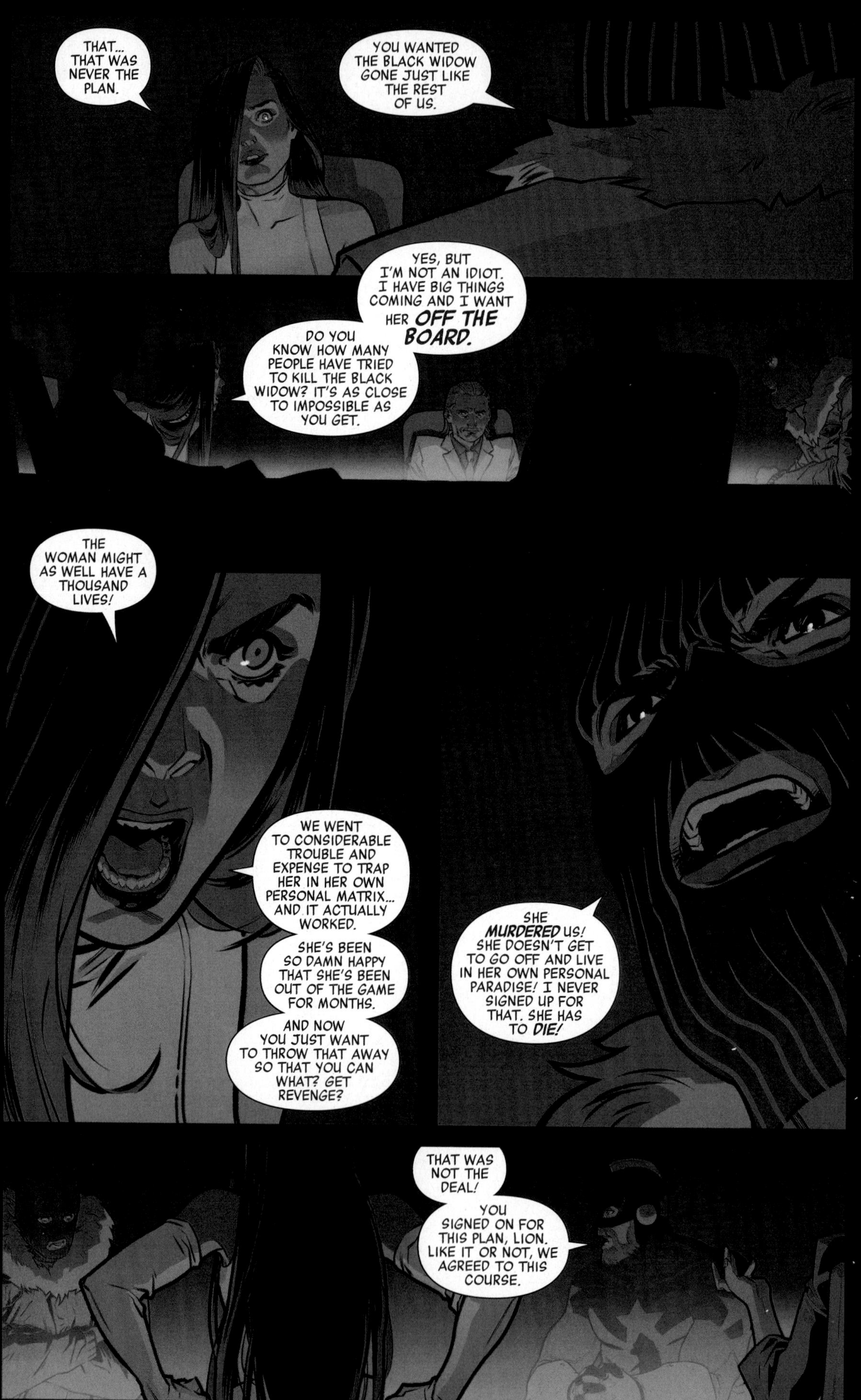
THAT... THAT WAS NEVER THE PLAN.
YOU WANTED THE BLACK WIDOW GONE JUST LIKE THE REST OF US.
YES, BUT I'M NOT AN IDIOT. I HAVE BIG THINGS COMING AND I WANT HER OFF THE BOARD.
DO YOU KNOW HOW MANY PEOPLE HAVE TRIED TO KILL THE BLACK WIDOW? IT'S AS CLOSE TO IMPOSSIBLE AS YOU GET.
THE WOMAN MIGHT AS WELL HAVE A THOUSAND LIVES!
WE WENT TO CONSIDERABLE TROUBLE AND EXPENSE TO TRAP HER IN HER OWN PERSONAL MATRIX... AND IT ACTUALLY WORKED.
SHE'S BEEN SO DAMN HAPPY THAT SHE'S BEEN OUT OF THE GAME FOR MONTHS.
AND NOW YOU JUST WANT TO THROW THAT AWAY SO THAT YOU CAN WHAT? GET REVENGE?
SHE MURDERED US! SHE DOESN'T GET TO GO OFF AND LIVE IN HER OWN PERSONAL PARADISE! I NEVER SIGNED UP FOR THAT. SHE HAS TO DIE!
THAT WAS NOT THE DEAL!
YOU SIGNED ON FOR THIS PLAN, LION. LIKE IT OR NOT, WE AGREED TO THIS COURSE.

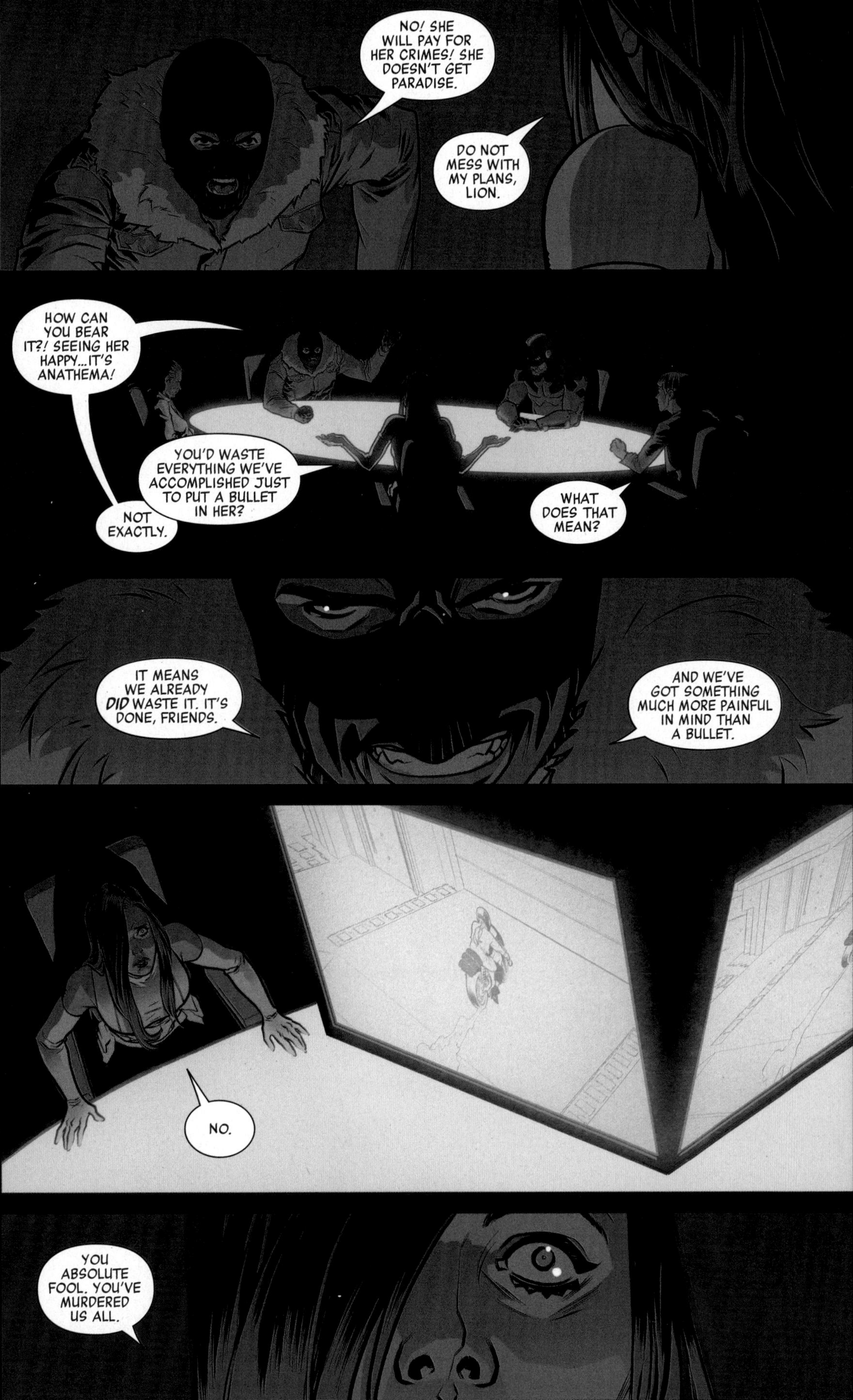
NO! SHE WILL PAY FOR HER CRIMES! SHE DOESN'T GET PARADISE.
DO NOT MESS WITH MY PLANS, LION.
HOW CAN YOU BEAR IT?! SEEING HER HAPPY...IT'S ANATHEMA!
YOU'D WASTE EVERYTHING WE'VE ACCOMPLISHED JUST TO PUT A BULLET IN HER?
NOT EXACTLY.
WHAT DOES THAT MEAN?
IT MEANS WE ALREADY *DID* WASTE IT. IT'S DONE, FRIENDS.
AND WE'VE GOT SOMETHING MUCH MORE PAINFUL IN MIND THAN A BULLET.
NO.
YOU ABSOLUTE FOOL. YOU'VE MURDERED US ALL.

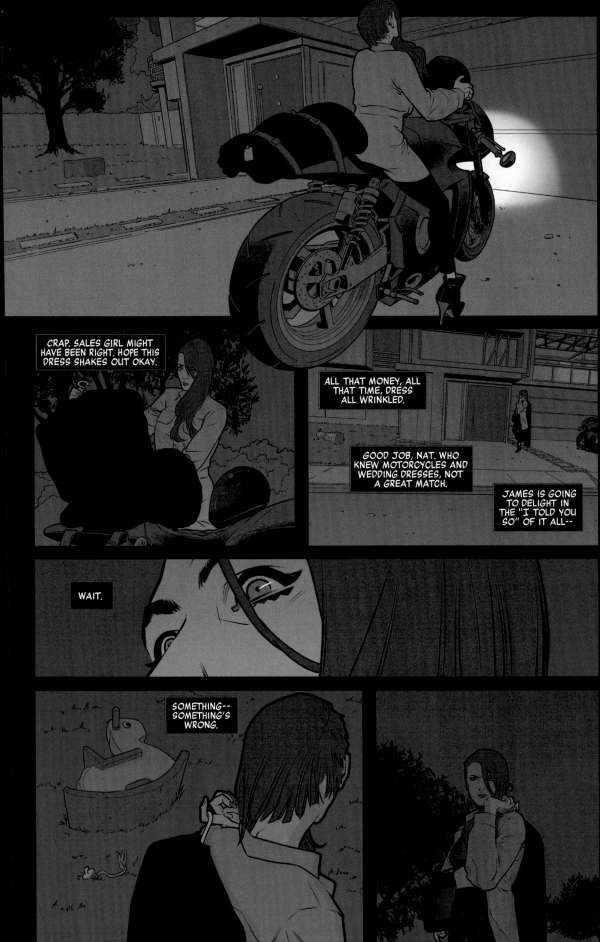

CRAP. SALES GIRL MIGHT HAVE BEEN RIGHT. HOPE THIS DRESS SHAKES OUT OKAY.

ALL THAT MONEY, ALL THAT TIME, DRESS ALL WRINKLED.

GOOD JOB, NAT. WHO KNEW MOTORCYCLES AND WEDDING DRESSES, NOT A GREAT MATCH.

JAMES IS GOING TO DELIGHT IN THE "I TOLD YOU SO" OF IT ALL--

WAIT.

SOMETHING-- SOMETHING'S WRONG.

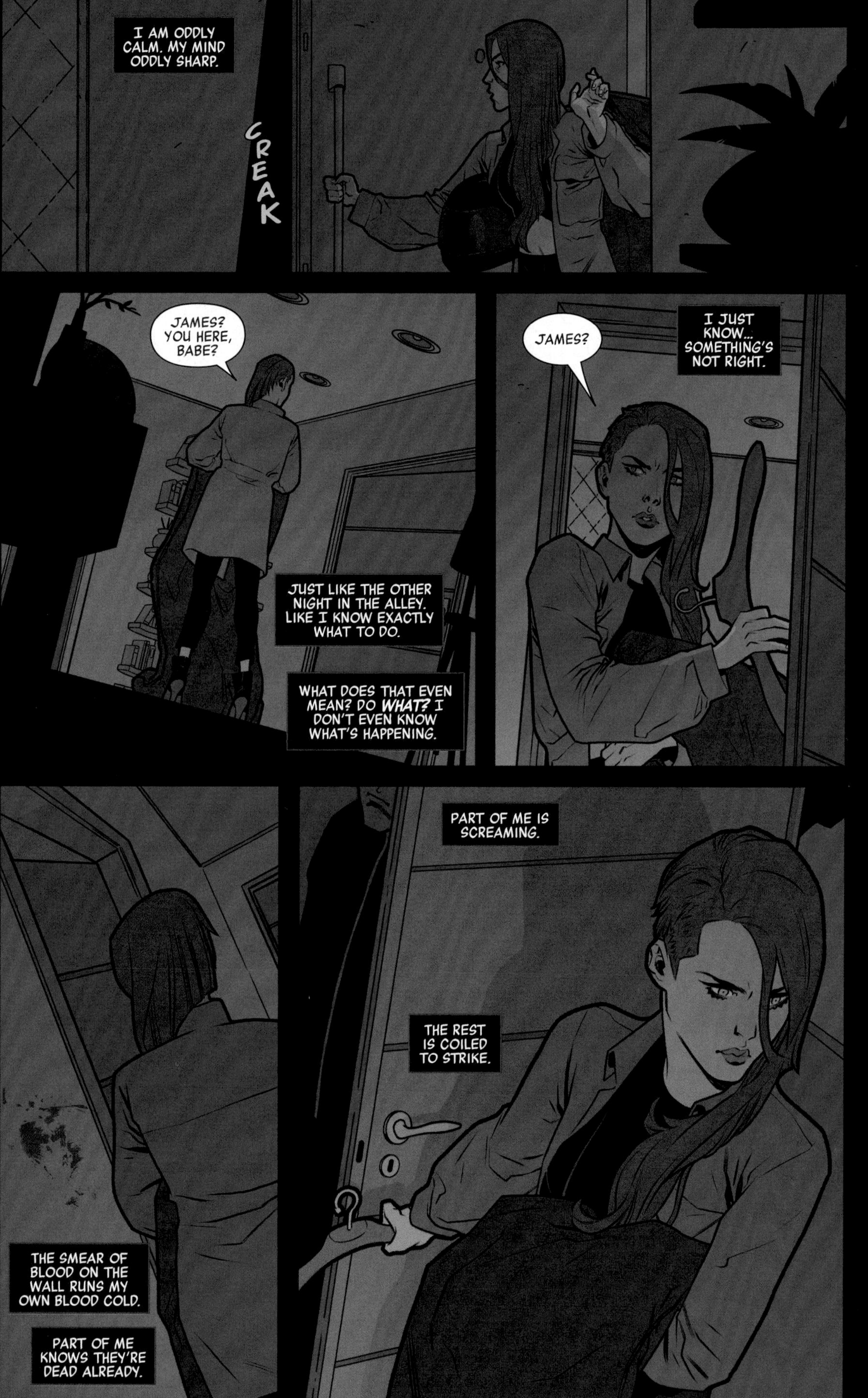
I AM ODDLY CALM. MY MIND ODDLY SHARP.
CREAK
JAMES? YOU HERE, BABE?
JUST LIKE THE OTHER NIGHT IN THE ALLEY. LIKE I KNOW EXACTLY WHAT TO DO.
WHAT DOES THAT EVEN MEAN? DO WHAT? I DON'T EVEN KNOW WHAT'S HAPPENING.
JAMES?
I JUST KNOW... SOMETHING'S NOT RIGHT.
THE SMEAR OF BLOOD ON THE WALL RUNS MY OWN BLOOD COLD.
PART OF ME KNOWS THEY'RE DEAD ALREADY.
PART OF ME IS SCREAMING.
THE REST IS COILED TO STRIKE.

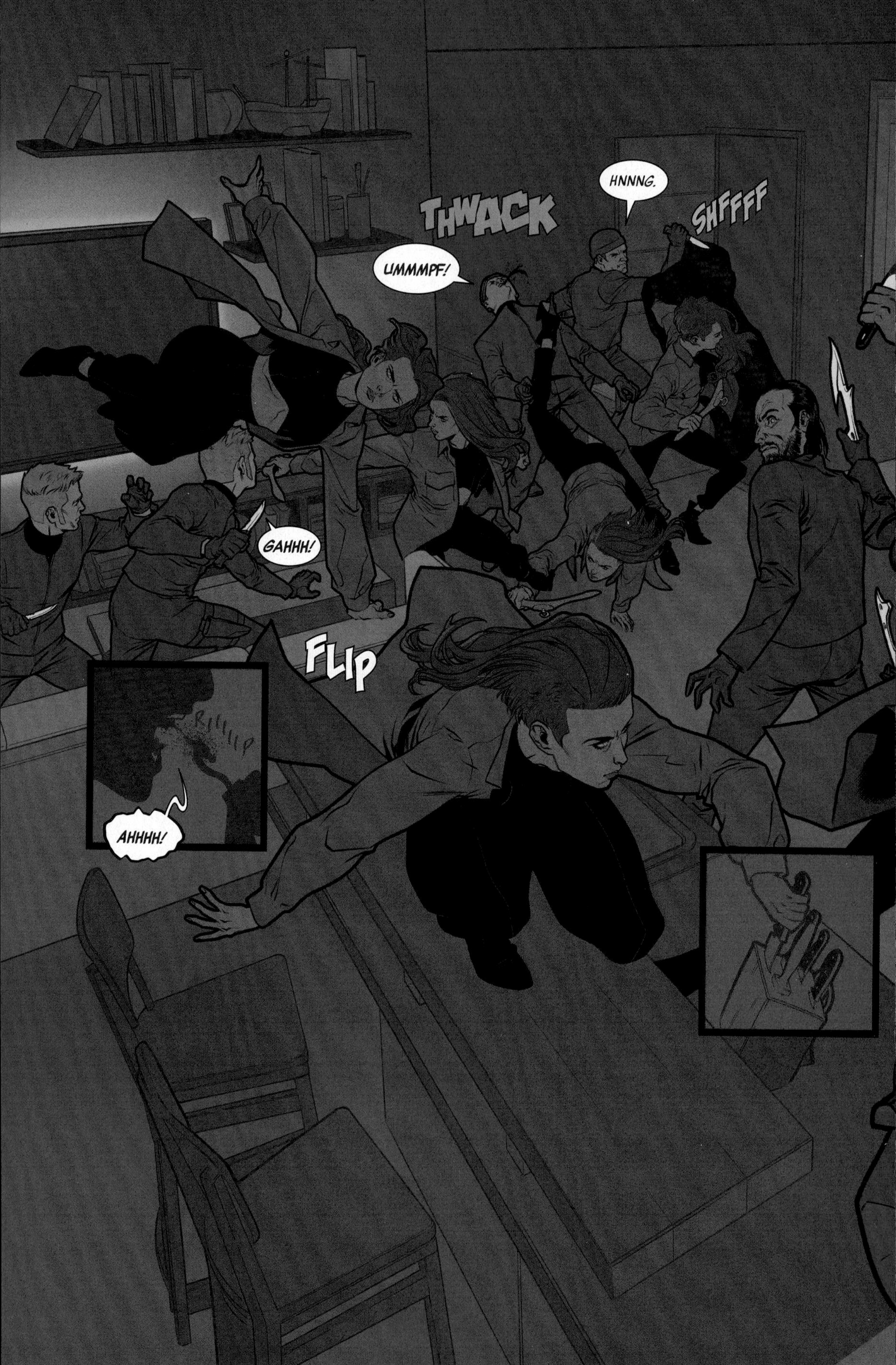
THWACK
UMMMPF!
HNNNG.
SHFFFF
GAHHH!
FLIP
RIIIIP
AHHHH!

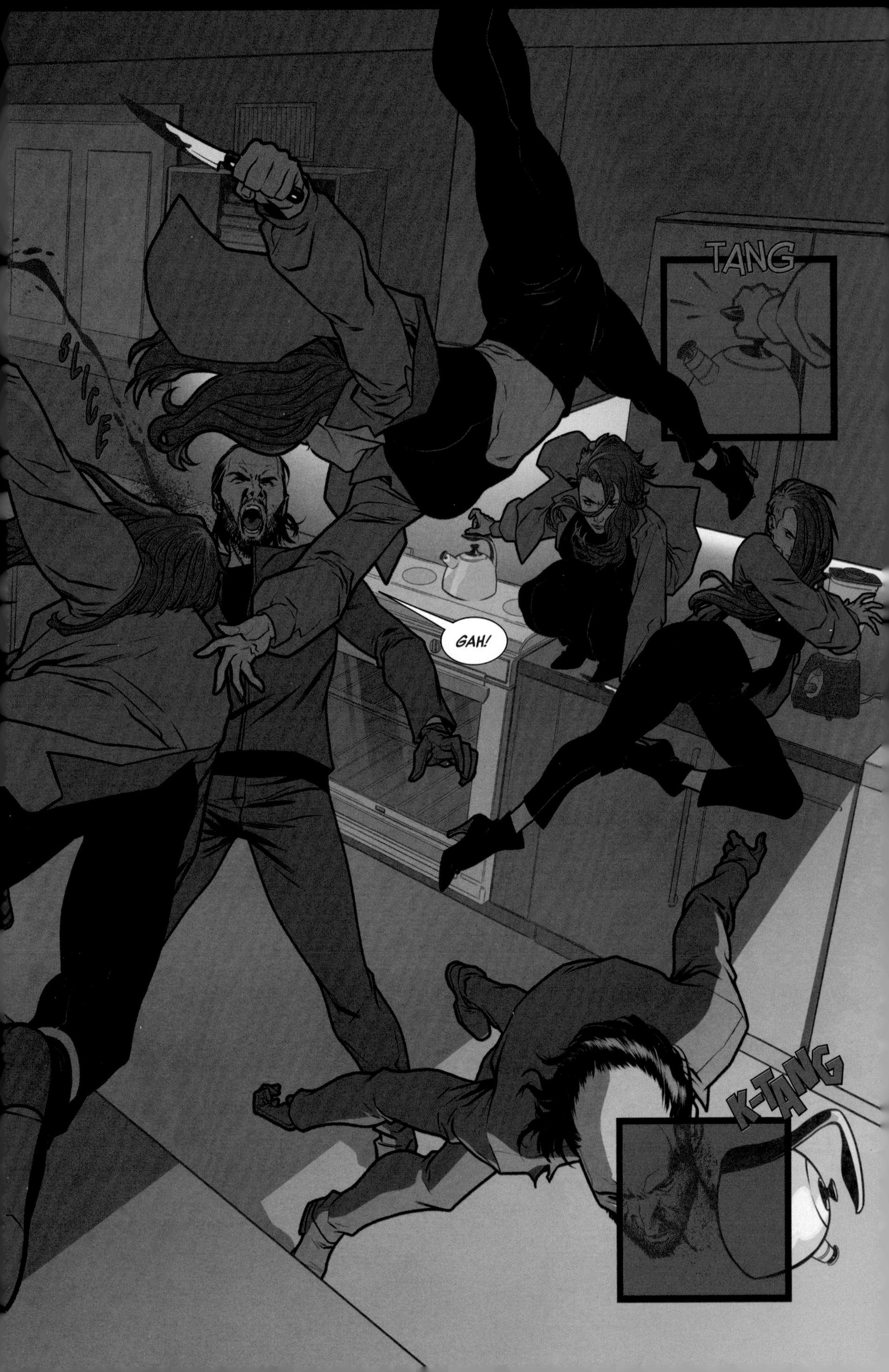
SLICE
TANG
GAH!
K-TANG

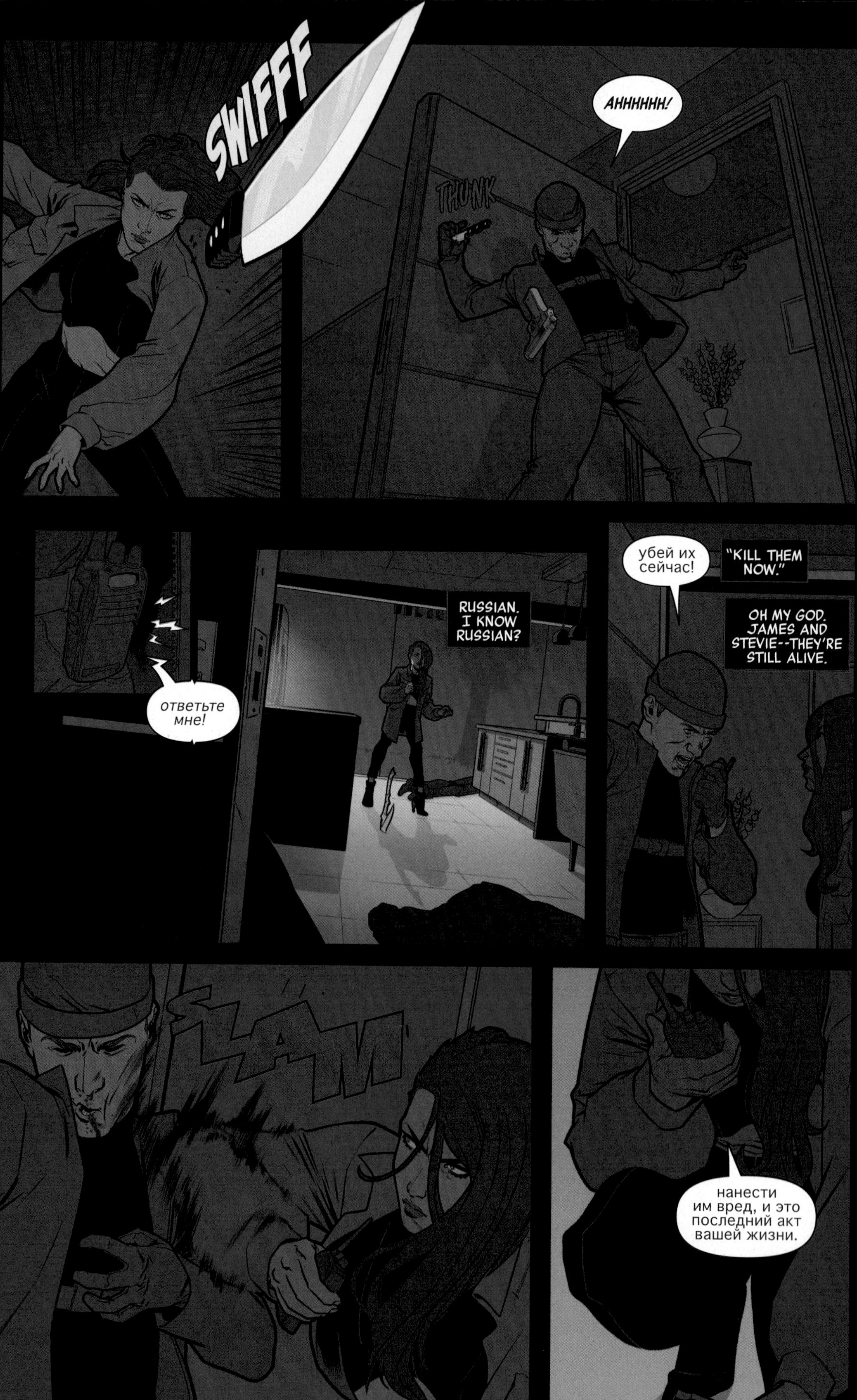
SWIFFF
AHHHHHH!
THUNK
ответьте
мне!
RUSSIAN.
I KNOW
RUSSIAN?
убей их
сейчас!
"KILL THEM
NOW."
OH MY GOD.
JAMES AND
STEVIE--THEY'RE
STILL ALIVE.
SLAM
нанести
им вред, и это
последний акт
вашей жизни.

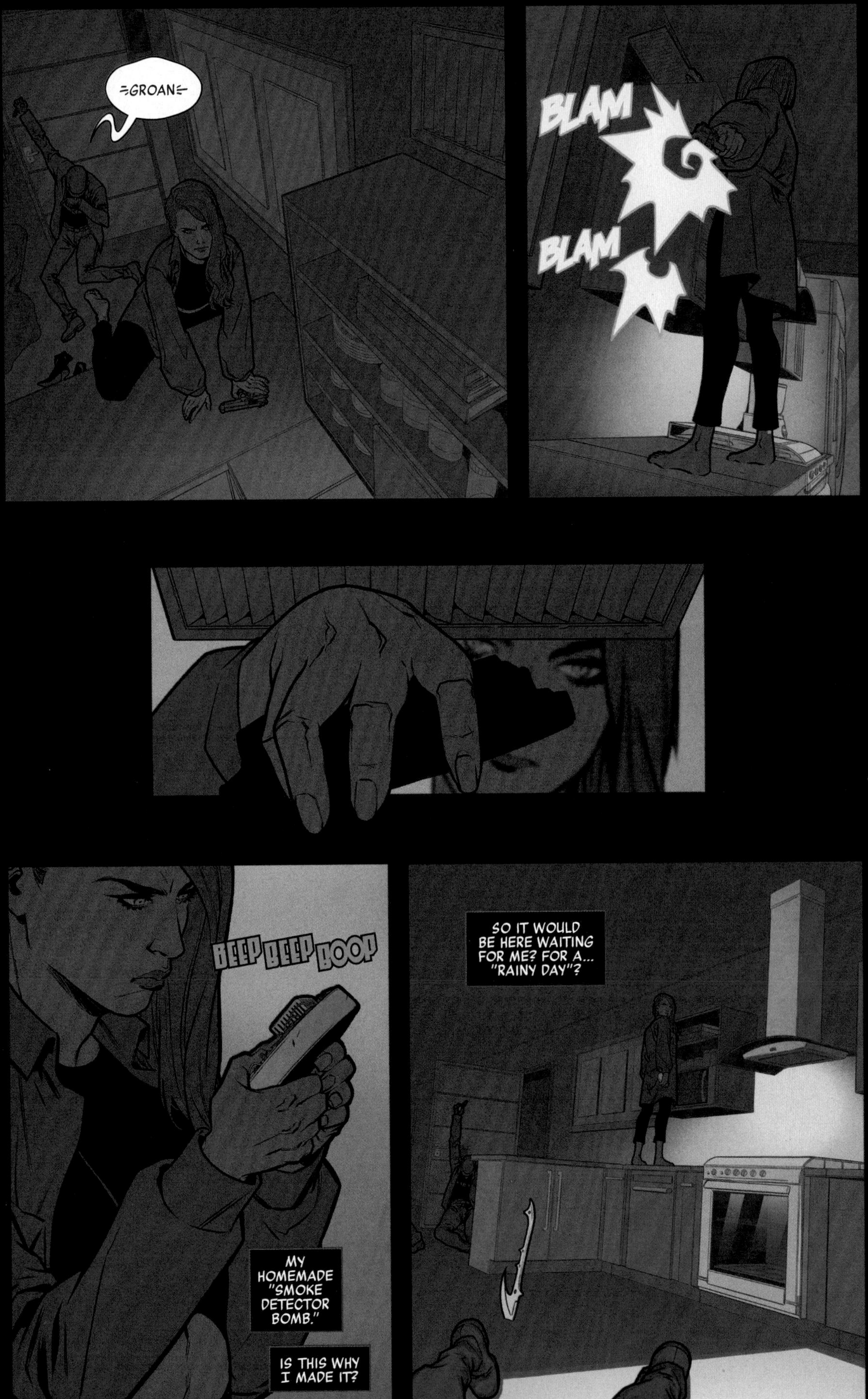

GROAN
BLAM
BLAM
BEEP BEEP BOOP
MY HOMEMADE "SMOKE DETECTOR BOMB."
IS THIS WHY I MADE IT?
SO IT WOULD BE HERE WAITING FOR ME? FOR A... "RAINY DAY"?

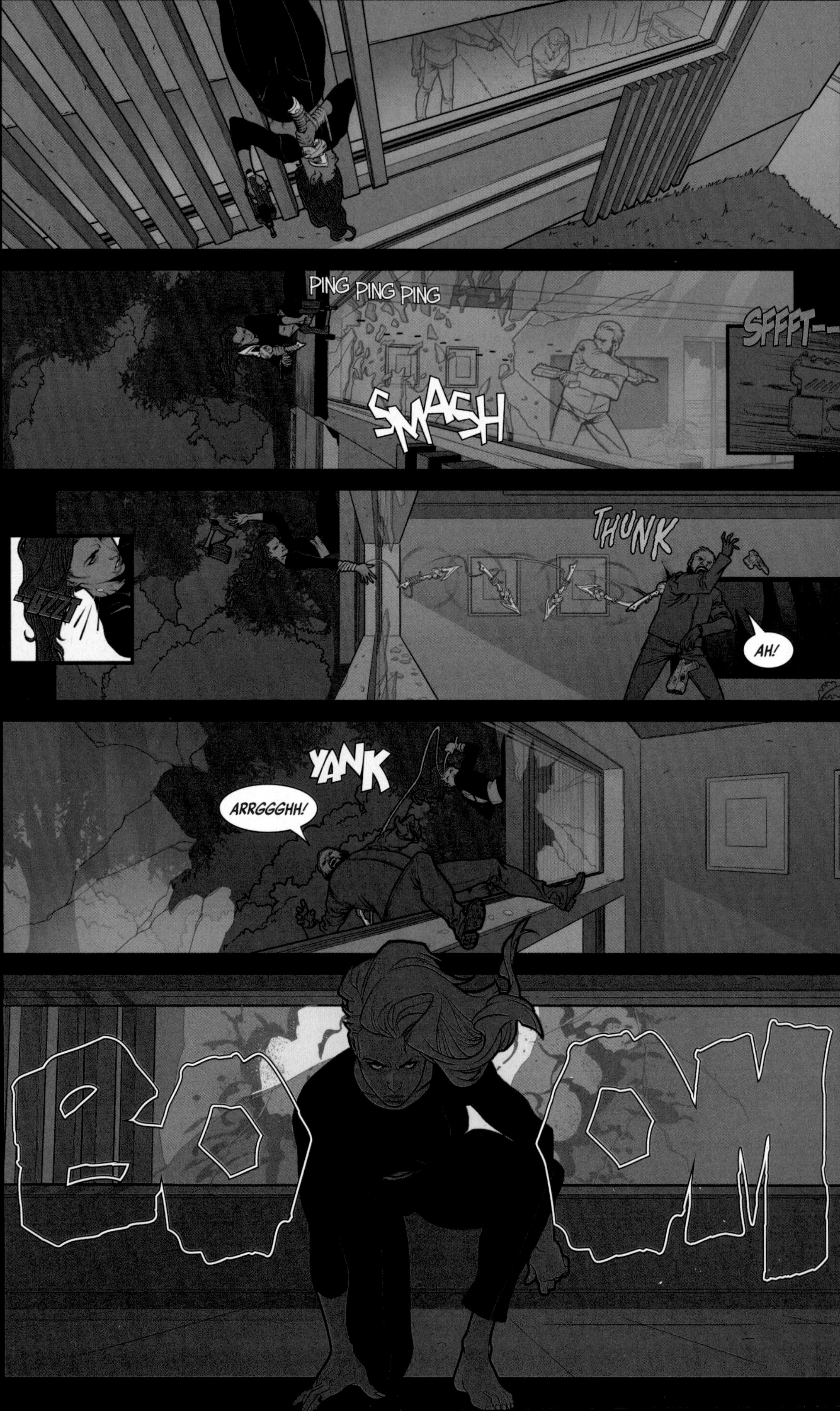
PING PING PING
SFFFT--
SMASH
BZZT
THUNK
AH!
YANK
ARRGGGHH!
BOOM

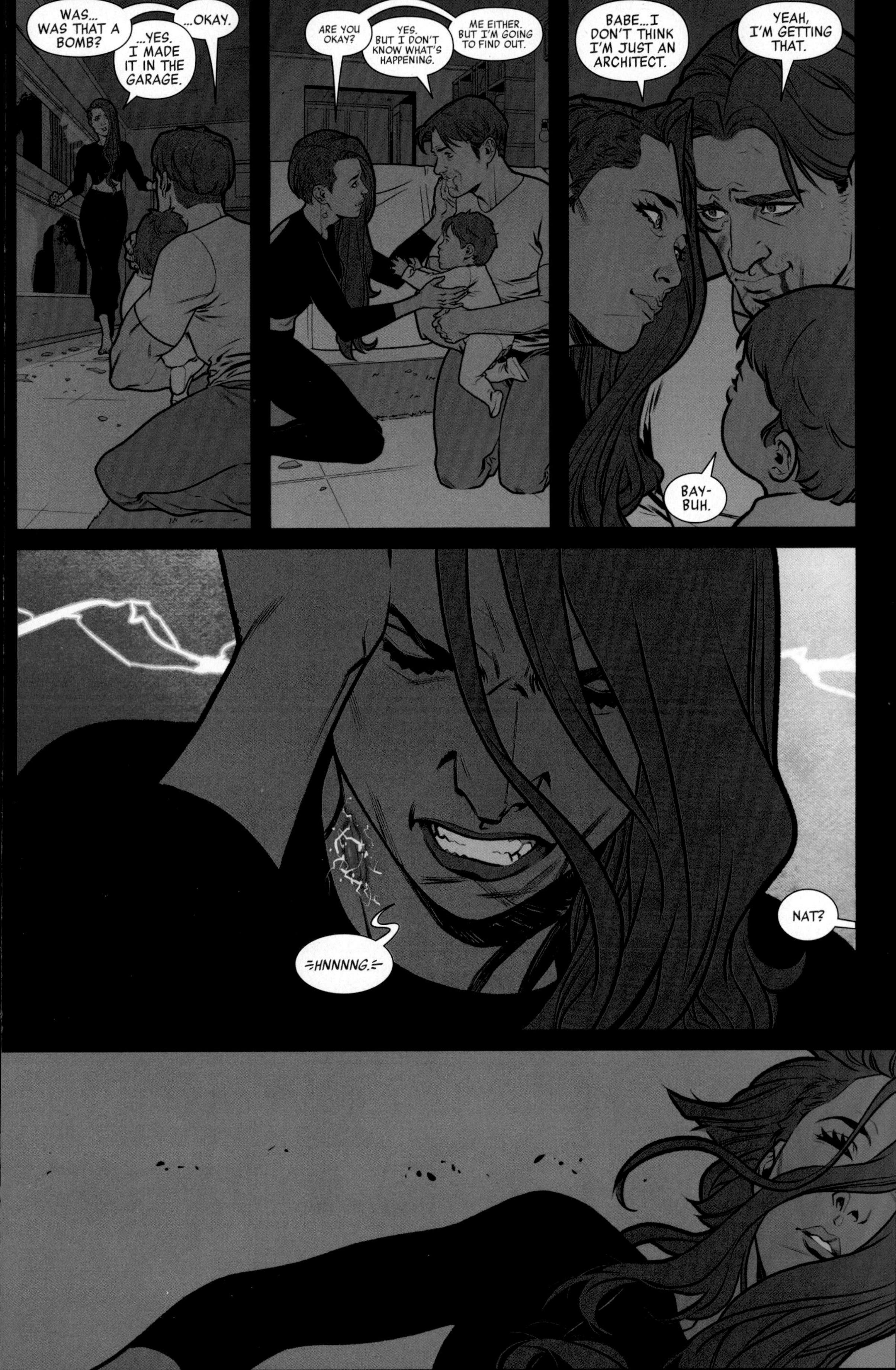
WAS... WAS THAT A BOMB?
...YES. I MADE IT IN THE GARAGE.
...OKAY.
ARE YOU OKAY?
YES. BUT I DON'T KNOW WHAT'S HAPPENING.
ME EITHER. BUT I'M GOING TO FIND OUT.
BABE...I DON'T THINK I'M JUST AN ARCHITECT.
YEAH, I'M GETTING THAT.
BAY-BUH.
NAT?
HNNNNG.

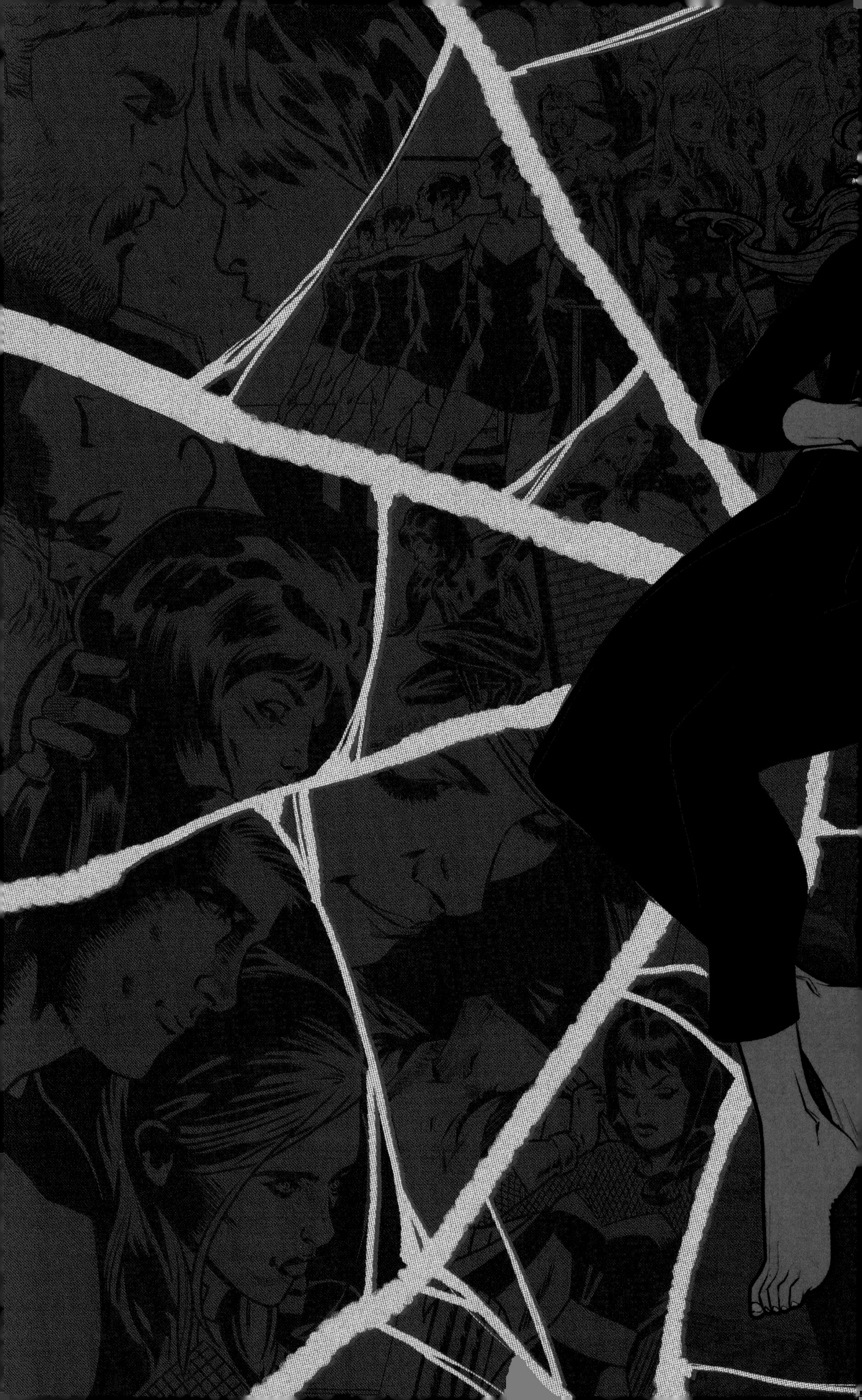

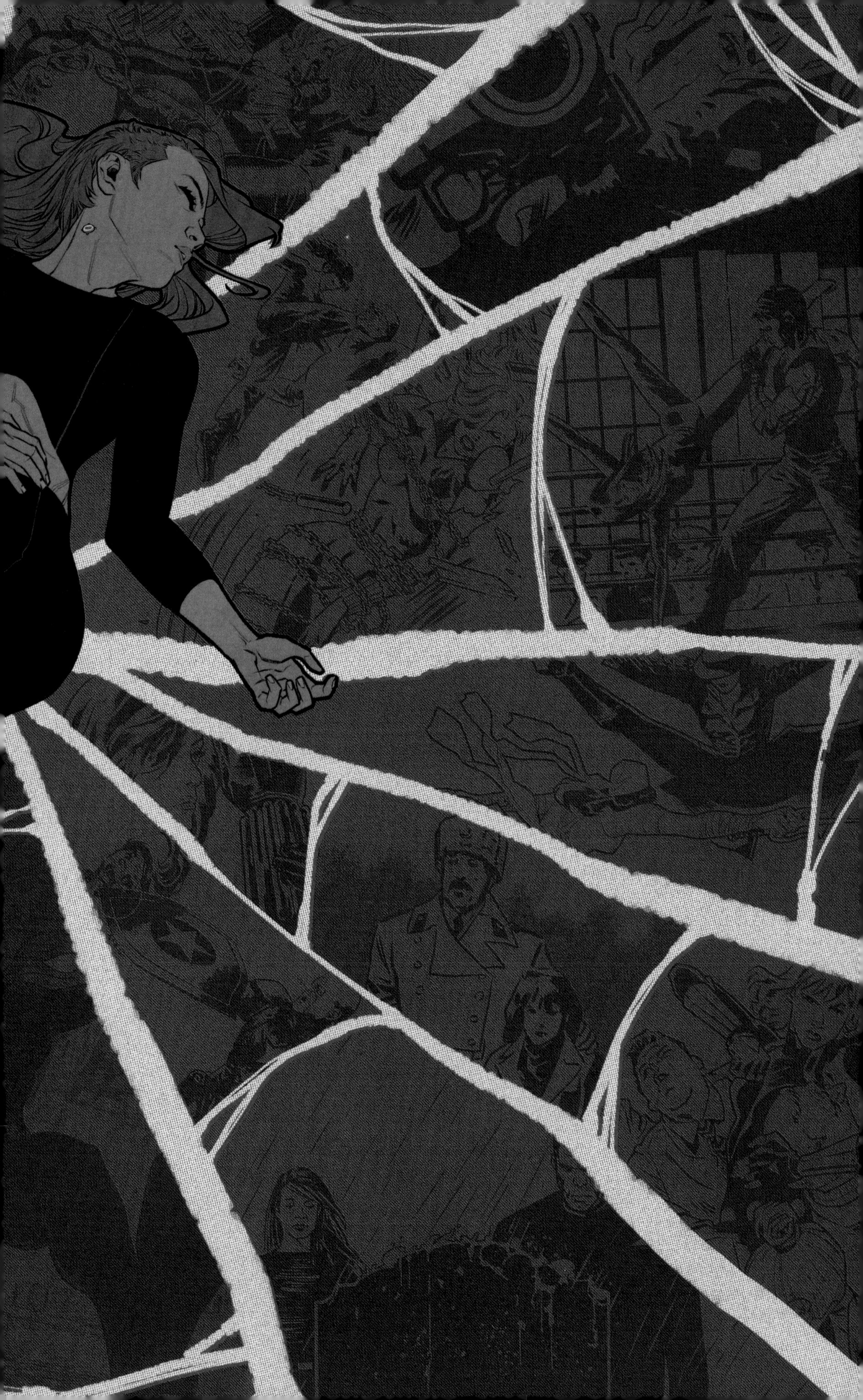

NATALIE... BABY. NAT, WAKE UP, HONEY. OH MY GOD.

MOMMA?

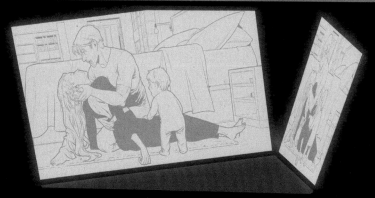

YOU BETTER HOPE THIS PROCESS KILLS HER, LION.

OR *SHE* WON'T HAVE TO KILL YOU, I'LL DO IT MYSELF.

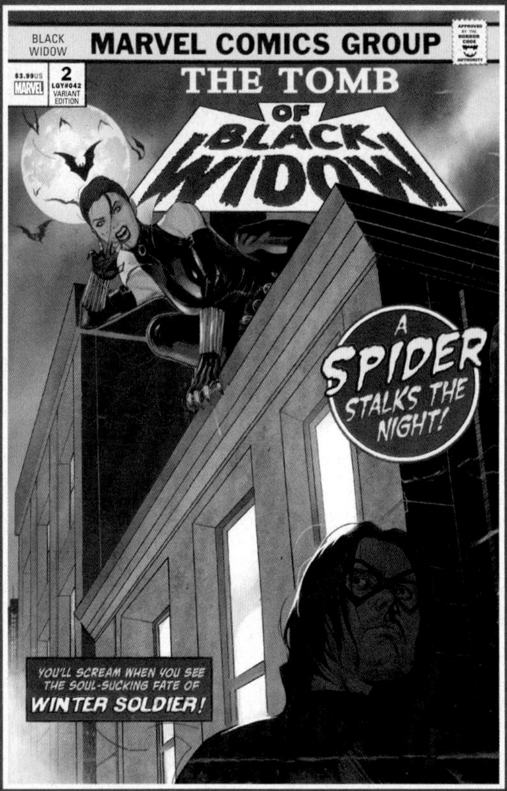
BLACK WIDOW
MARVEL COMICS GROUP
$3.99US
2
LGY#042
VARIANT EDITION
THE TOMB OF BLACK WIDOW
A SPIDER STALKS THE NIGHT!
YOU'LL SCREAM WHEN YOU SEE THE SOUL-SUCKING FATE OF WINTER SOLDIER!

#2 HORROR VARIANT BY JOSHUA "SWAY" SWABY

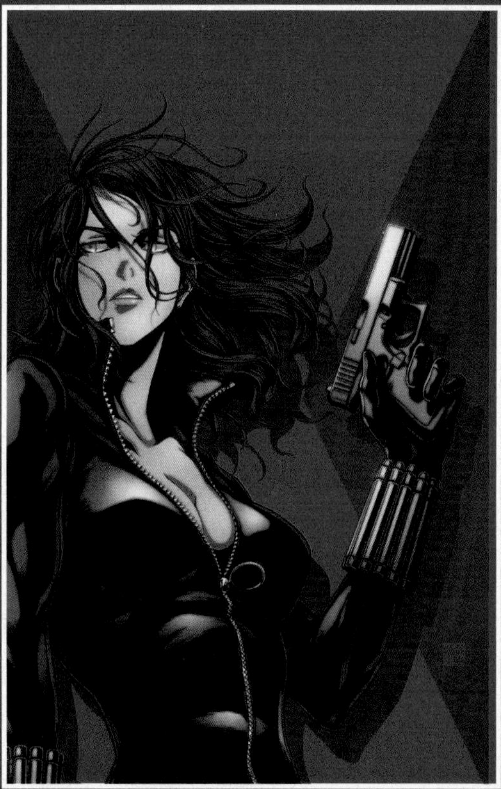

#2 VARIANT BY TAKASHI OKAZAKI & JORDIE BELLAIRE

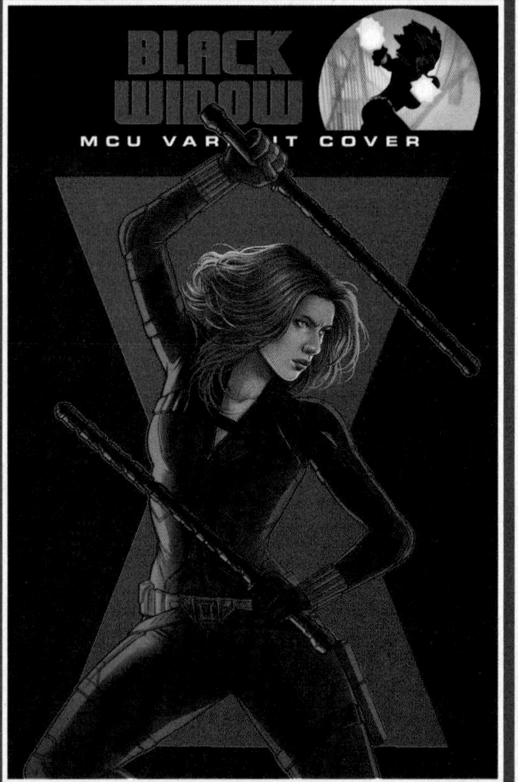
BLACK WIDOW

#3 MCU VARIANT BY JEN BARTEL

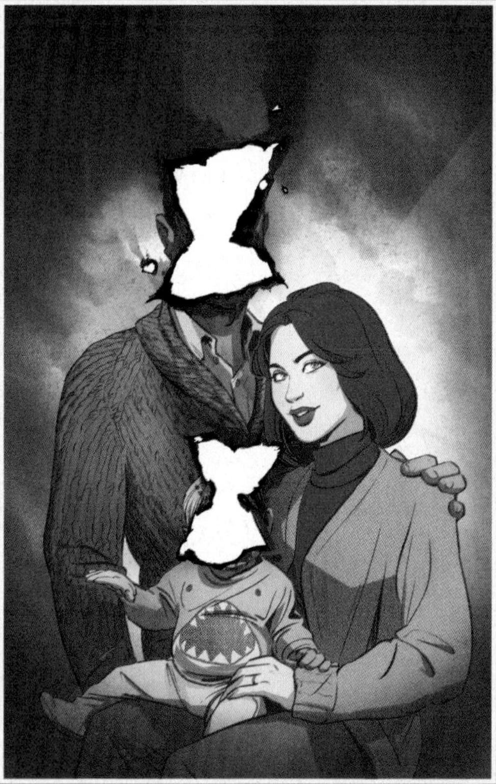

#3 VARIANT BY ANNIE WU

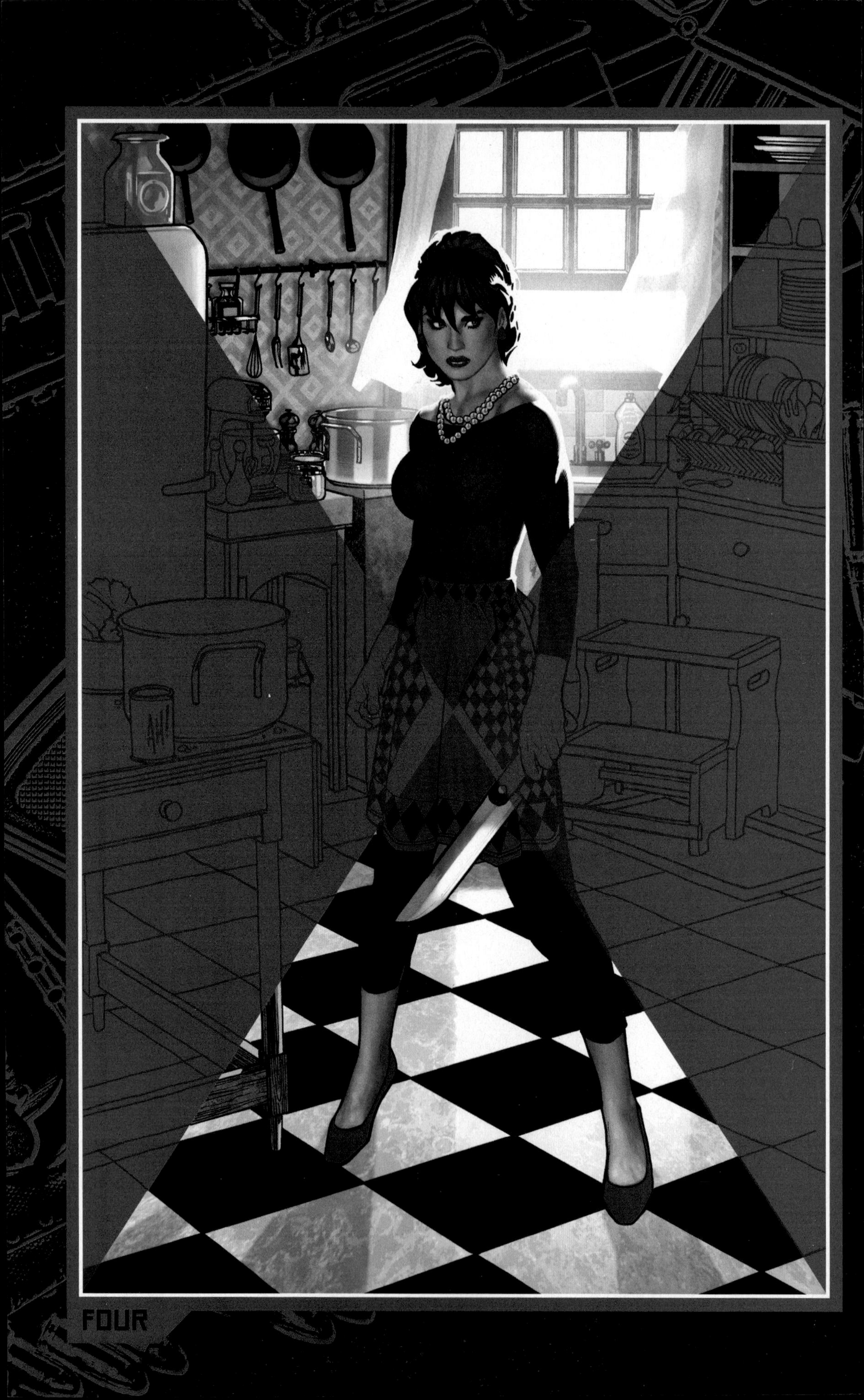
AH!

FOUR

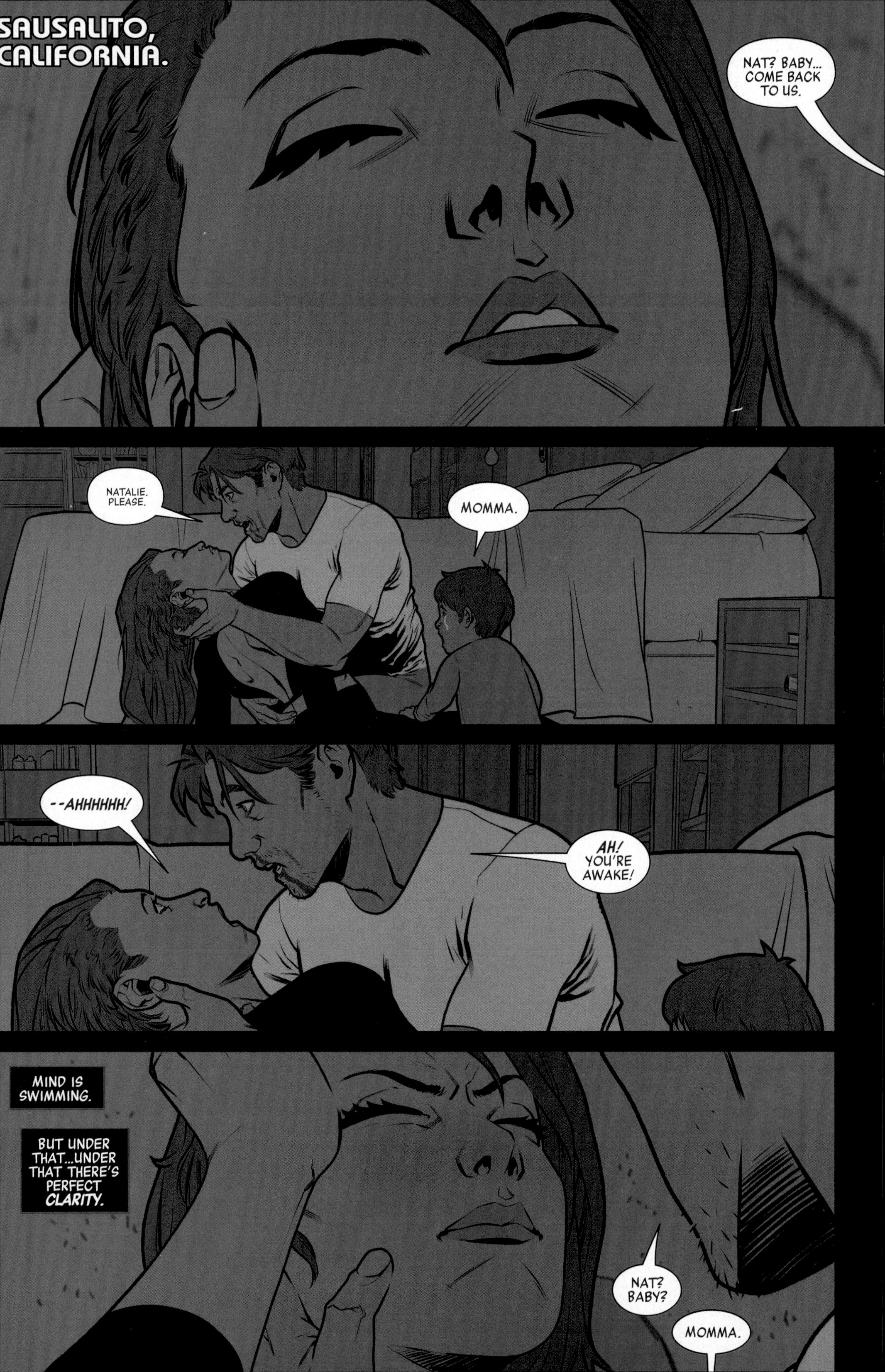
SAUSALITO, CALIFORNIA.
NAT? BABY... COME BACK TO US.
NATALIE. PLEASE.
MOMMA.
--AHHHHHH!
AH! YOU'RE AWAKE!
MIND IS SWIMMING.
BUT UNDER THAT...UNDER THAT THERE'S PERFECT CLARITY.
NAT? BABY?
MOMMA.

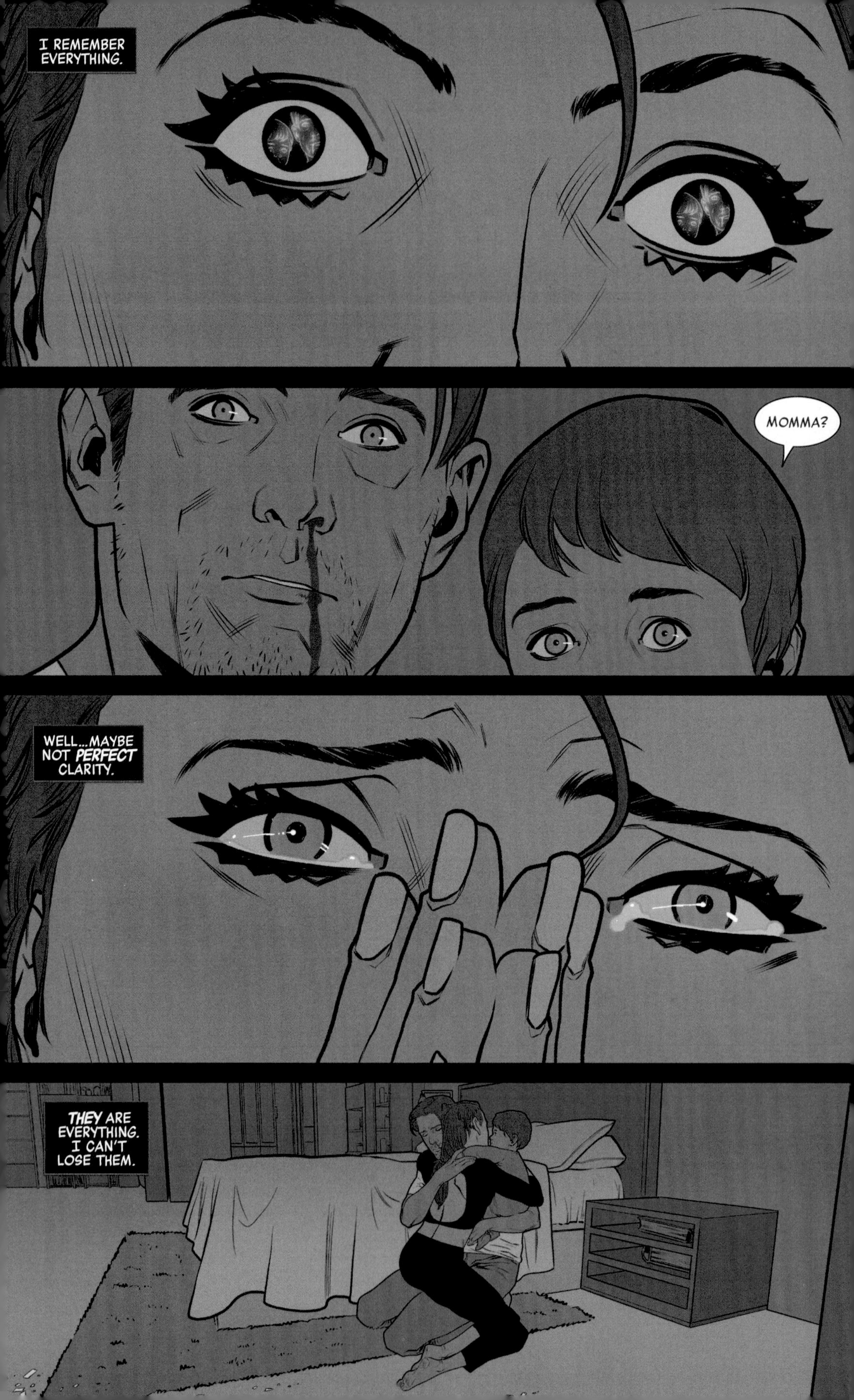
I REMEMBER EVERYTHING.
MOMMA?
WELL...MAYBE NOT PERFECT CLARITY.
THEY ARE EVERYTHING. I CAN'T LOSE THEM.

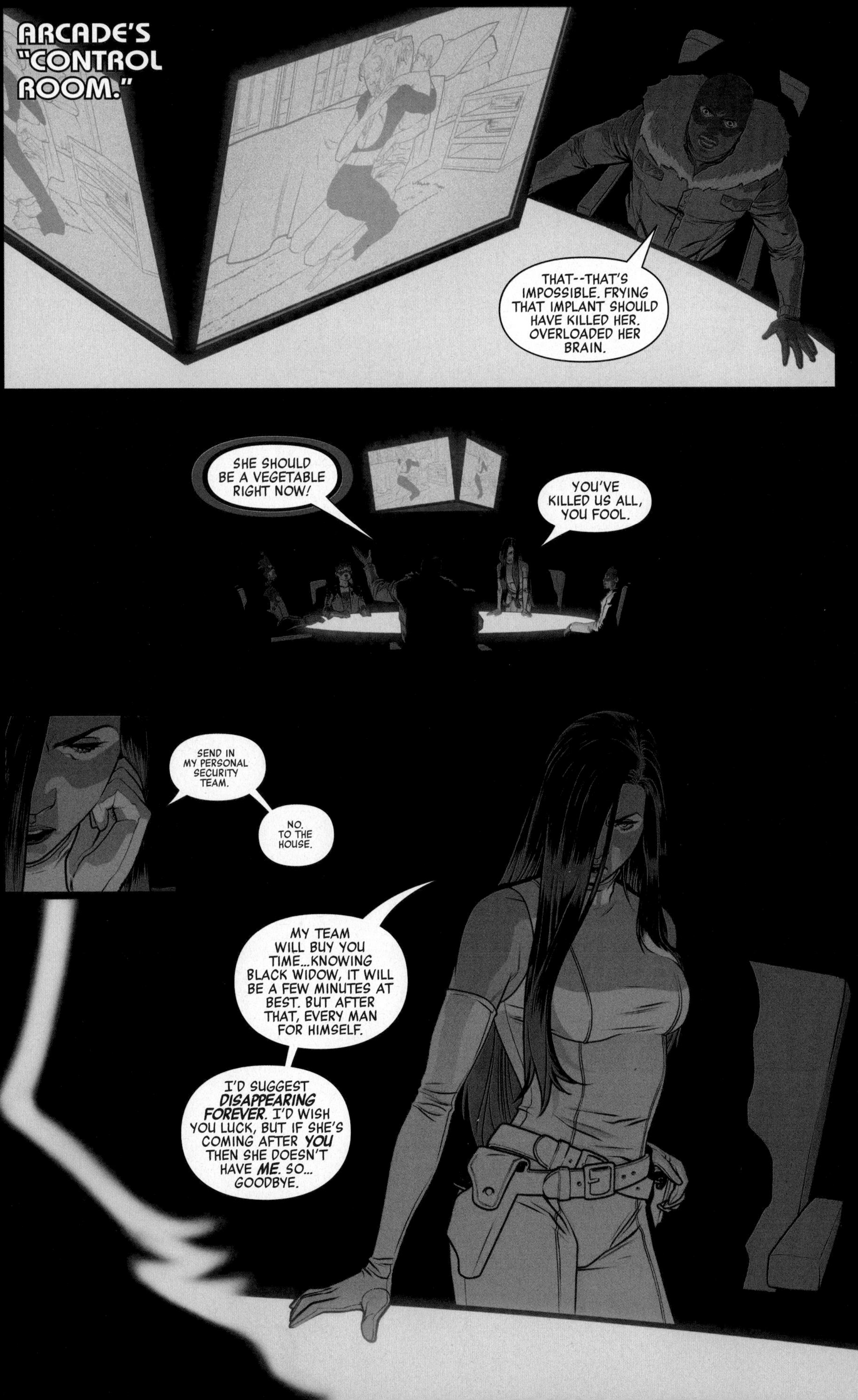

ARCADE'S "CONTROL ROOM."
THAT--THAT'S IMPOSSIBLE. FRYING THAT IMPLANT SHOULD HAVE KILLED HER. OVERLOADED HER BRAIN.
SHE SHOULD BE A VEGETABLE RIGHT NOW!
YOU'VE KILLED US ALL, YOU FOOL.
SEND IN MY PERSONAL SECURITY TEAM.
NO. TO THE HOUSE.
MY TEAM WILL BUY YOU TIME...KNOWING BLACK WIDOW, IT WILL BE A FEW MINUTES AT BEST. BUT AFTER THAT, EVERY MAN FOR HIMSELF.
I'D SUGGEST DISAPPEARING FOREVER. I'D WISH YOU LUCK, BUT IF SHE'S COMING AFTER YOU THEN SHE DOESN'T HAVE ME. SO... GOODBYE.

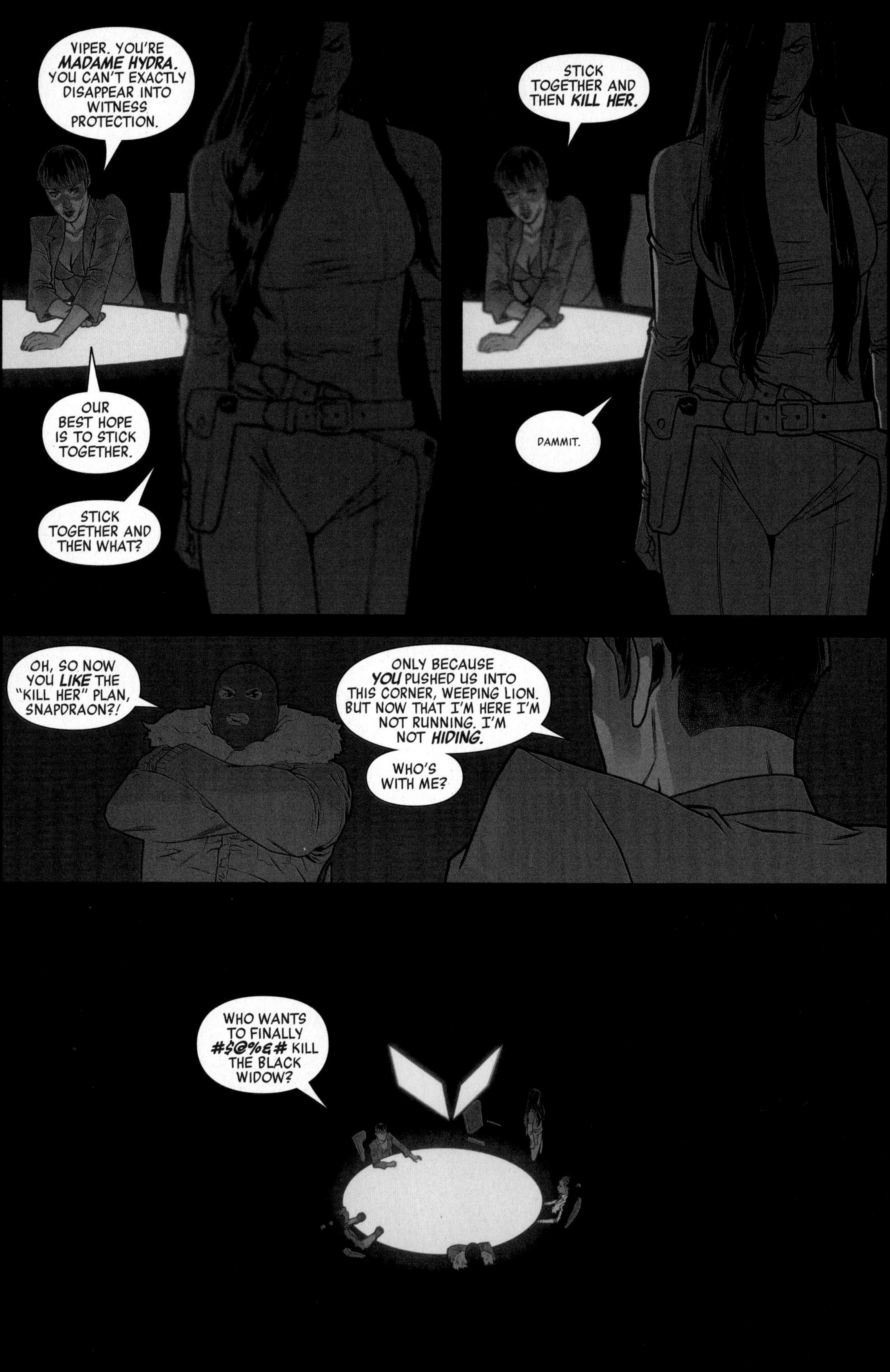
VIPER. YOU'RE **MADAME HYDRA.** YOU CAN'T EXACTLY DISAPPEAR INTO WITNESS PROTECTION.
OUR BEST HOPE IS TO STICK TOGETHER.
STICK TOGETHER AND THEN WHAT?
STICK TOGETHER AND THEN **KILL HER.**
DAMMIT.
OH, SO NOW YOU **LIKE** THE "KILL HER" PLAN, SNAPDRAON?!
ONLY BECAUSE **YOU** PUSHED US INTO THIS CORNER, WEEPING LION. BUT NOW THAT I'M HERE I'M NOT RUNNING. I'M NOT **HIDING.**
WHO'S WITH ME?
WHO WANTS TO FINALLY **#$@%&#** KILL THE BLACK WIDOW?

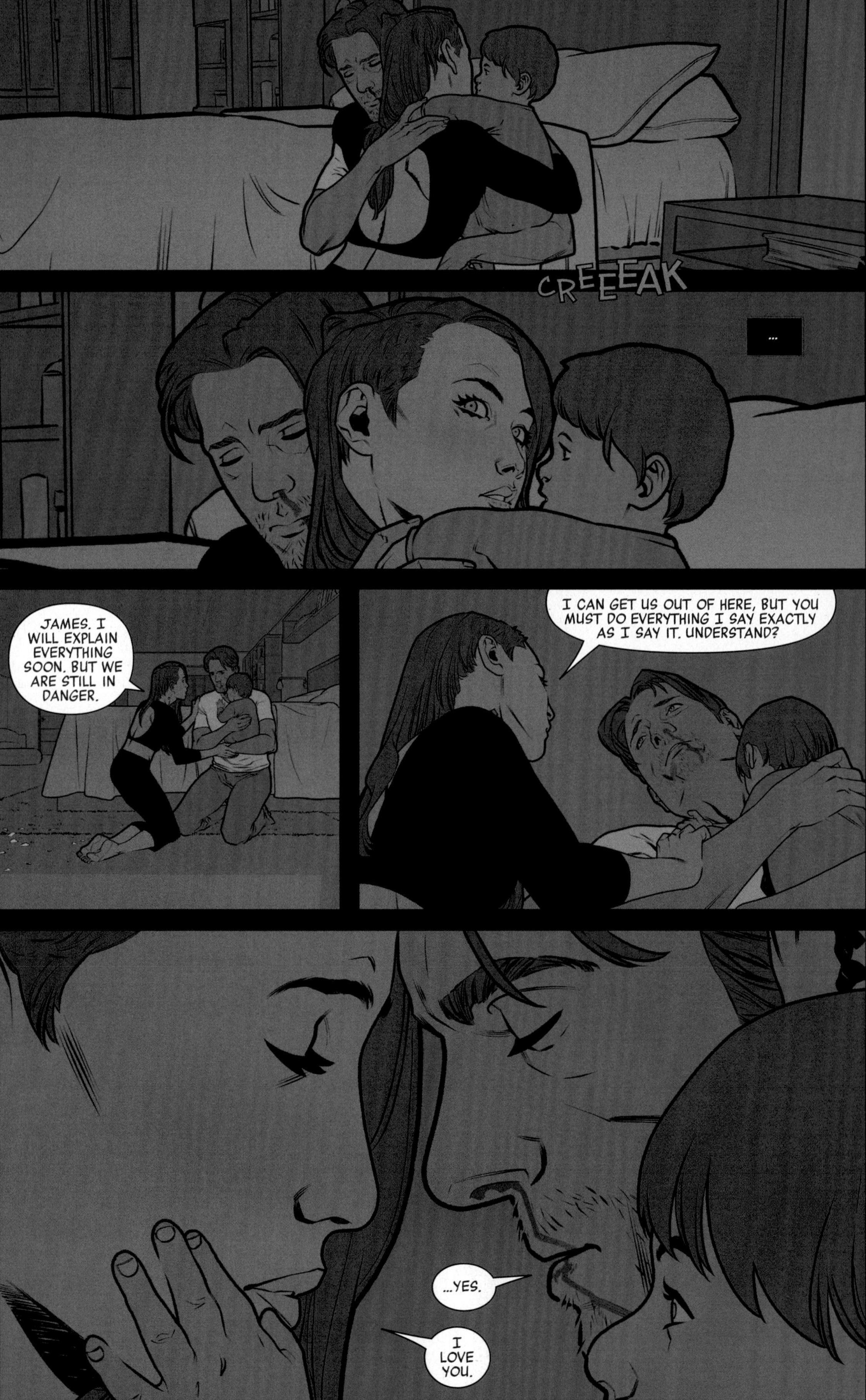

CREEEAK
...
JAMES. I WILL EXPLAIN EVERYTHING SOON. BUT WE ARE STILL IN DANGER.
I CAN GET US OUT OF HERE, BUT YOU MUST DO EVERYTHING I SAY EXACTLY AS I SAY IT. UNDERSTAND?
...YES.
I LOVE YOU.

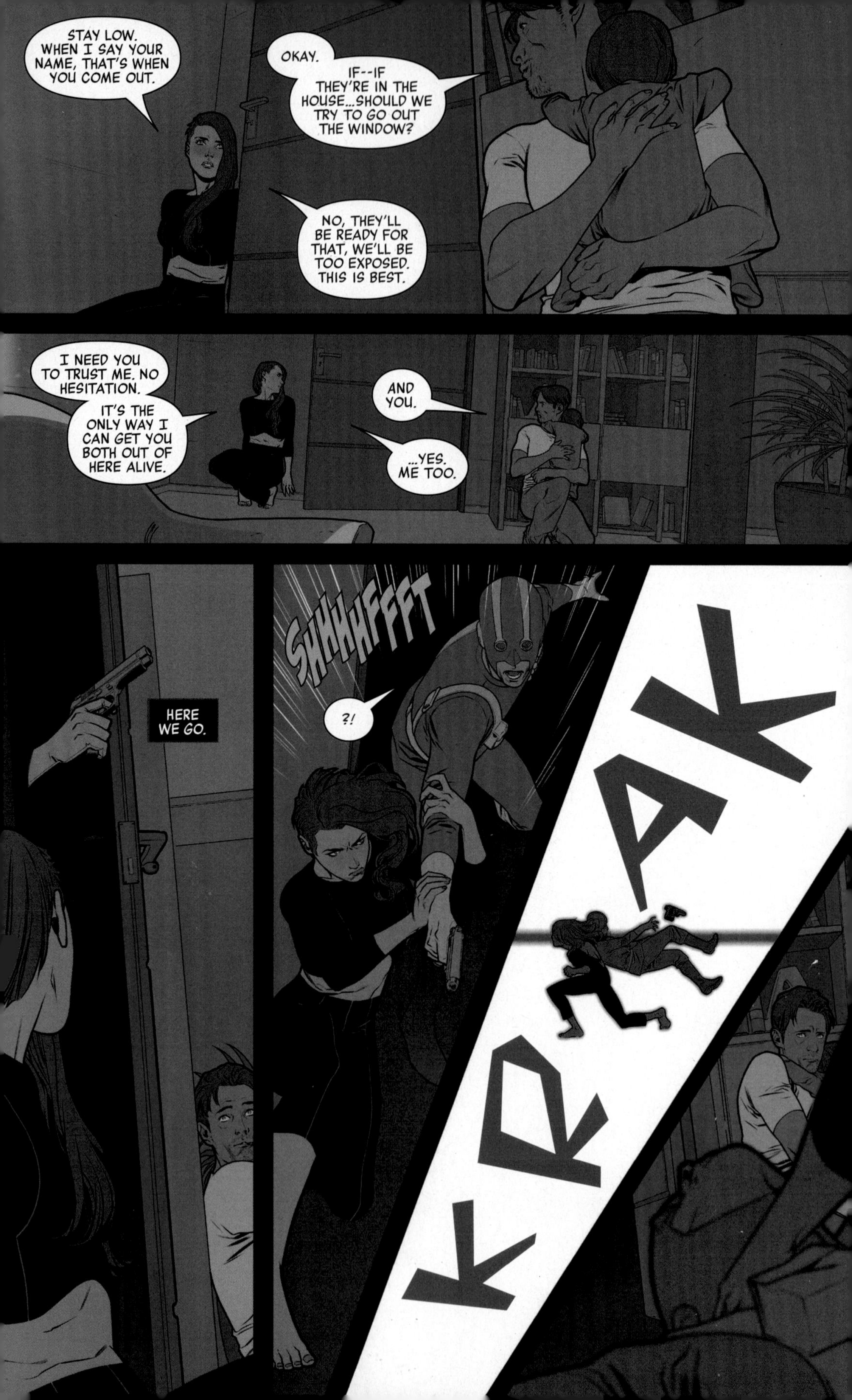
STAY LOW. WHEN I SAY YOUR NAME, THAT'S WHEN YOU COME OUT.
OKAY.
IF--IF THEY'RE IN THE HOUSE...SHOULD WE TRY TO GO OUT THE WINDOW?
NO, THEY'LL BE READY FOR THAT, WE'LL BE TOO EXPOSED. THIS IS BEST.
I NEED YOU TO TRUST ME. NO HESITATION.
IT'S THE ONLY WAY I CAN GET YOU BOTH OUT OF HERE ALIVE.
AND YOU.
...YES. ME TOO.
HERE WE GO.
SHHHHFFFT
?!
KRAK

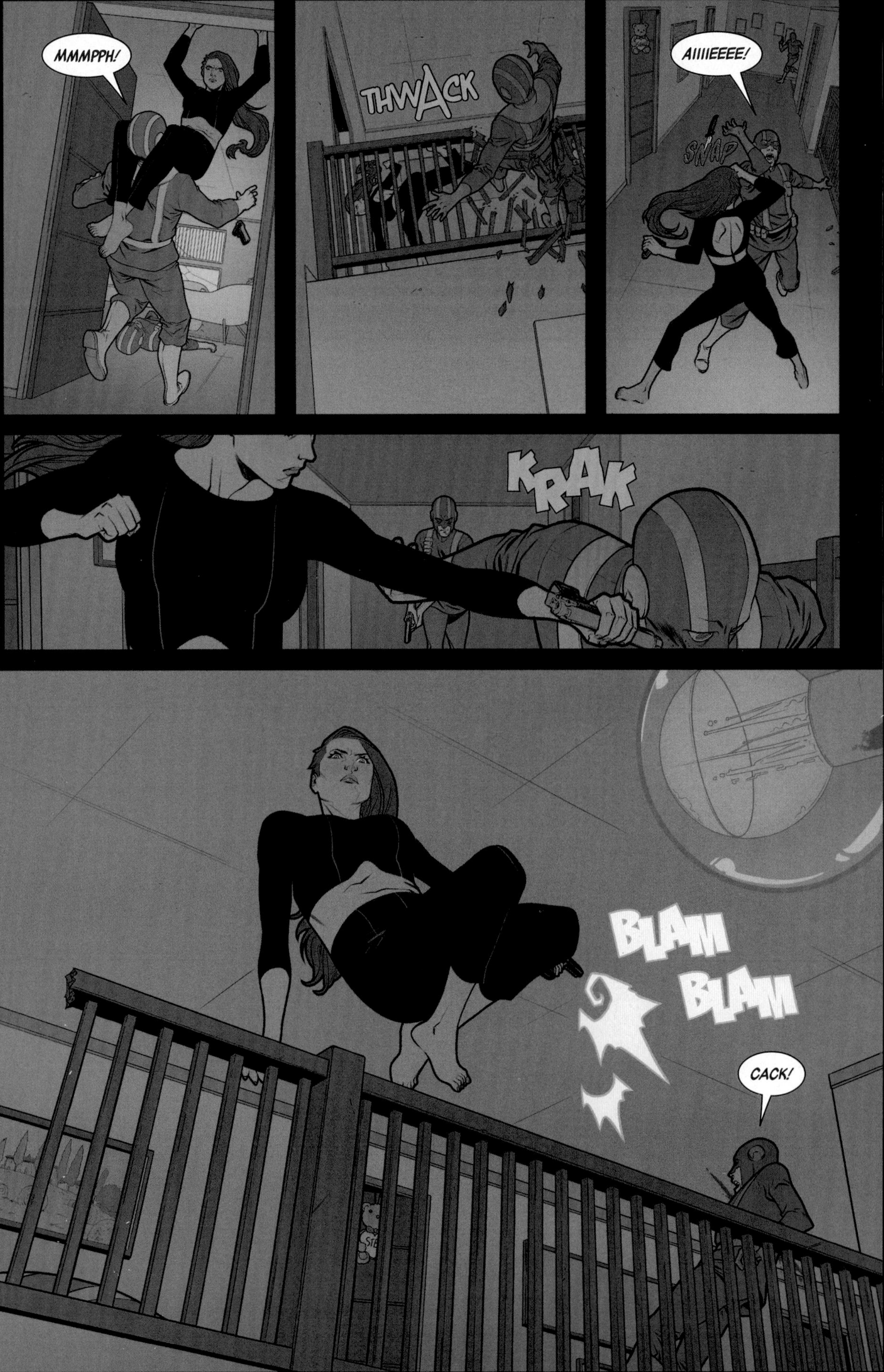
MMMPPH!
THWACK
AIIIIEEEE!
SNAP
KRAK
BLAM
BLAM
CACK!

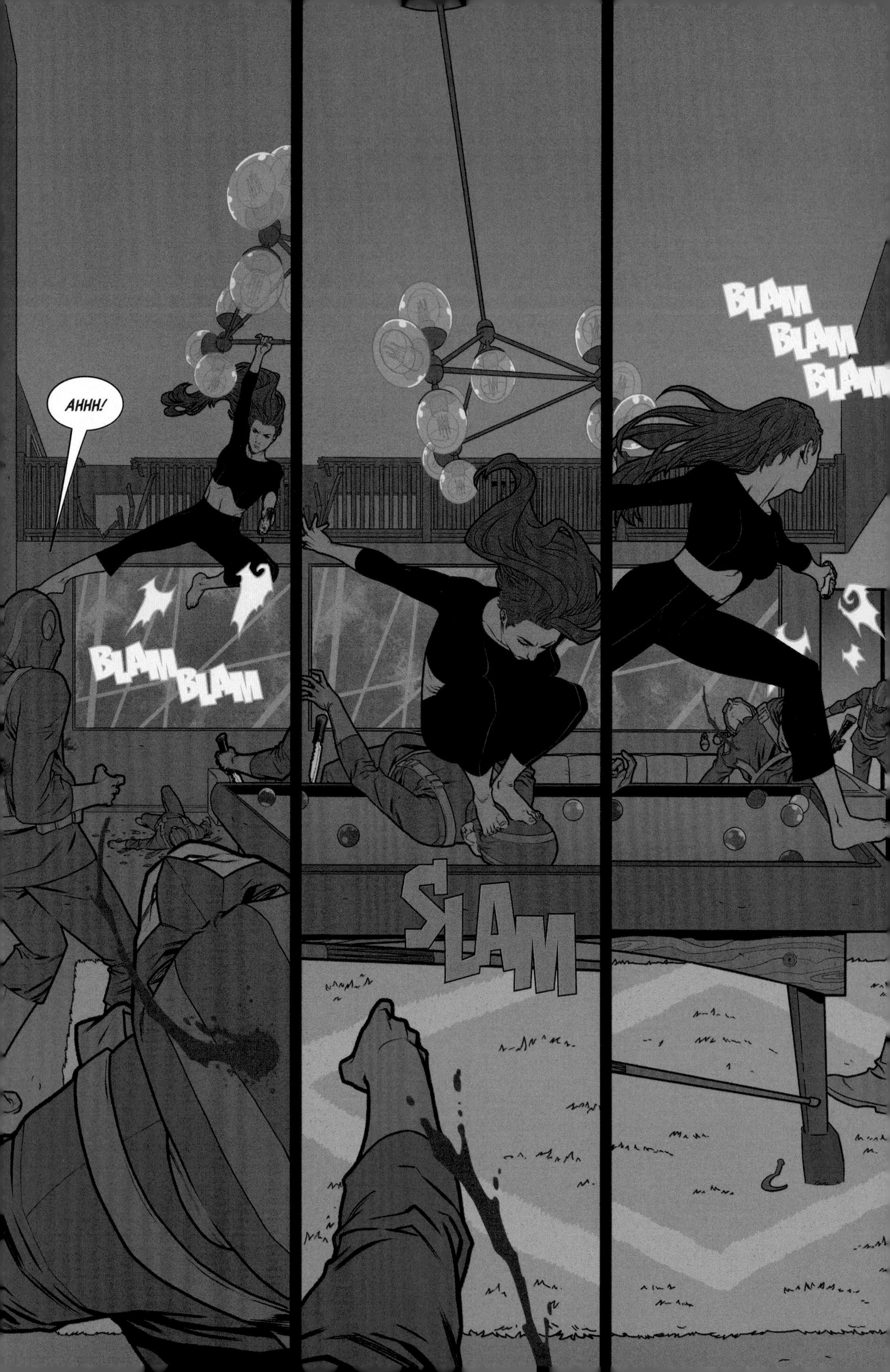
AHHH!
BLAM BLAM
SLAM
BLAM
BLAM
BLAM

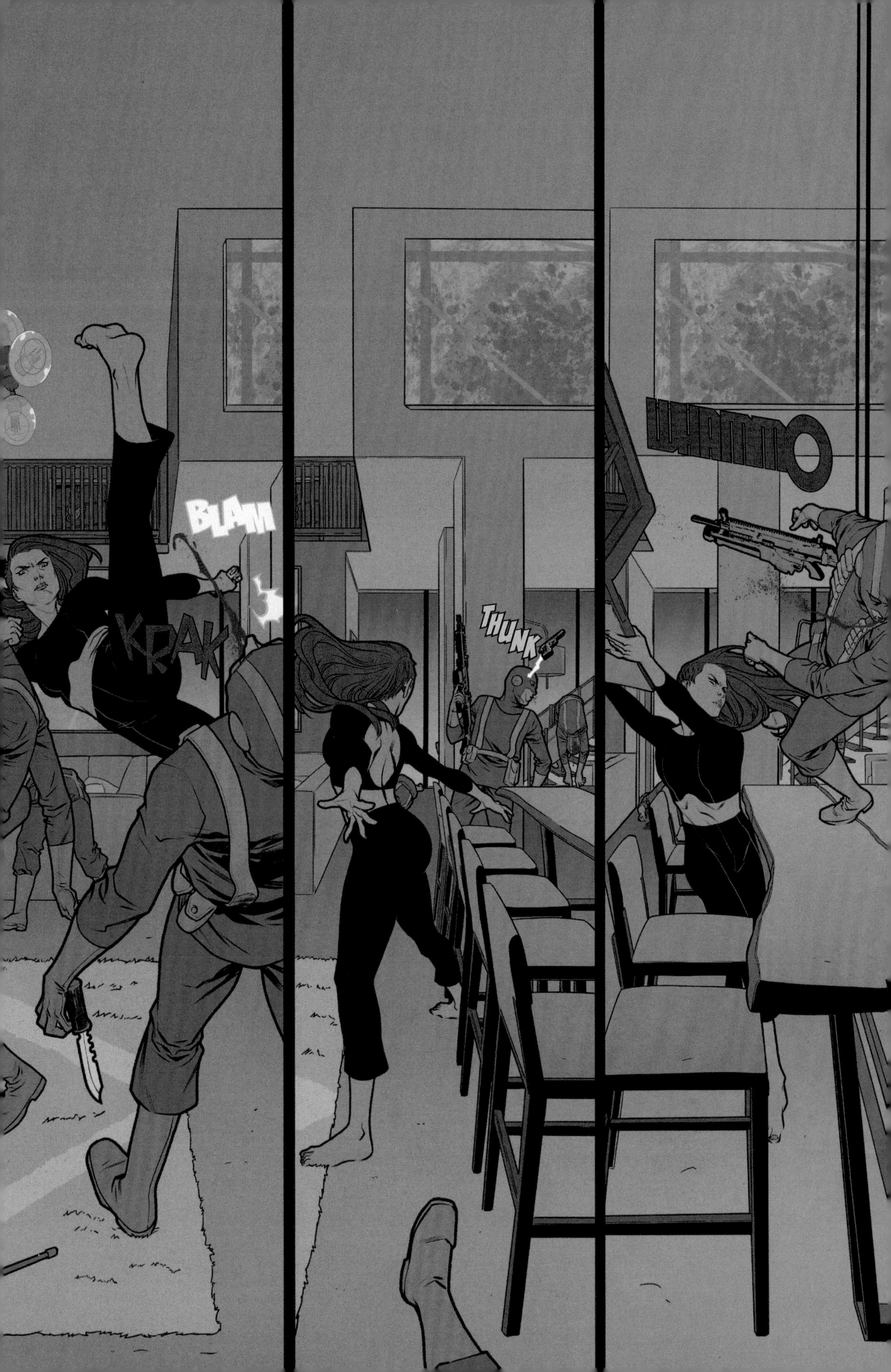
BLAM
KRAK
THUNK
WHAMMO

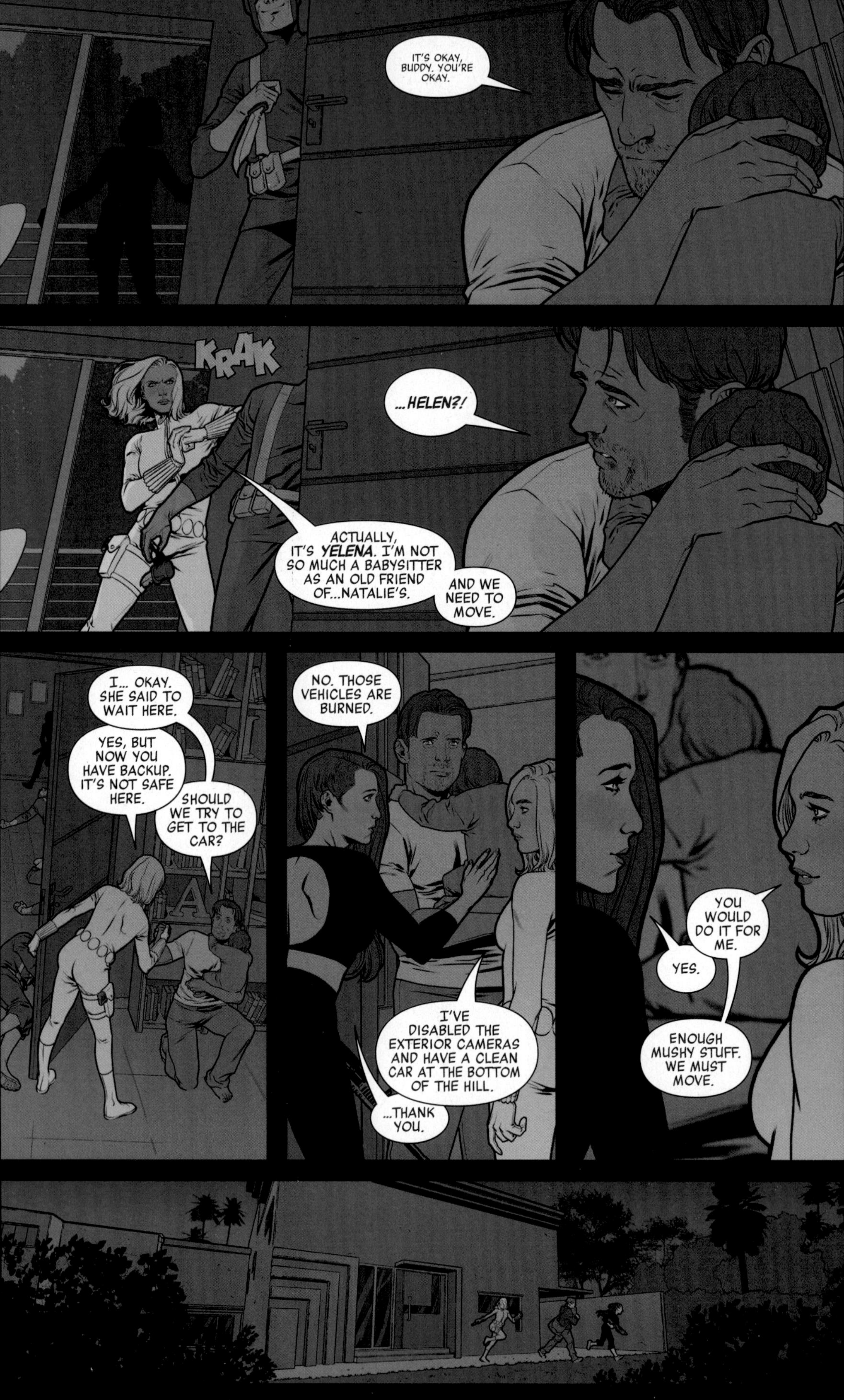
IT'S OKAY, BUDDY. YOU'RE OKAY.
KRAK
...HELEN?!
ACTUALLY, IT'S YELENA. I'M NOT SO MUCH A BABYSITTER AS AN OLD FRIEND OF...NATALIE'S.
AND WE NEED TO MOVE.
I... OKAY. SHE SAID TO WAIT HERE.
YES, BUT NOW YOU HAVE BACKUP. IT'S NOT SAFE HERE.
SHOULD WE TRY TO GET TO THE CAR?
NO. THOSE VEHICLES ARE BURNED.
I'VE DISABLED THE EXTERIOR CAMERAS AND HAVE A CLEAN CAR AT THE BOTTOM OF THE HILL.
...THANK YOU.
YOU WOULD DO IT FOR ME.
YES.
ENOUGH MUSHY STUFF. WE MUST MOVE.

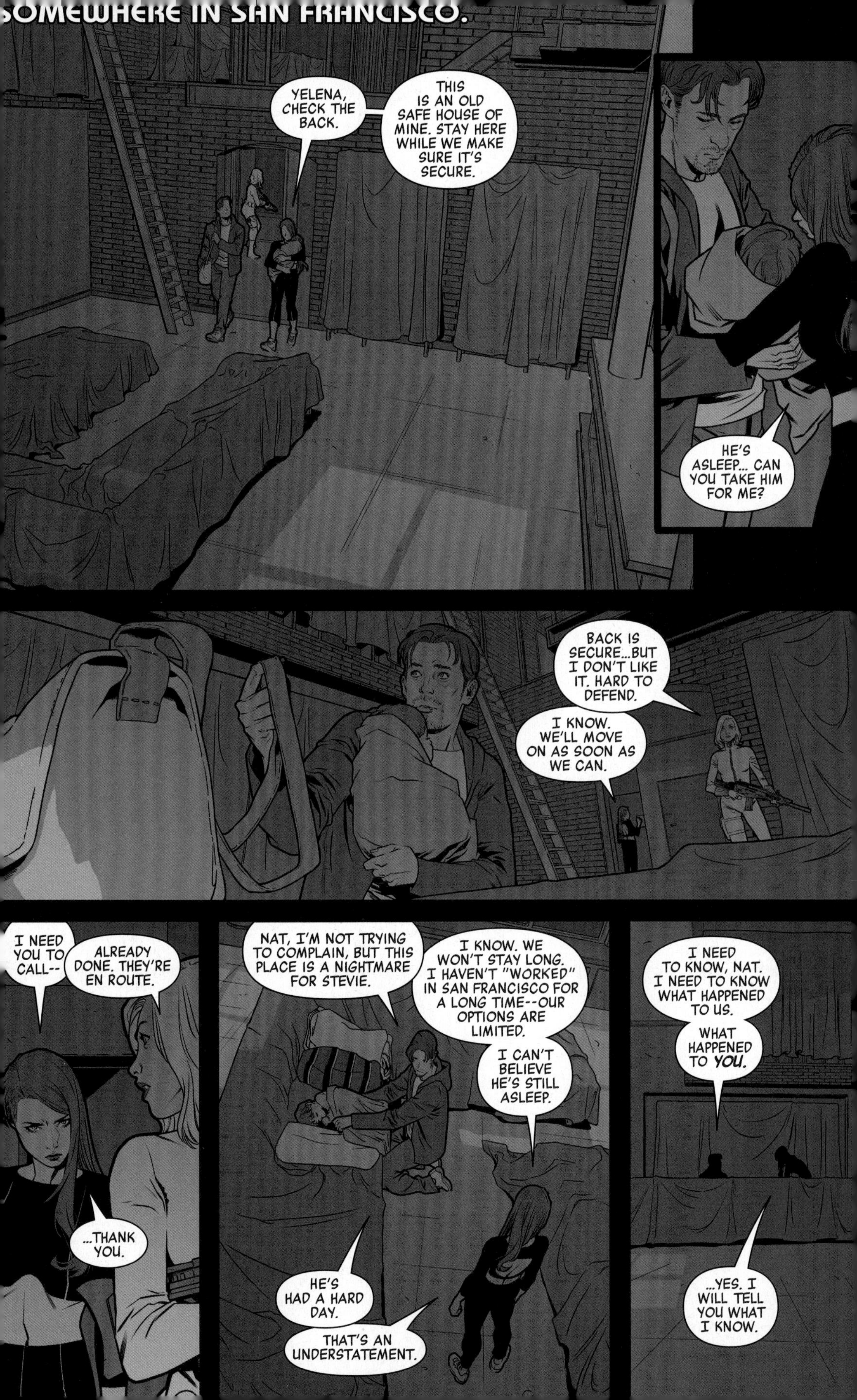
SOMEWHERE IN SAN FRANCISCO.
YELENA, CHECK THE BACK.
THIS IS AN OLD SAFE HOUSE OF MINE. STAY HERE WHILE WE MAKE SURE IT'S SECURE.
HE'S ASLEEP... CAN YOU TAKE HIM FOR ME?
BACK IS SECURE...BUT I DON'T LIKE IT. HARD TO DEFEND.
I KNOW. WE'LL MOVE ON AS SOON AS WE CAN.
I NEED YOU TO CALL--
ALREADY DONE. THEY'RE EN ROUTE.
...THANK YOU.
NAT, I'M NOT TRYING TO COMPLAIN, BUT THIS PLACE IS A NIGHTMARE FOR STEVIE.
I KNOW. WE WON'T STAY LONG. I HAVEN'T "WORKED" IN SAN FRANCISCO FOR A LONG TIME--OUR OPTIONS ARE LIMITED.
I CAN'T BELIEVE HE'S STILL ASLEEP.
HE'S HAD A HARD DAY.
THAT'S AN UNDERSTATEMENT.
I NEED TO KNOW, NAT. I NEED TO KNOW WHAT HAPPENED TO US.
WHAT HAPPENED TO *YOU.*
...YES. I WILL TELL YOU WHAT I KNOW.

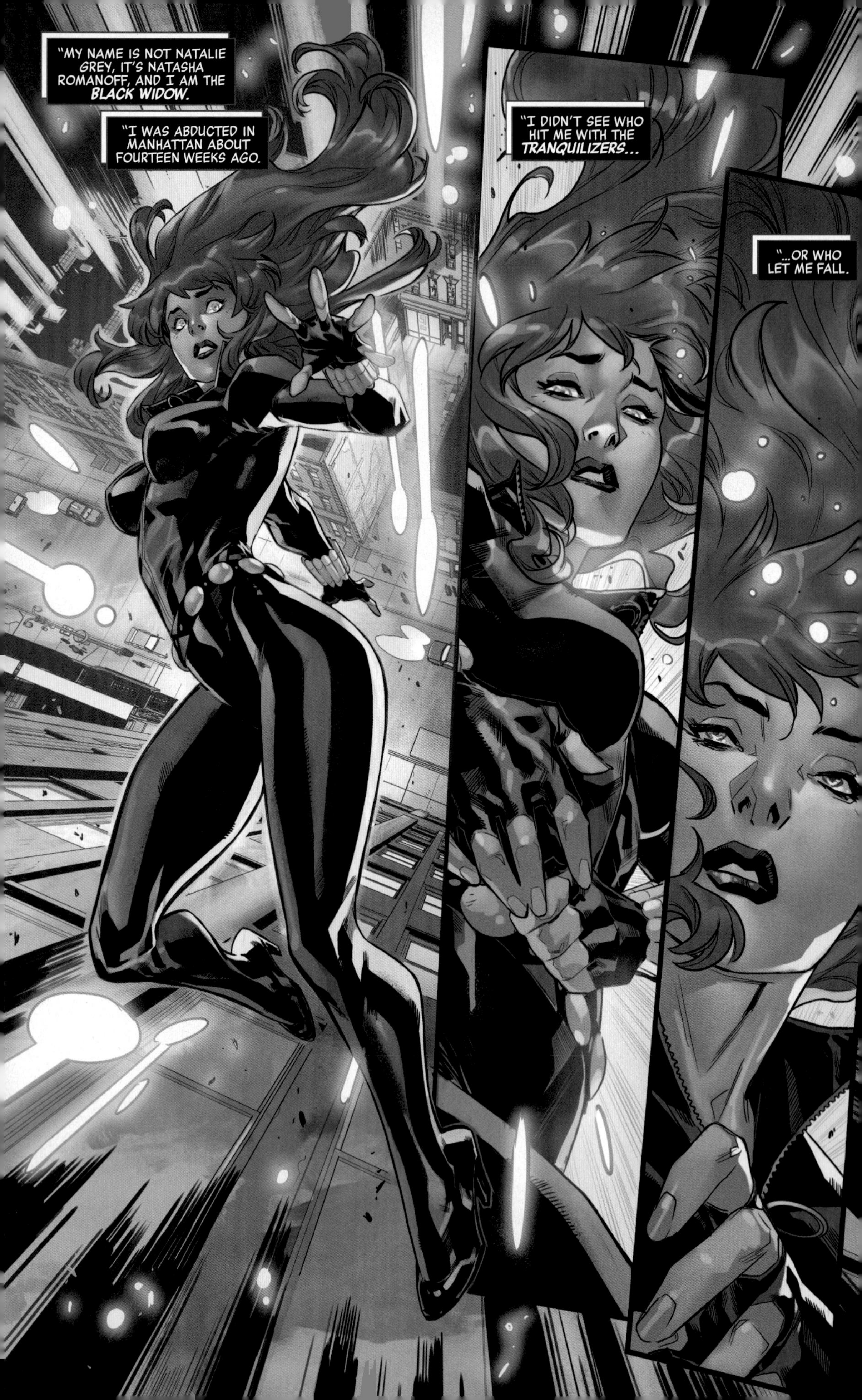
"MY NAME IS NOT NATALIE GREY, IT'S NATASHA ROMANOFF, AND I AM THE BLACK WIDOW.
"I WAS ABDUCTED IN MANHATTAN ABOUT FOURTEEN WEEKS AGO.
"I DIDN'T SEE WHO HIT ME WITH THE TRANQUILIZERS...
"...OR WHO LET ME FALL.

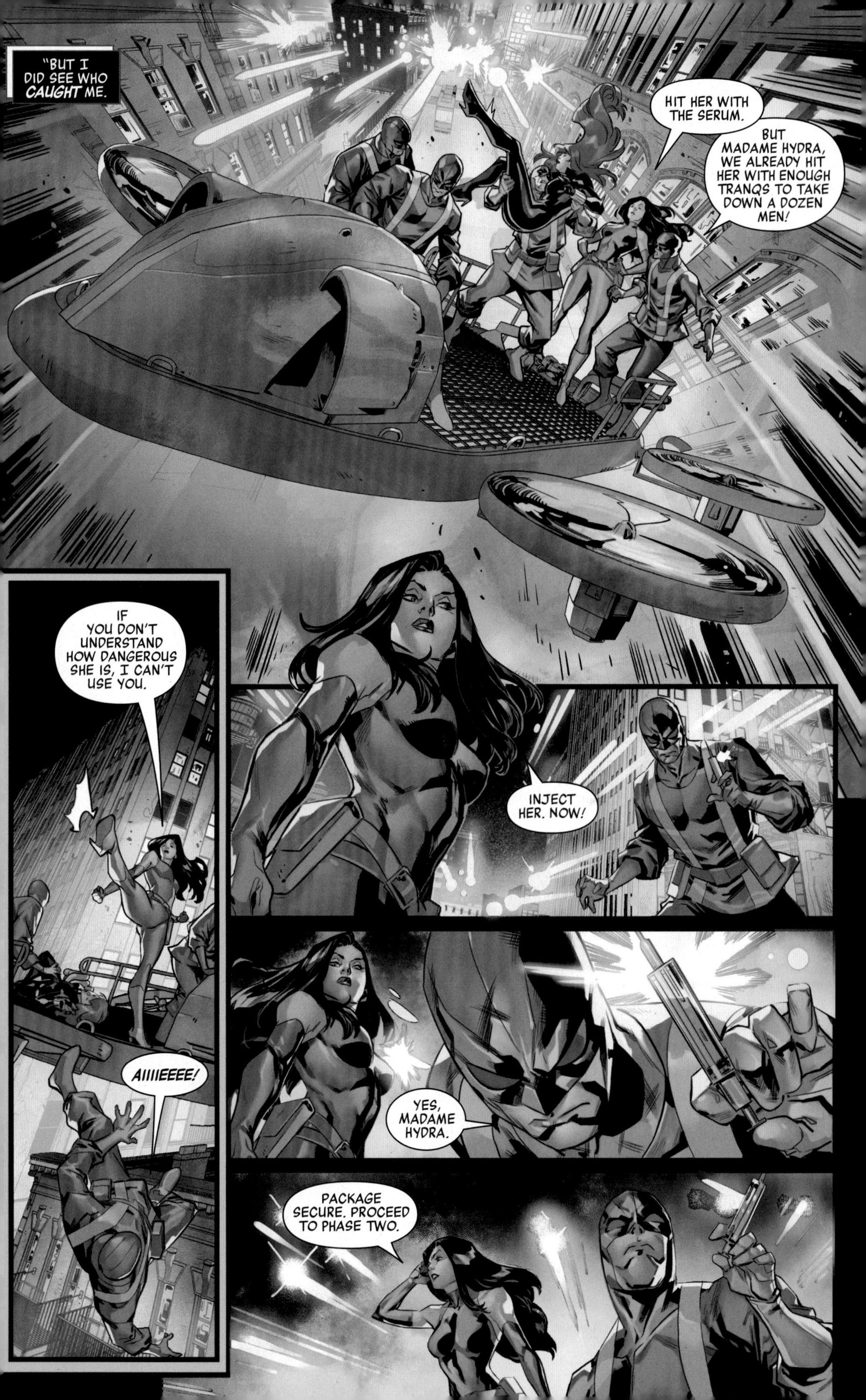
"BUT I DID SEE WHO CAUGHT ME.
HIT HER WITH THE SERUM.
BUT MADAME HYDRA, WE ALREADY HIT HER WITH ENOUGH TRANQS TO TAKE DOWN A DOZEN MEN!
IF YOU DON'T UNDERSTAND HOW DANGEROUS SHE IS, I CAN'T USE YOU.
AIIIEEEE!
INJECT HER. NOW!
YES, MADAME HYDRA.
PACKAGE SECURE. PROCEED TO PHASE TWO.

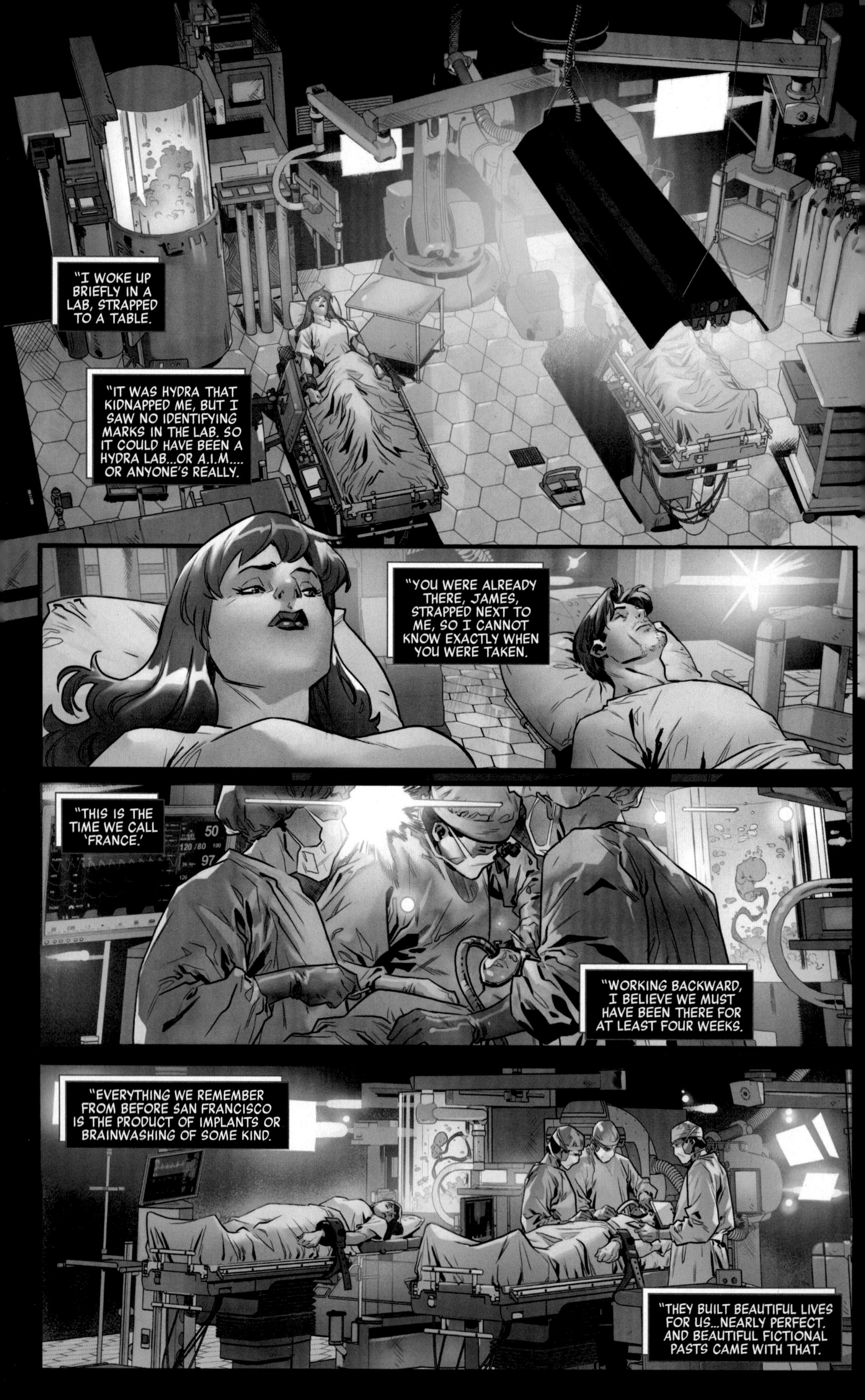
"I WOKE UP BRIEFLY IN A LAB, STRAPPED TO A TABLE.
"IT WAS HYDRA THAT KIDNAPPED ME, BUT I SAW NO IDENTIFYING MARKS IN THE LAB. SO IT COULD HAVE BEEN A HYDRA LAB...OR A.I.M.... OR ANYONE'S REALLY.
"YOU WERE ALREADY THERE, JAMES, STRAPPED NEXT TO ME, SO I CANNOT KNOW EXACTLY WHEN YOU WERE TAKEN.
"THIS IS THE TIME WE CALL 'FRANCE.'
"WORKING BACKWARD, I BELIEVE WE MUST HAVE BEEN THERE FOR AT LEAST FOUR WEEKS.
"EVERYTHING WE REMEMBER FROM BEFORE SAN FRANCISCO IS THE PRODUCT OF IMPLANTS OR BRAINWASHING OF SOME KIND.
"THEY BUILT BEAUTIFUL LIVES FOR US...NEARLY PERFECT. AND BEAUTIFUL FICTIONAL PASTS CAME WITH THAT.

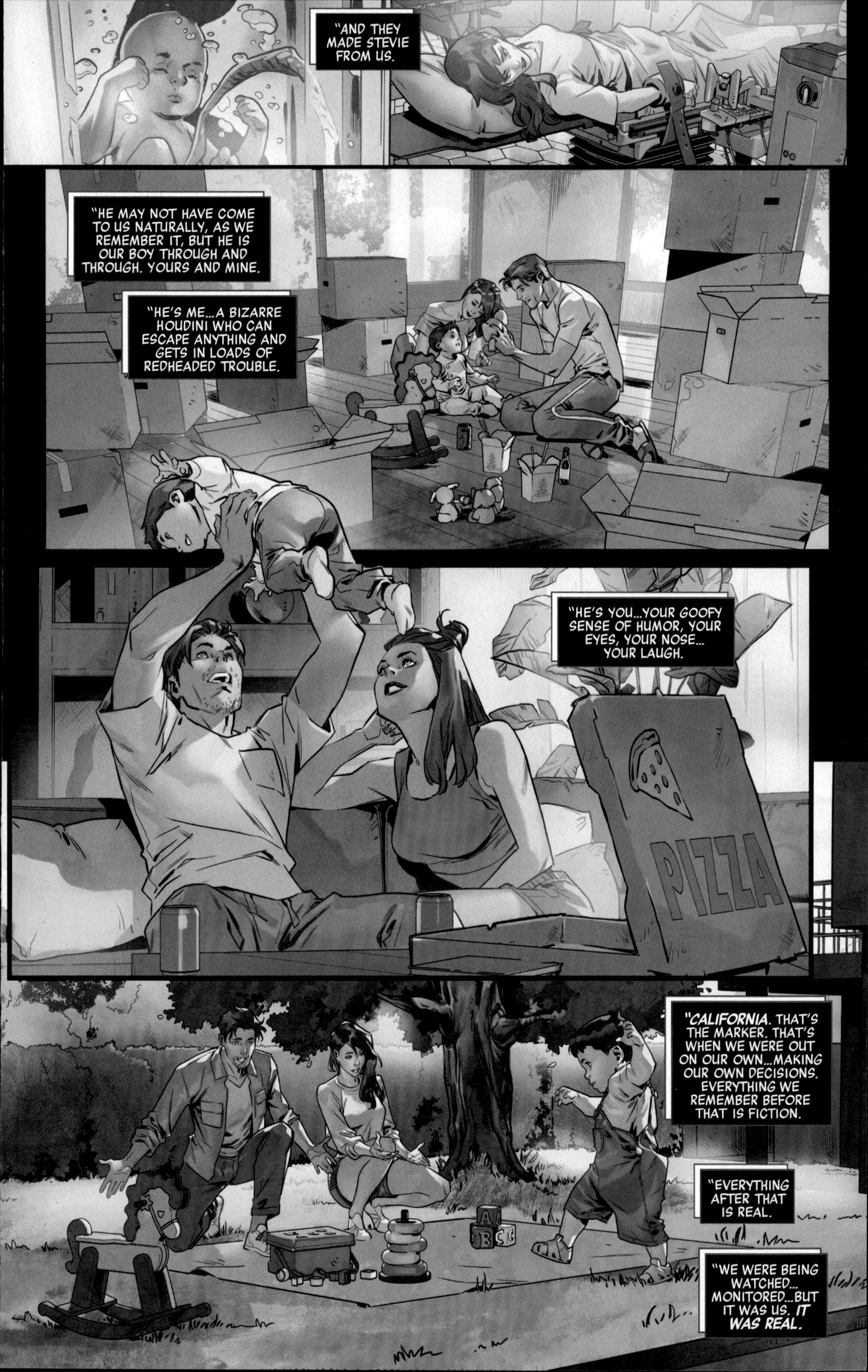
"AND THEY MADE STEVIE FROM US.
"HE MAY NOT HAVE COME TO US NATURALLY, AS WE REMEMBER IT, BUT HE IS OUR BOY THROUGH AND THROUGH. YOURS AND MINE.
"HE'S ME...A BIZARRE HOUDINI WHO CAN ESCAPE ANYTHING AND GETS IN LOADS OF REDHEADED TROUBLE.
"HE'S YOU...YOUR GOOFY SENSE OF HUMOR, YOUR EYES, YOUR NOSE... YOUR LAUGH.
PIZZA
"*CALIFORNIA*. THAT'S THE MARKER. THAT'S WHEN WE WERE OUT ON OUR OWN...MAKING OUR OWN DECISIONS. EVERYTHING WE REMEMBER BEFORE THAT IS FICTION.
"EVERYTHING AFTER THAT IS REAL.
"WE WERE BEING WATCHED... MONITORED...BUT IT WAS US. *IT WAS REAL.*

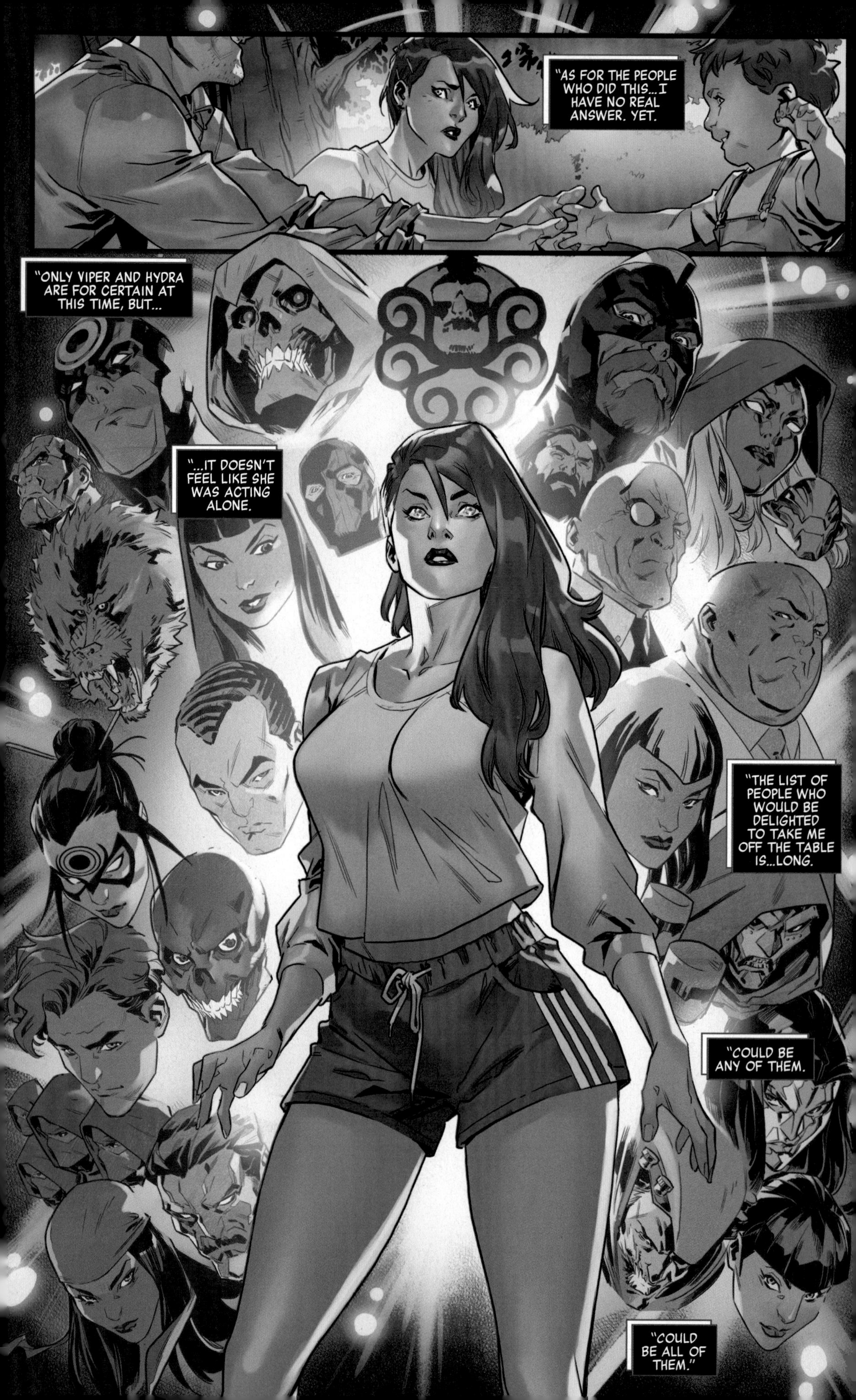
"AS FOR THE PEOPLE WHO DID THIS...I HAVE NO REAL ANSWER. YET.
"ONLY VIPER AND HYDRA ARE FOR CERTAIN AT THIS TIME, BUT...
"...IT DOESN'T FEEL LIKE SHE WAS ACTING ALONE.
"THE LIST OF PEOPLE WHO WOULD BE DELIGHTED TO TAKE ME OFF THE TABLE IS...LONG.
"COULD BE ANY OF THEM.
"COULD BE ALL OF THEM."

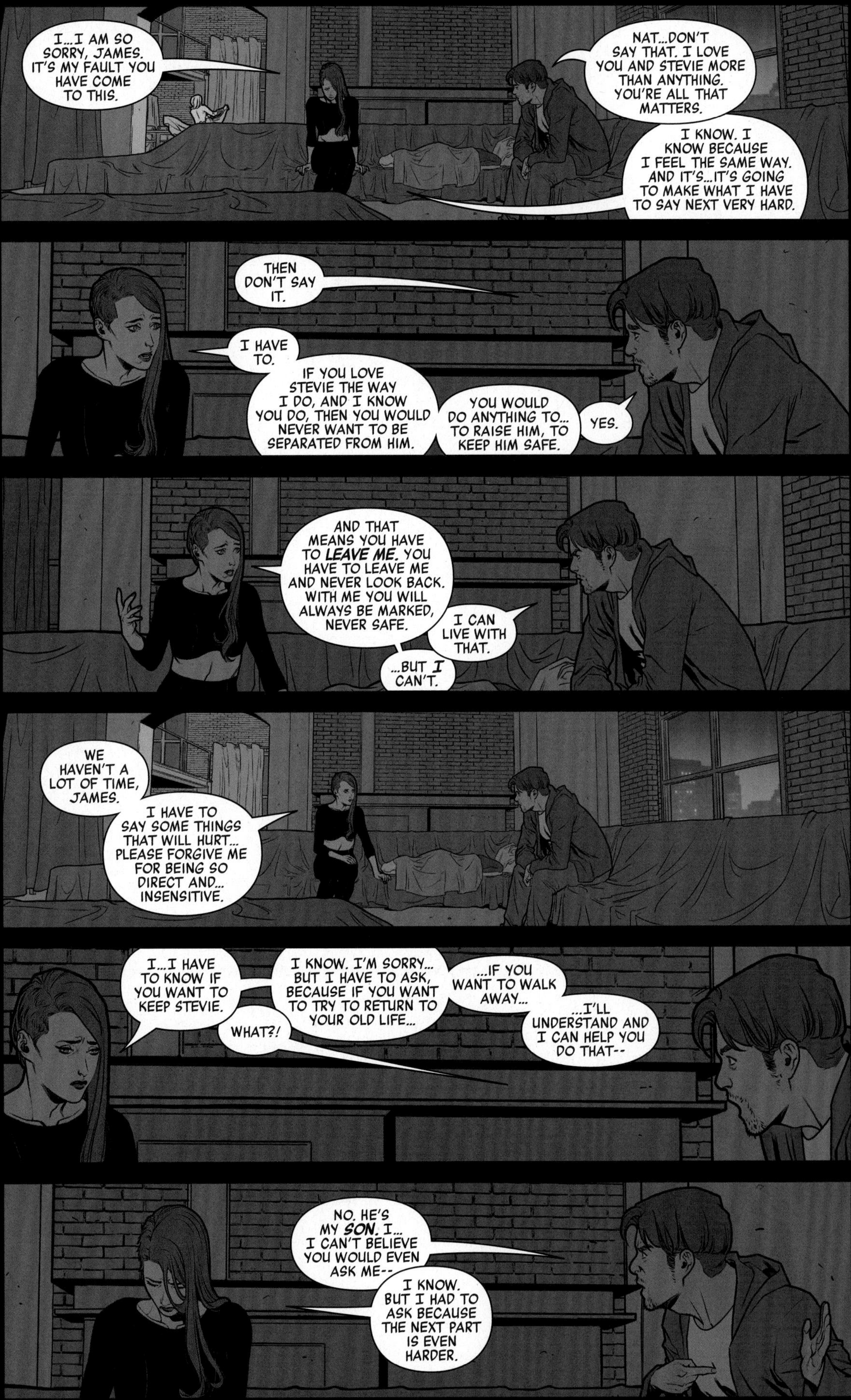
I...I AM SO SORRY, JAMES. IT'S MY FAULT YOU HAVE COME TO THIS.
NAT...DON'T SAY THAT. I LOVE YOU AND STEVIE MORE THAN ANYTHING. YOU'RE ALL THAT MATTERS.
I KNOW. I KNOW BECAUSE I FEEL THE SAME WAY. AND IT'S...IT'S GOING TO MAKE WHAT I HAVE TO SAY NEXT VERY HARD.
THEN DON'T SAY IT.
I HAVE TO.
IF YOU LOVE STEVIE THE WAY I DO, AND I KNOW YOU DO, THEN YOU WOULD NEVER WANT TO BE SEPARATED FROM HIM.
YOU WOULD DO ANYTHING TO... TO RAISE HIM, TO KEEP HIM SAFE.
YES.
AND THAT MEANS YOU HAVE TO LEAVE ME. YOU HAVE TO LEAVE ME AND NEVER LOOK BACK. WITH ME YOU WILL ALWAYS BE MARKED, NEVER SAFE.
I CAN LIVE WITH THAT.
...BUT I CAN'T.
WE HAVEN'T A LOT OF TIME, JAMES.
I HAVE TO SAY SOME THINGS THAT WILL HURT... PLEASE FORGIVE ME FOR BEING SO DIRECT AND... INSENSITIVE.
I...I HAVE TO KNOW IF YOU WANT TO KEEP STEVIE.
WHAT?!
I KNOW. I'M SORRY... BUT I HAVE TO ASK, BECAUSE IF YOU WANT TO TRY TO RETURN TO YOUR OLD LIFE...
...IF YOU WANT TO WALK AWAY...
...I'LL UNDERSTAND AND I CAN HELP YOU DO THAT--
NO. HE'S MY SON. I... I CAN'T BELIEVE YOU WOULD EVEN ASK ME--
I KNOW. BUT I HAD TO ASK BECAUSE THE NEXT PART IS EVEN HARDER.

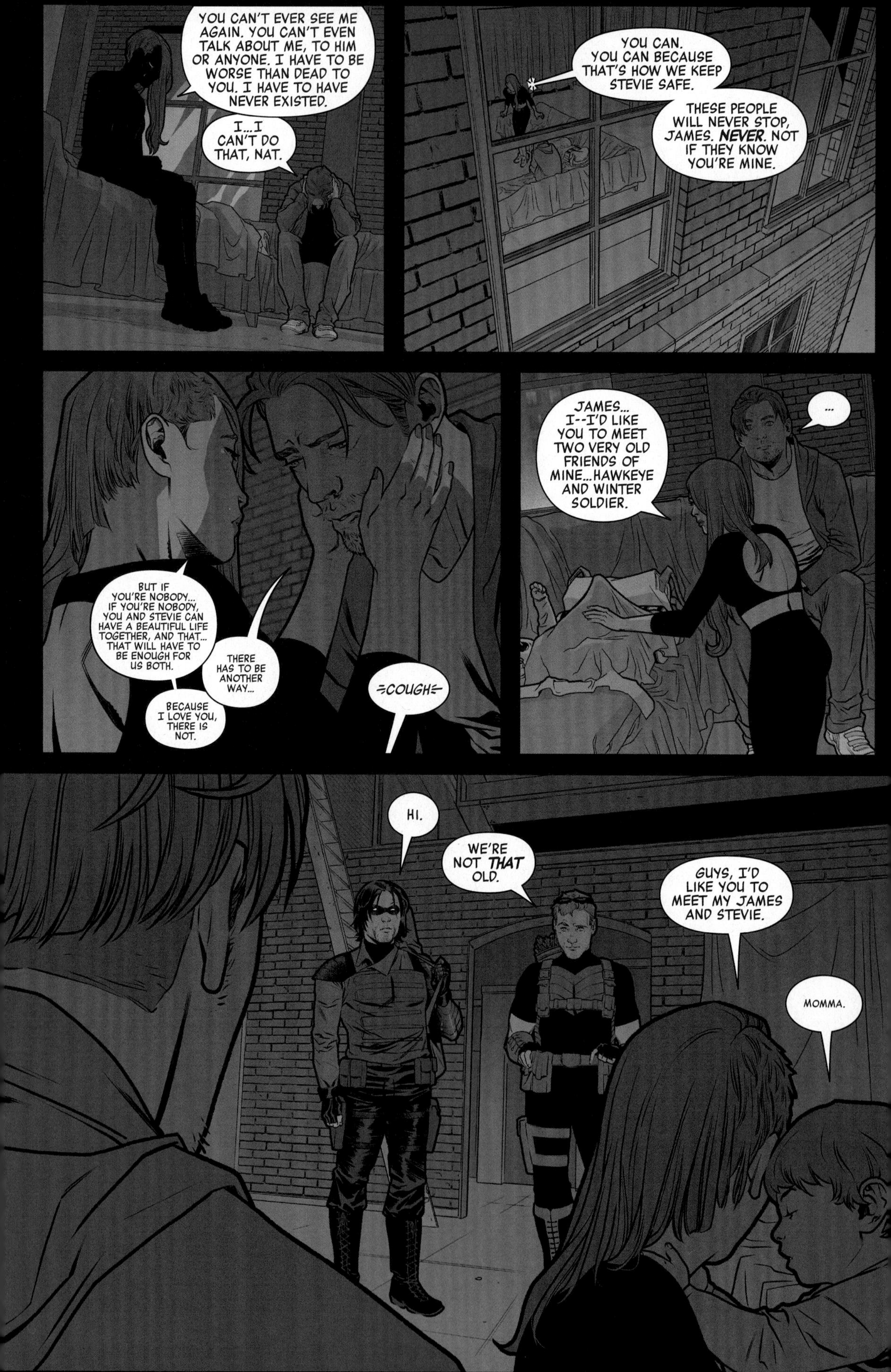
YOU CAN'T EVER SEE ME AGAIN. YOU CAN'T EVEN TALK ABOUT ME, TO HIM OR ANYONE. I HAVE TO BE WORSE THAN DEAD TO YOU. I HAVE TO HAVE NEVER EXISTED.
I...I CAN'T DO THAT, NAT.
YOU CAN. YOU CAN BECAUSE THAT'S HOW WE KEEP STEVIE SAFE.
THESE PEOPLE WILL NEVER STOP, JAMES. NEVER. NOT IF THEY KNOW YOU'RE MINE.
BUT IF YOU'RE NOBODY... IF YOU'RE NOBODY, YOU AND STEVIE CAN HAVE A BEAUTIFUL LIFE TOGETHER, AND THAT... THAT WILL HAVE TO BE ENOUGH FOR US BOTH.
THERE HAS TO BE ANOTHER WAY...
BECAUSE I LOVE YOU, THERE IS NOT.
=COUGH=
JAMES... I--I'D LIKE YOU TO MEET TWO VERY OLD FRIENDS OF MINE...HAWKEYE AND WINTER SOLDIER.
...
HI.
WE'RE NOT THAT OLD.
GUYS, I'D LIKE YOU TO MEET MY JAMES AND STEVIE.
MOMMA.

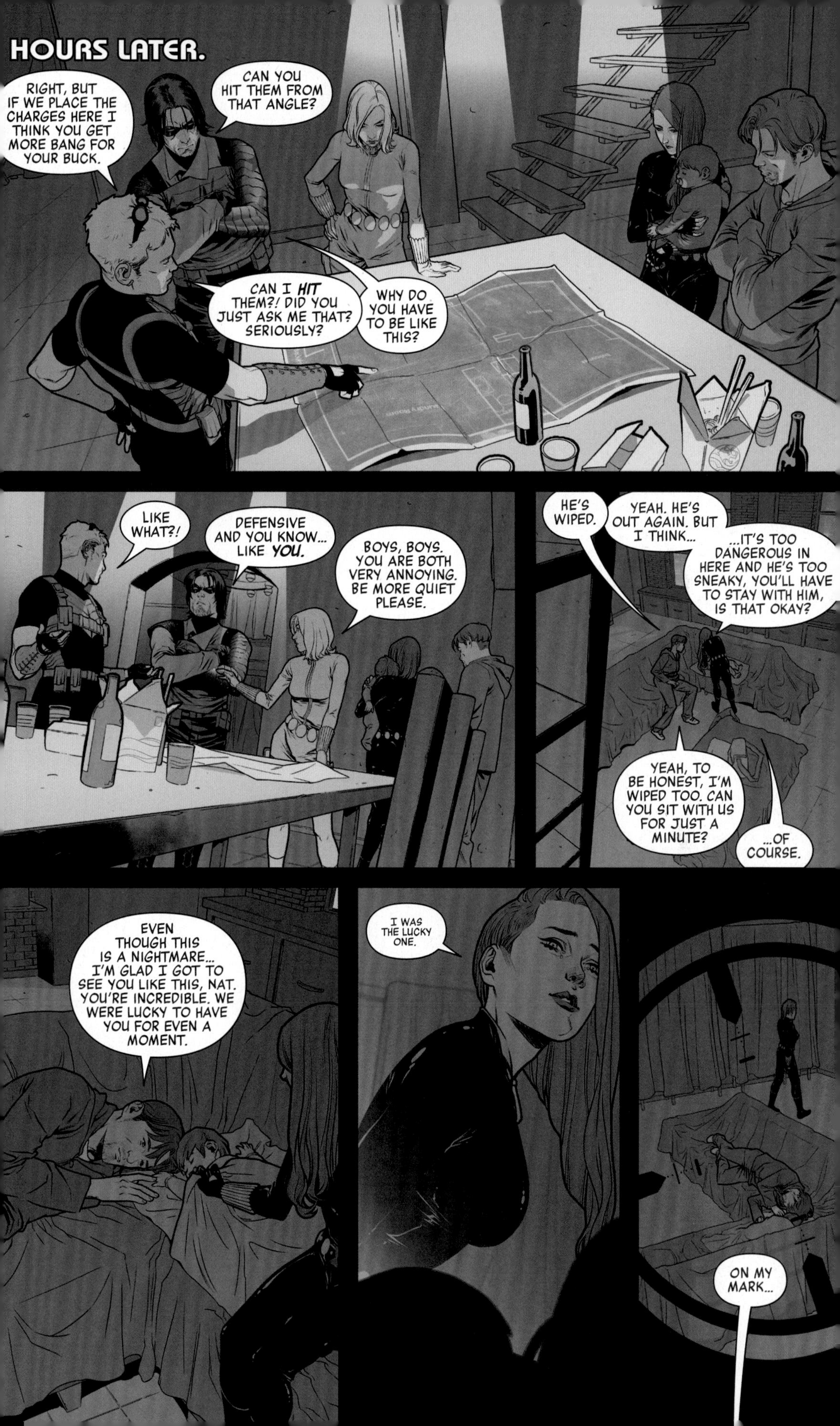
HOURS LATER.
RIGHT, BUT IF WE PLACE THE CHARGES HERE I THINK YOU GET MORE BANG FOR YOUR BUCK.
CAN YOU HIT THEM FROM THAT ANGLE?
CAN I HIT THEM?! DID YOU JUST ASK ME THAT? SERIOUSLY?
WHY DO YOU HAVE TO BE LIKE THIS?
LIKE WHAT?!
DEFENSIVE AND YOU KNOW... LIKE YOU.
BOYS, BOYS. YOU ARE BOTH VERY ANNOYING. BE MORE QUIET PLEASE.
HE'S WIPED.
YEAH. HE'S OUT AGAIN. BUT I THINK...
...IT'S TOO DANGEROUS IN HERE AND HE'S TOO SNEAKY, YOU'LL HAVE TO STAY WITH HIM, IS THAT OKAY?
YEAH, TO BE HONEST, I'M WIPED TOO. CAN YOU SIT WITH US FOR JUST A MINUTE?
...OF COURSE.
EVEN THOUGH THIS IS A NIGHTMARE... I'M GLAD I GOT TO SEE YOU LIKE THIS, NAT. YOU'RE INCREDIBLE. WE WERE LUCKY TO HAVE YOU FOR EVEN A MOMENT.
I WAS THE LUCKY ONE.
ON MY MARK...

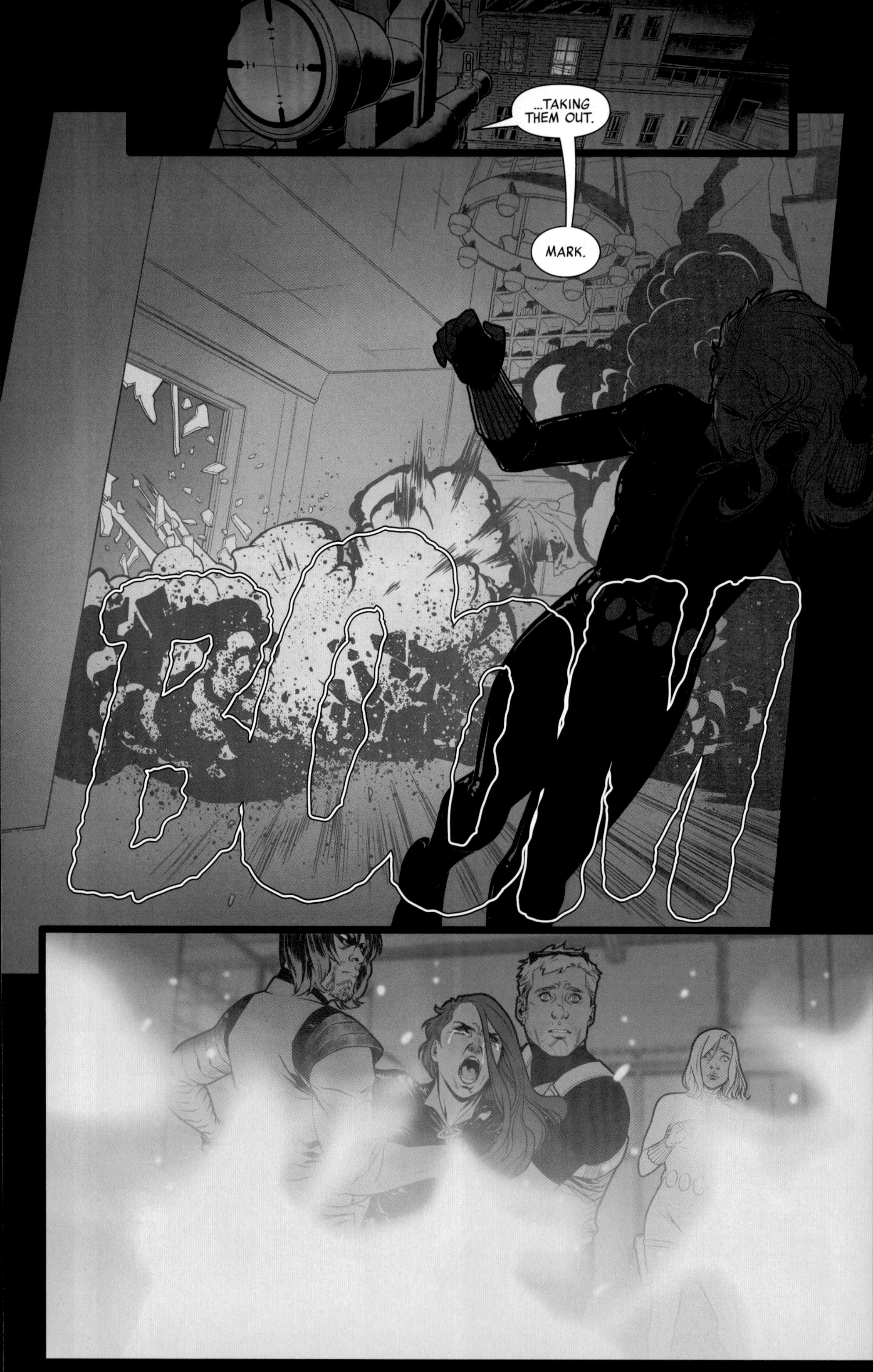
...TAKING THEM OUT.
MARK.
BOOM

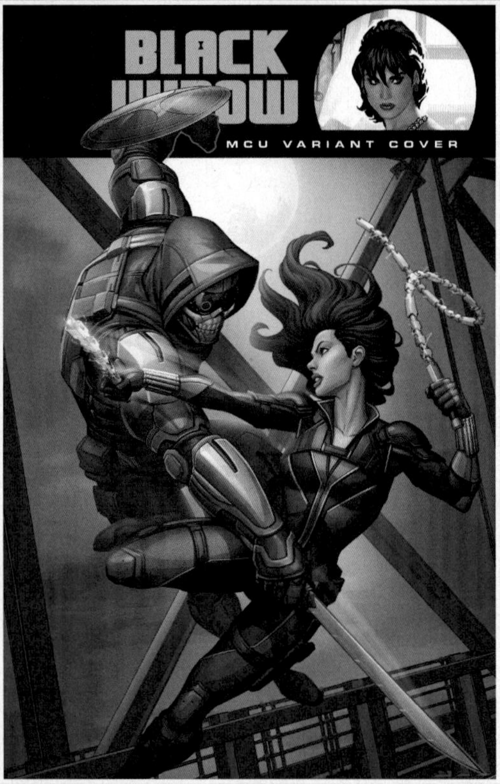
BLACK WIDOW
MCU VARIANT COVER

#4 MCU VARIANT BY PATRICK BROWN

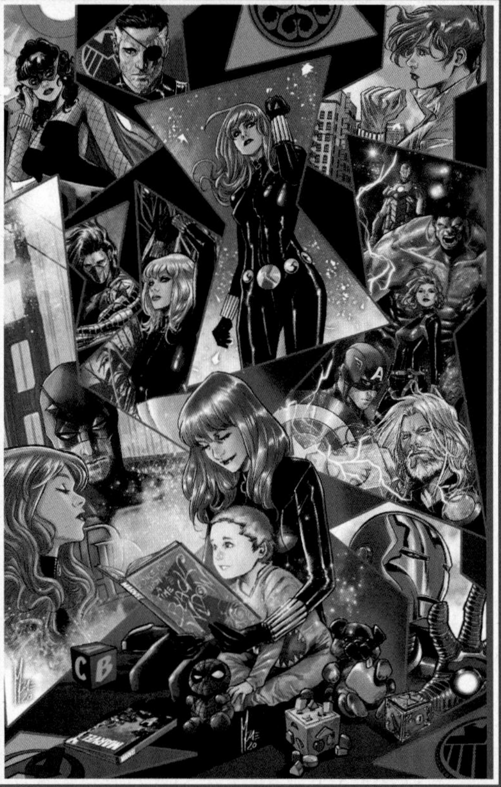

#4 VARIANT BY MARCO CHECCHETTO

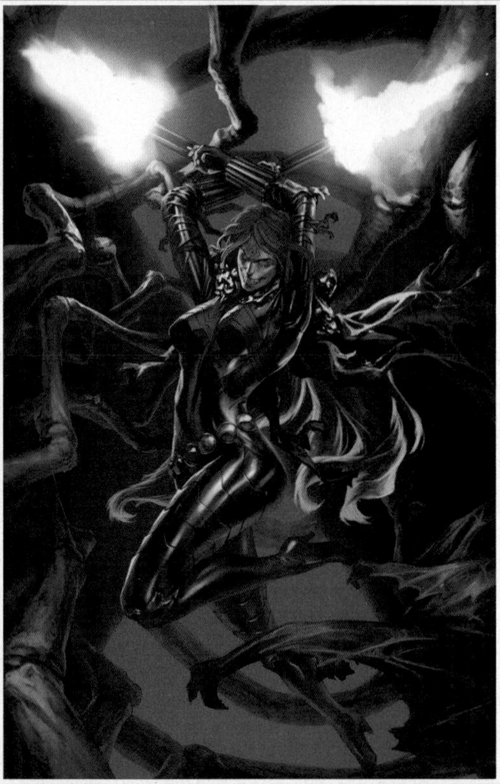

SKAN

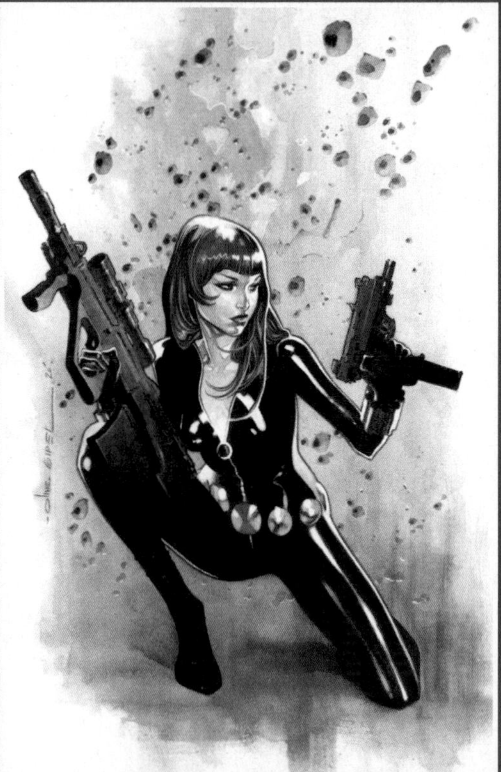

#5 VARIANT BY OLIVIER COIPEL

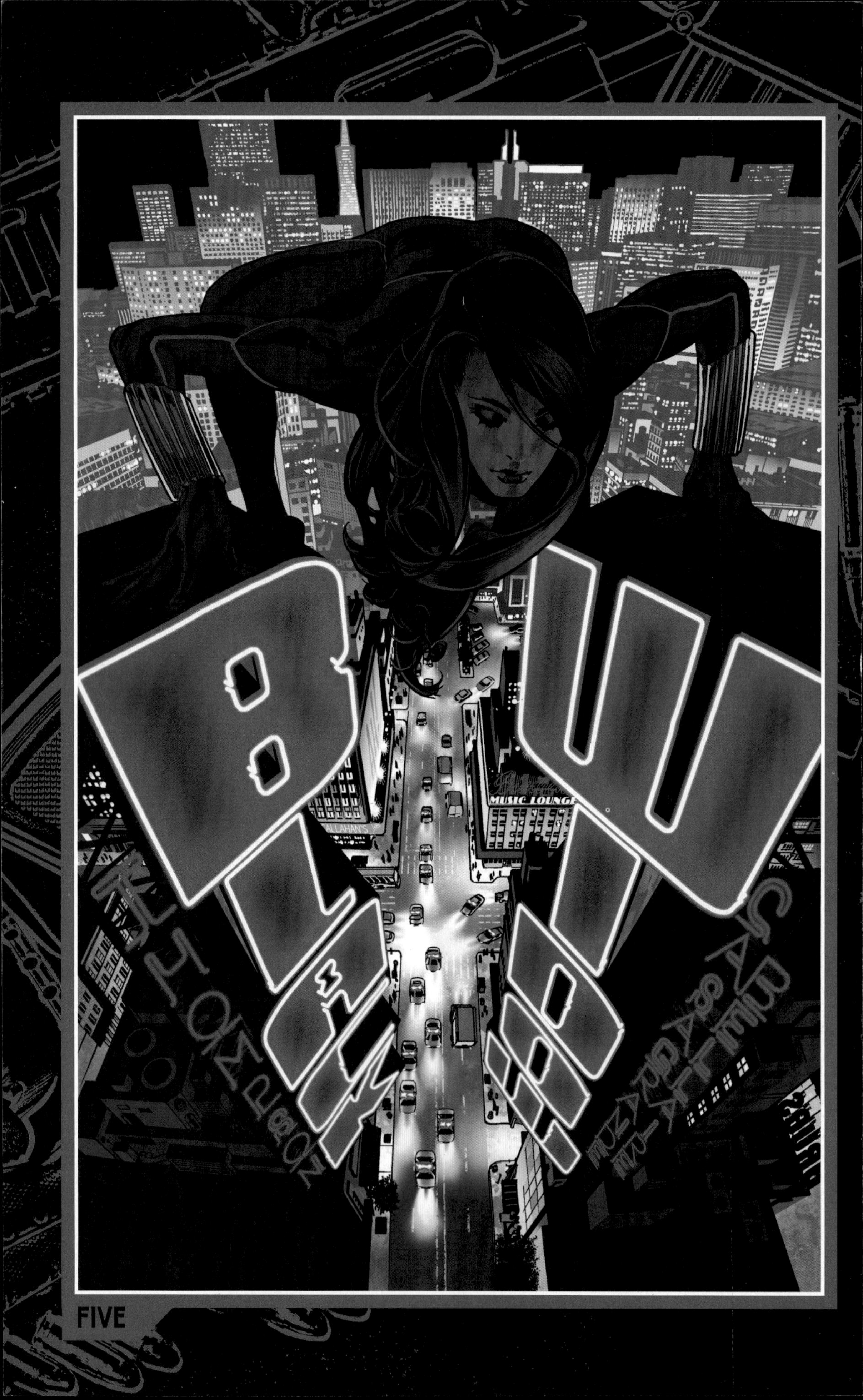
MUSIC LOUNGE

FIVE

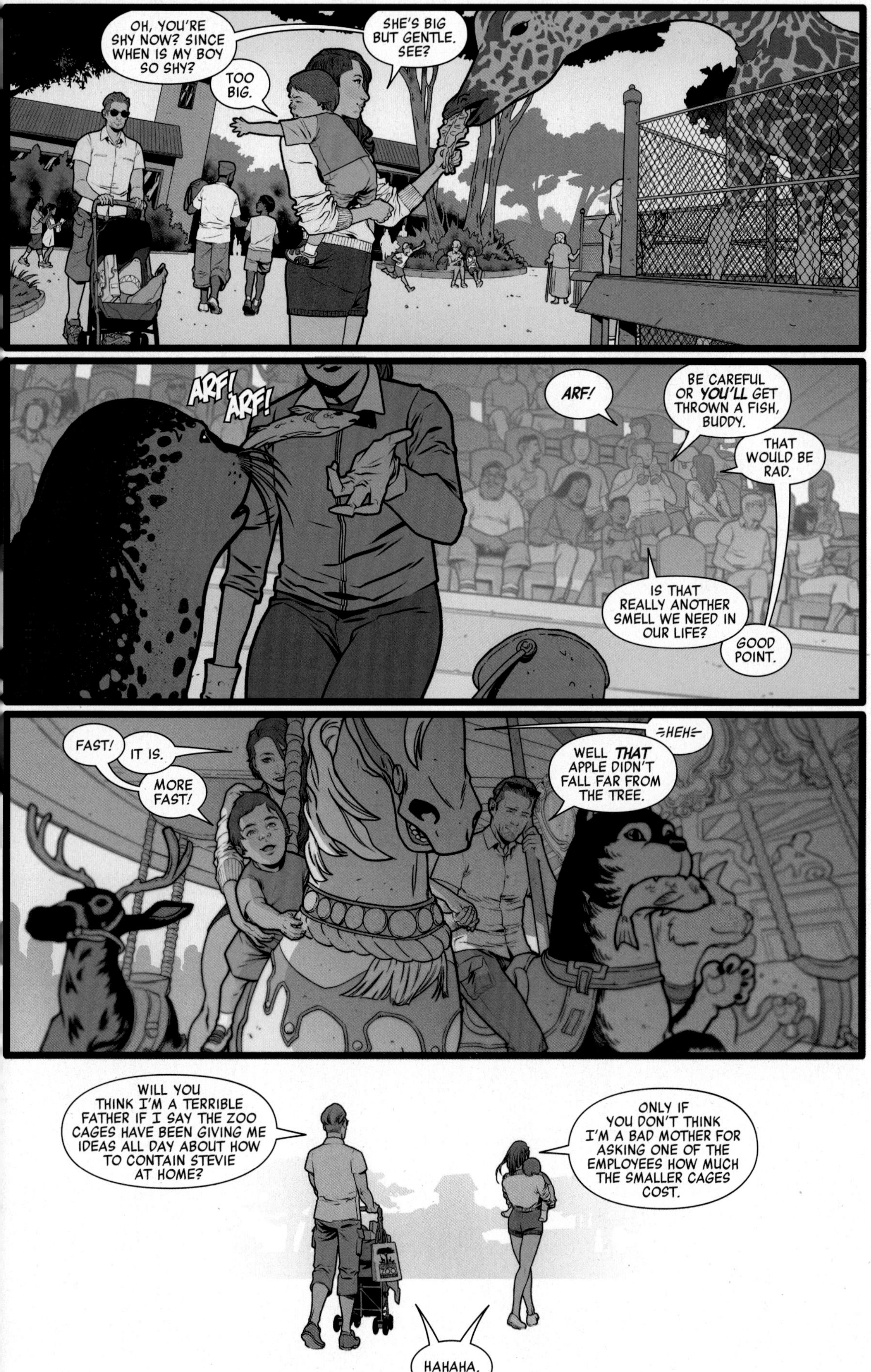

OH, YOU'RE SHY NOW? SINCE WHEN IS MY BOY SO SHY?
TOO BIG.
SHE'S BIG BUT GENTLE. SEE?
ARF! ARF!
ARF!
BE CAREFUL OR YOU'LL GET THROWN A FISH, BUDDY.
THAT WOULD BE RAD.
IS THAT REALLY ANOTHER SMELL WE NEED IN OUR LIFE?
GOOD POINT.
FAST!
IT IS.
MORE FAST!
HEH
WELL THAT APPLE DIDN'T FALL FAR FROM THE TREE.
WILL YOU THINK I'M A TERRIBLE FATHER IF I SAY THE ZOO CAGES HAVE BEEN GIVING ME IDEAS ALL DAY ABOUT HOW TO CONTAIN STEVIE AT HOME?
ONLY IF YOU DON'T THINK I'M A BAD MOTHER FOR ASKING ONE OF THE EMPLOYEES HOW MUCH THE SMALLER CAGES COST.
HAHAHA.

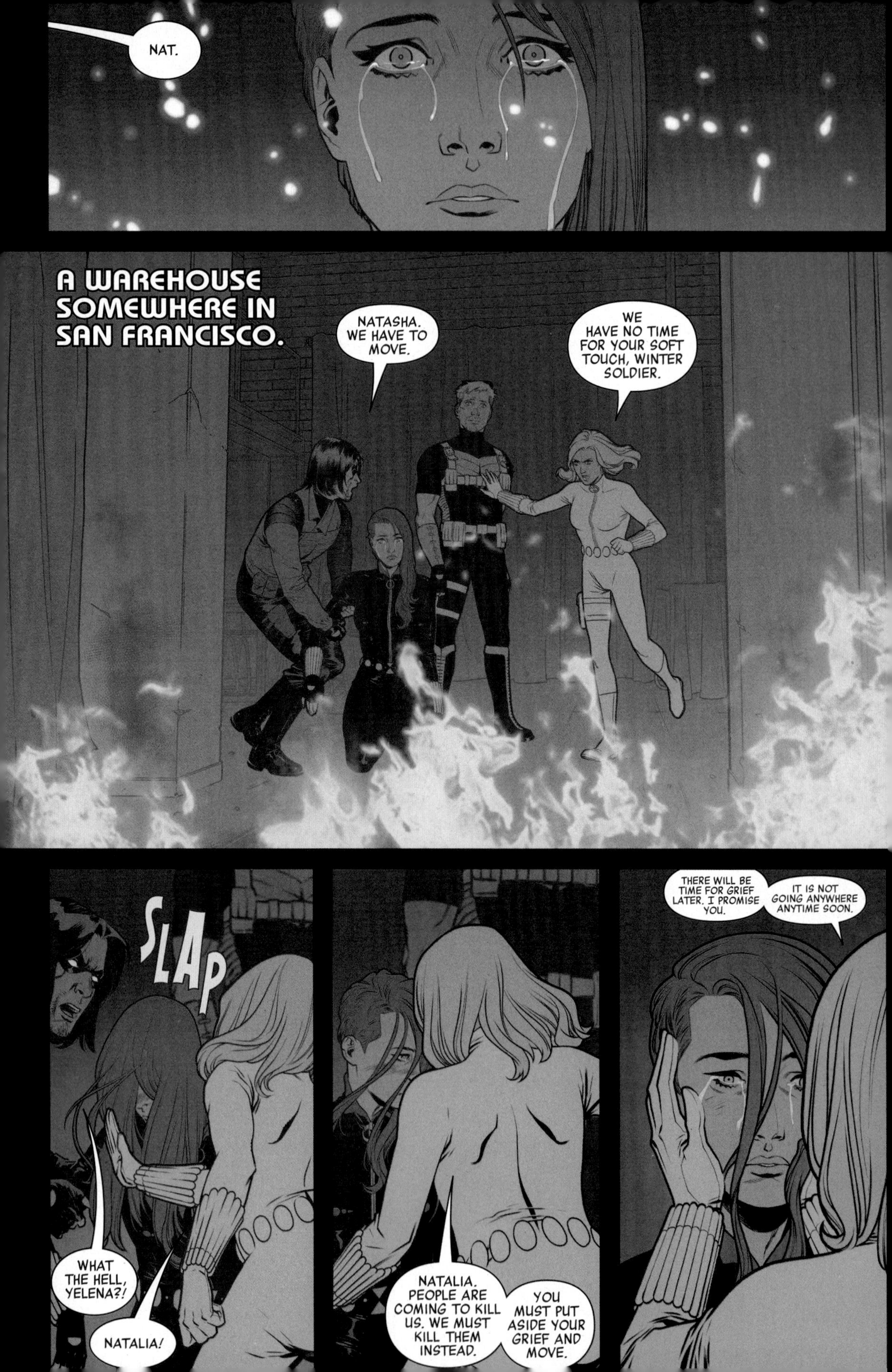
NAT.
A WAREHOUSE SOMEWHERE IN SAN FRANCISCO.
NATASHA. WE HAVE TO MOVE.
WE HAVE NO TIME FOR YOUR SOFT TOUCH, WINTER SOLDIER.
SLAP
WHAT THE HELL, YELENA?!
NATALIA!
NATALIA. PEOPLE ARE COMING TO KILL US. WE MUST KILL THEM INSTEAD.
YOU MUST PUT ASIDE YOUR GRIEF AND MOVE.
THERE WILL BE TIME FOR GRIEF LATER. I PROMISE YOU.
IT IS NOT GOING ANYWHERE ANYTIME SOON.

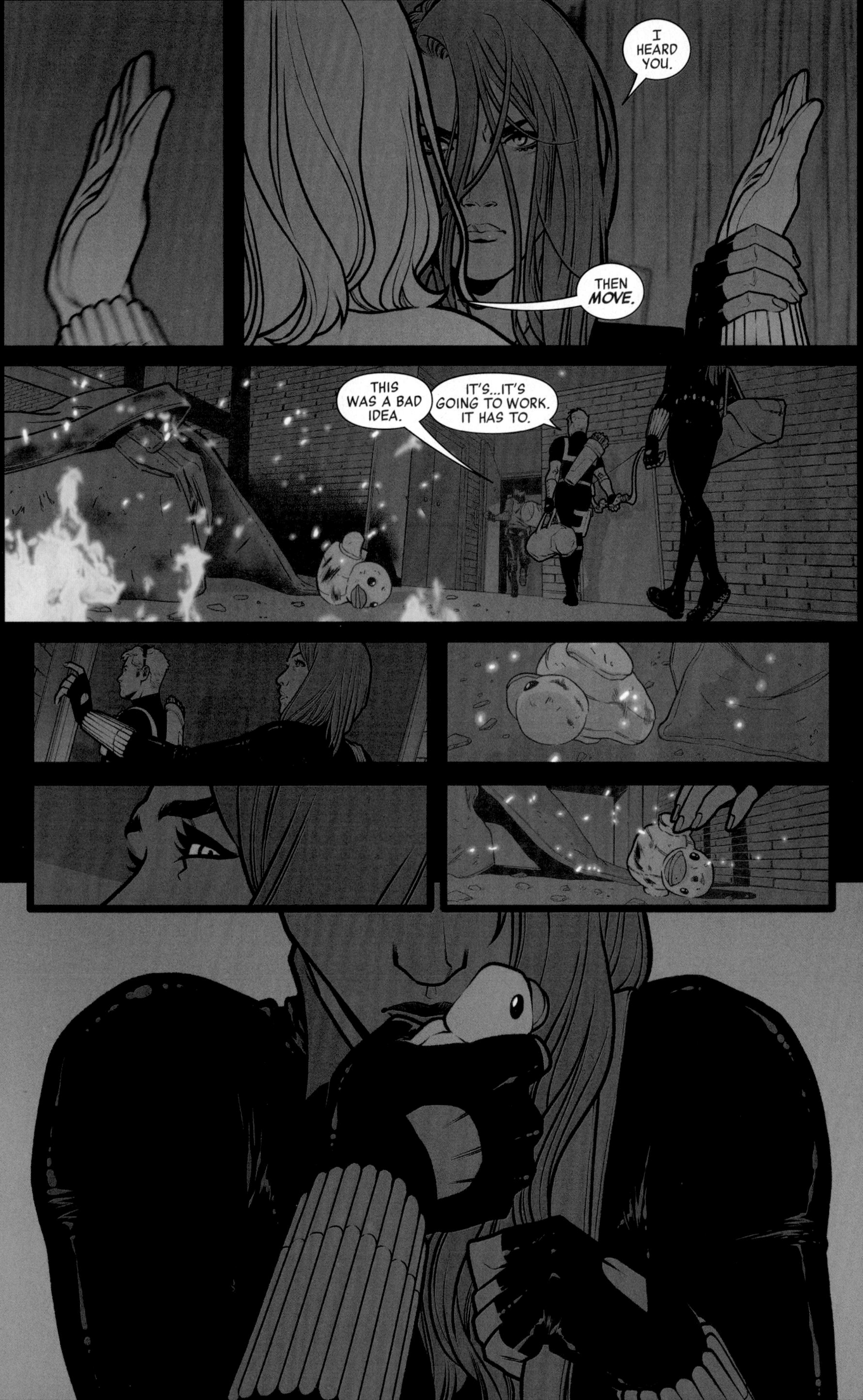
I HEARD YOU.
THEN MOVE.
THIS WAS A BAD IDEA.
IT'S...IT'S GOING TO WORK. IT HAS TO.

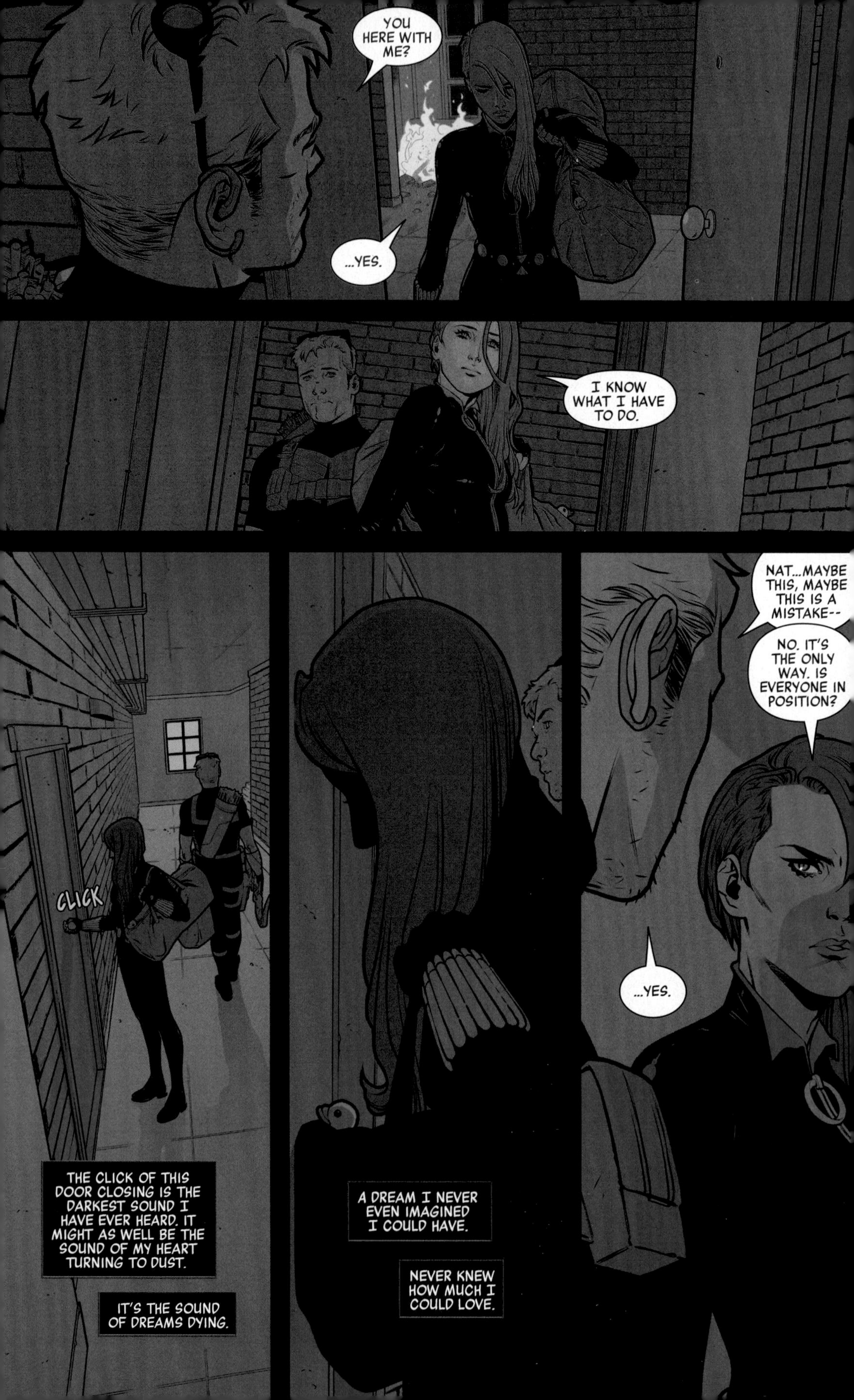
YOU HERE WITH ME?
...YES.
I KNOW WHAT I HAVE TO DO.
CLICK
THE CLICK OF THIS DOOR CLOSING IS THE DARKEST SOUND I HAVE EVER HEARD. IT MIGHT AS WELL BE THE SOUND OF MY HEART TURNING TO DUST.
IT'S THE SOUND OF DREAMS DYING.
A DREAM I NEVER EVEN IMAGINED I COULD HAVE.
NEVER KNEW HOW MUCH I COULD LOVE.
NAT...MAYBE THIS, MAYBE THIS IS A MISTAKE--
NO. IT'S THE ONLY WAY. IS EVERYONE IN POSITION?
...YES.

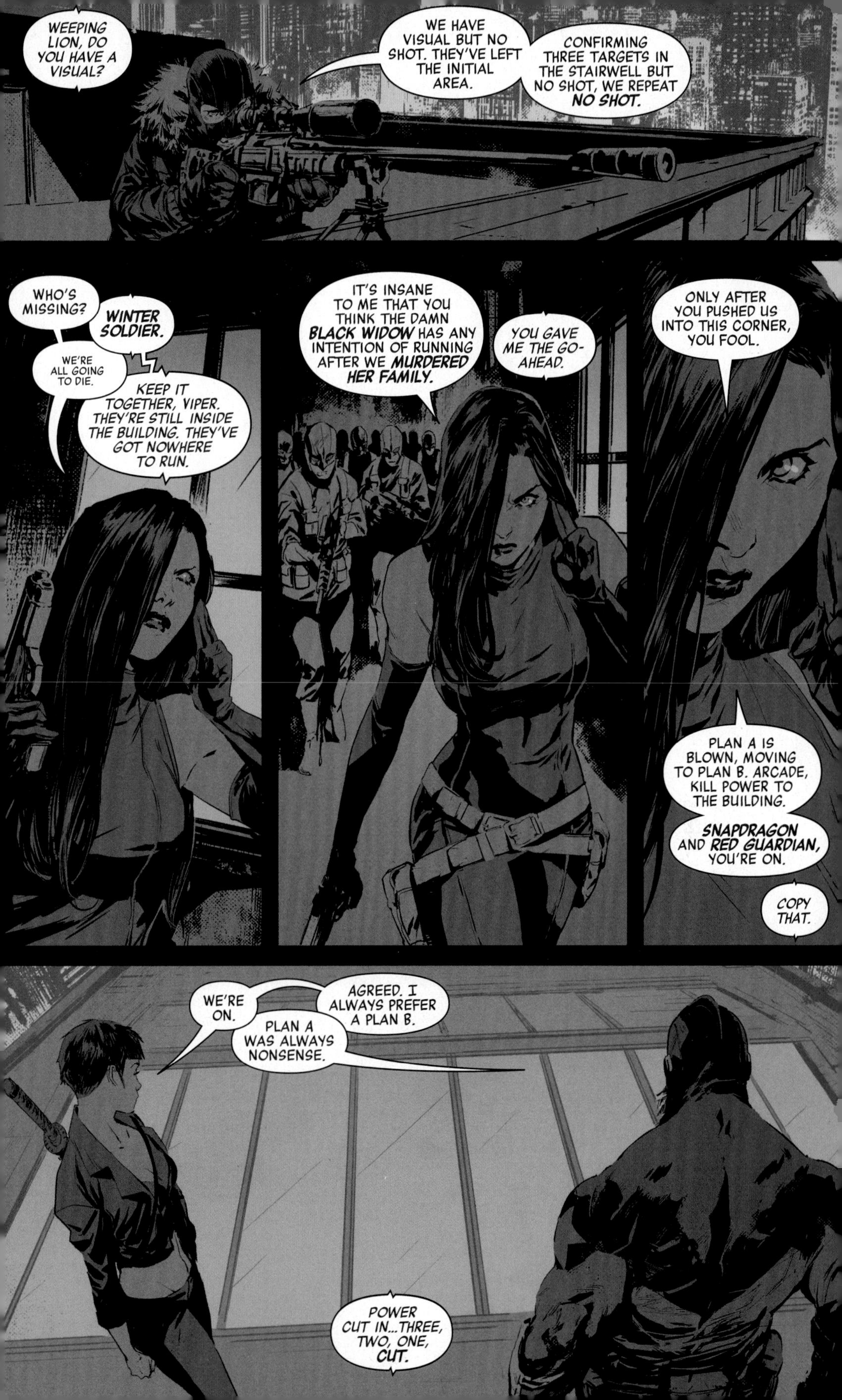

WEEPING LION, DO YOU HAVE A VISUAL?
WE HAVE VISUAL BUT NO SHOT. THEY'VE LEFT THE INITIAL AREA.
CONFIRMING THREE TARGETS IN THE STAIRWELL BUT NO SHOT, WE REPEAT NO SHOT.
WHO'S MISSING?
WINTER SOLDIER.
WE'RE ALL GOING TO DIE.
KEEP IT TOGETHER, VIPER. THEY'RE STILL INSIDE THE BUILDING. THEY'VE GOT NOWHERE TO RUN.
IT'S INSANE TO ME THAT YOU THINK THE DAMN BLACK WIDOW HAS ANY INTENTION OF RUNNING AFTER WE MURDERED HER FAMILY.
YOU GAVE ME THE GO-AHEAD.
ONLY AFTER YOU PUSHED US INTO THIS CORNER, YOU FOOL.
PLAN A IS BLOWN, MOVING TO PLAN B. ARCADE, KILL POWER TO THE BUILDING.
SNAPDRAGON AND RED GUARDIAN, YOU'RE ON.
COPY THAT.
WE'RE ON.
AGREED. I ALWAYS PREFER A PLAN B.
PLAN A WAS ALWAYS NONSENSE.
POWER CUT IN...THREE, TWO, ONE, CUT.

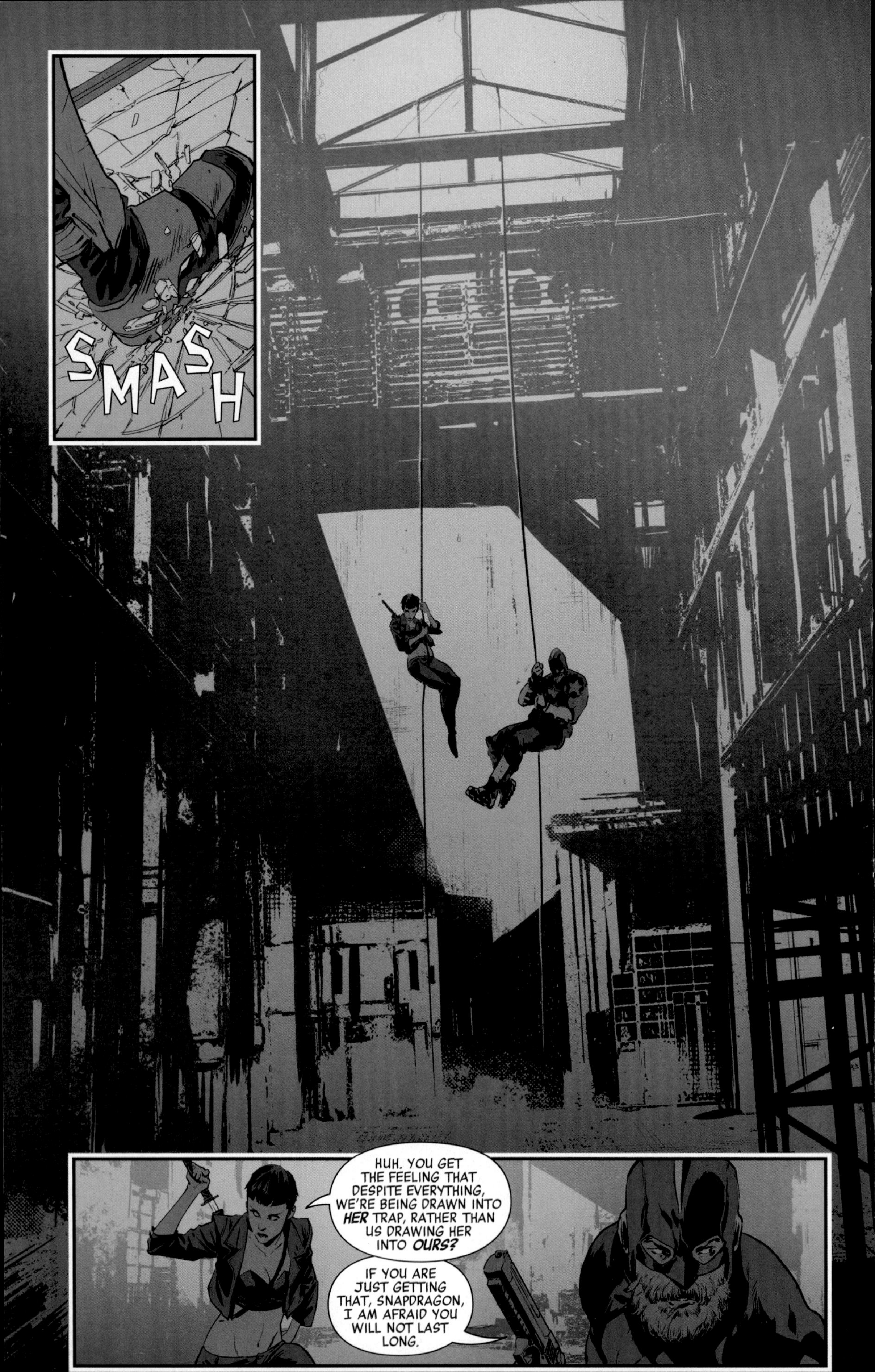
SMASH
HUH. YOU GET THE FEELING THAT DESPITE EVERYTHING, WE'RE BEING DRAWN INTO HER TRAP, RATHER THAN US DRAWING HER INTO OURS?
IF YOU ARE JUST GETTING THAT, SNAPDRAGON, I AM AFRAID YOU WILL NOT LAST LONG.

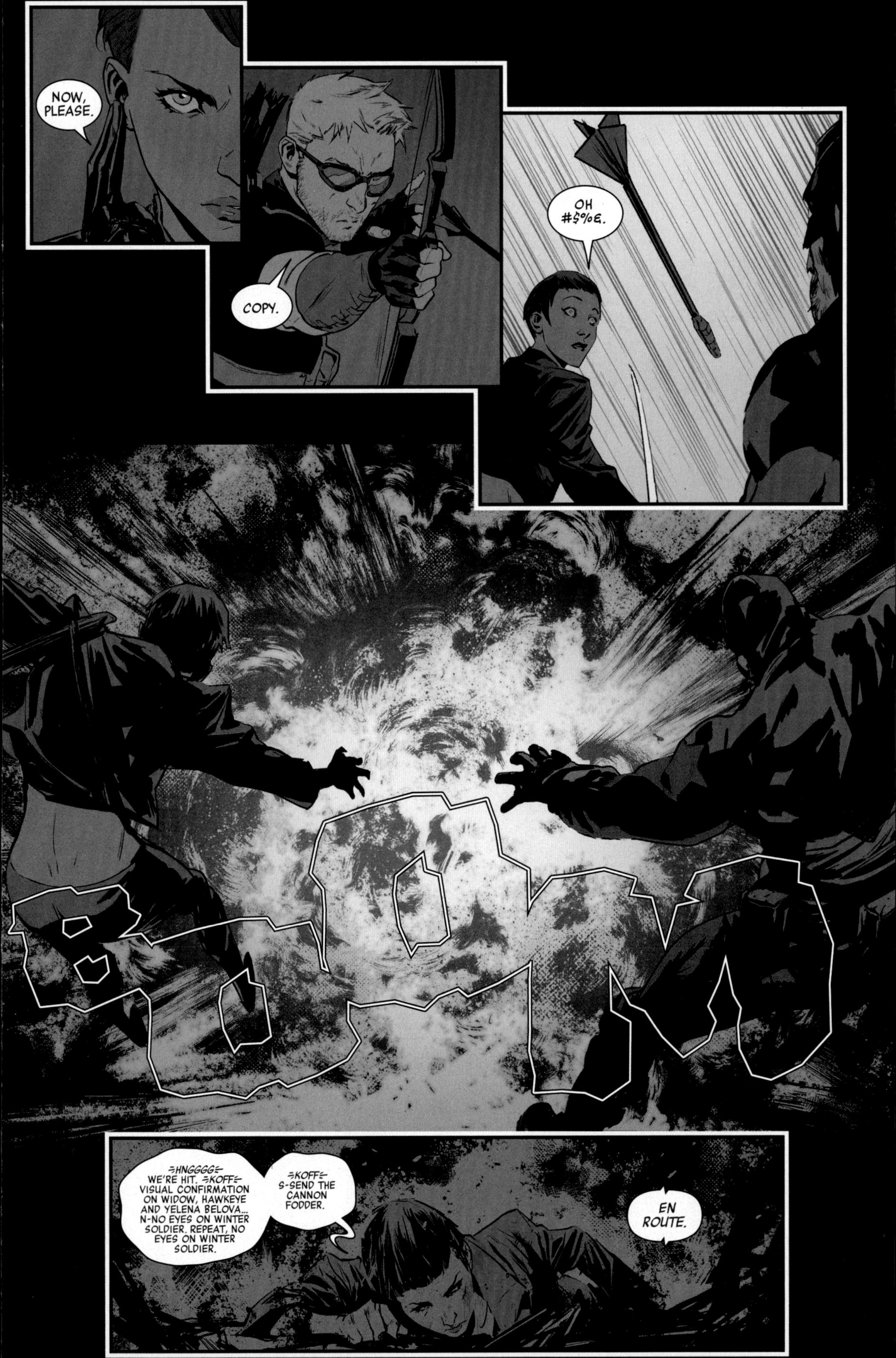
NOW, PLEASE.
COPY.
OH #$%&.
BOOM
HNGGGG WE'RE HIT. KOFF VISUAL CONFIRMATION ON WIDOW, HAWKEYE AND YELENA BELOVA... N-NO EYES ON WINTER SOLDIER. REPEAT, NO EYES ON WINTER SOLDIER.
KOFF S-SEND THE CANNON FODDER.
EN ROUTE.

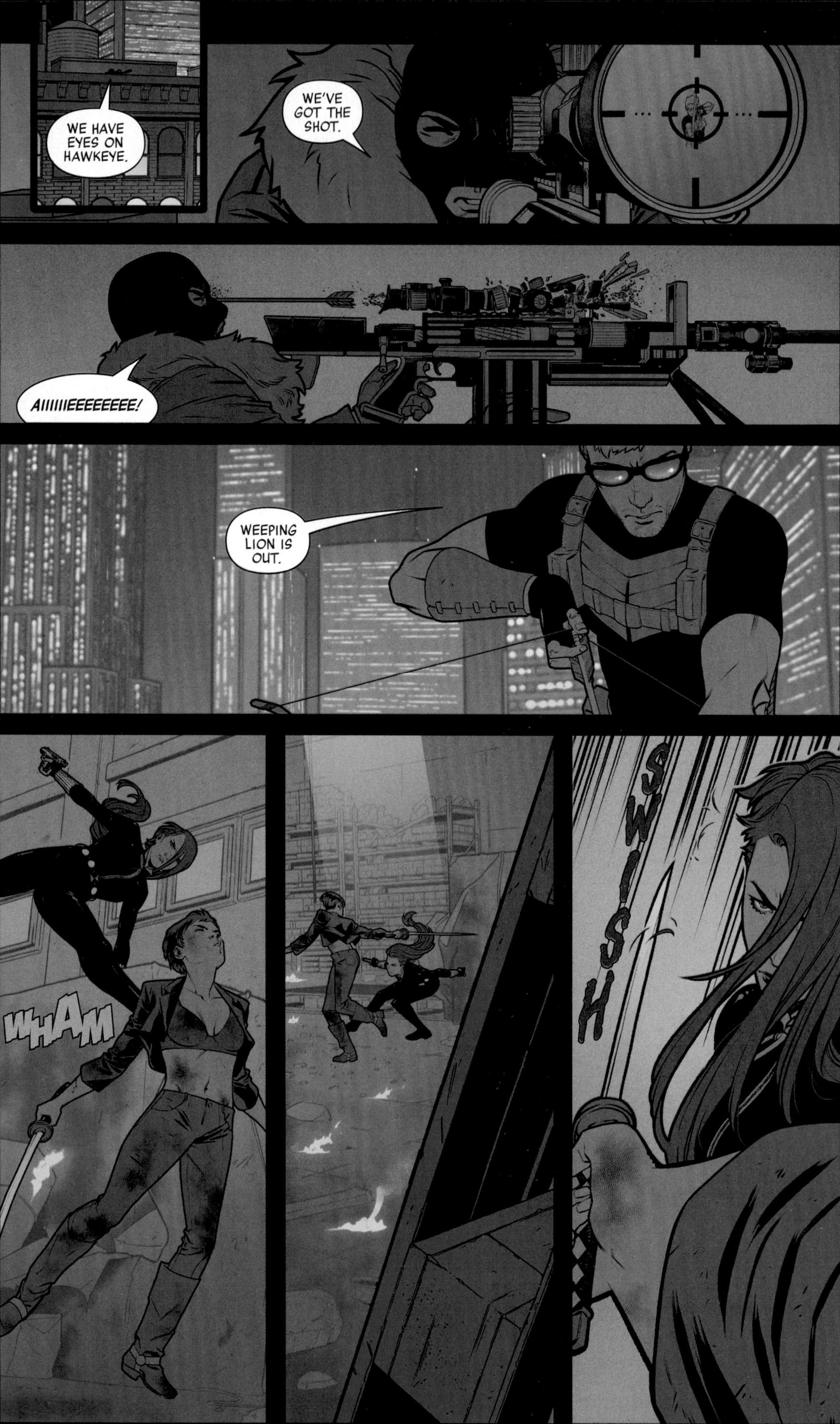
WE HAVE EYES ON HAWKEYE.
WE'VE GOT THE SHOT.
AIIIIIEEEEEEEE!
WEEPING LION IS OUT.
WHAM
SWISH

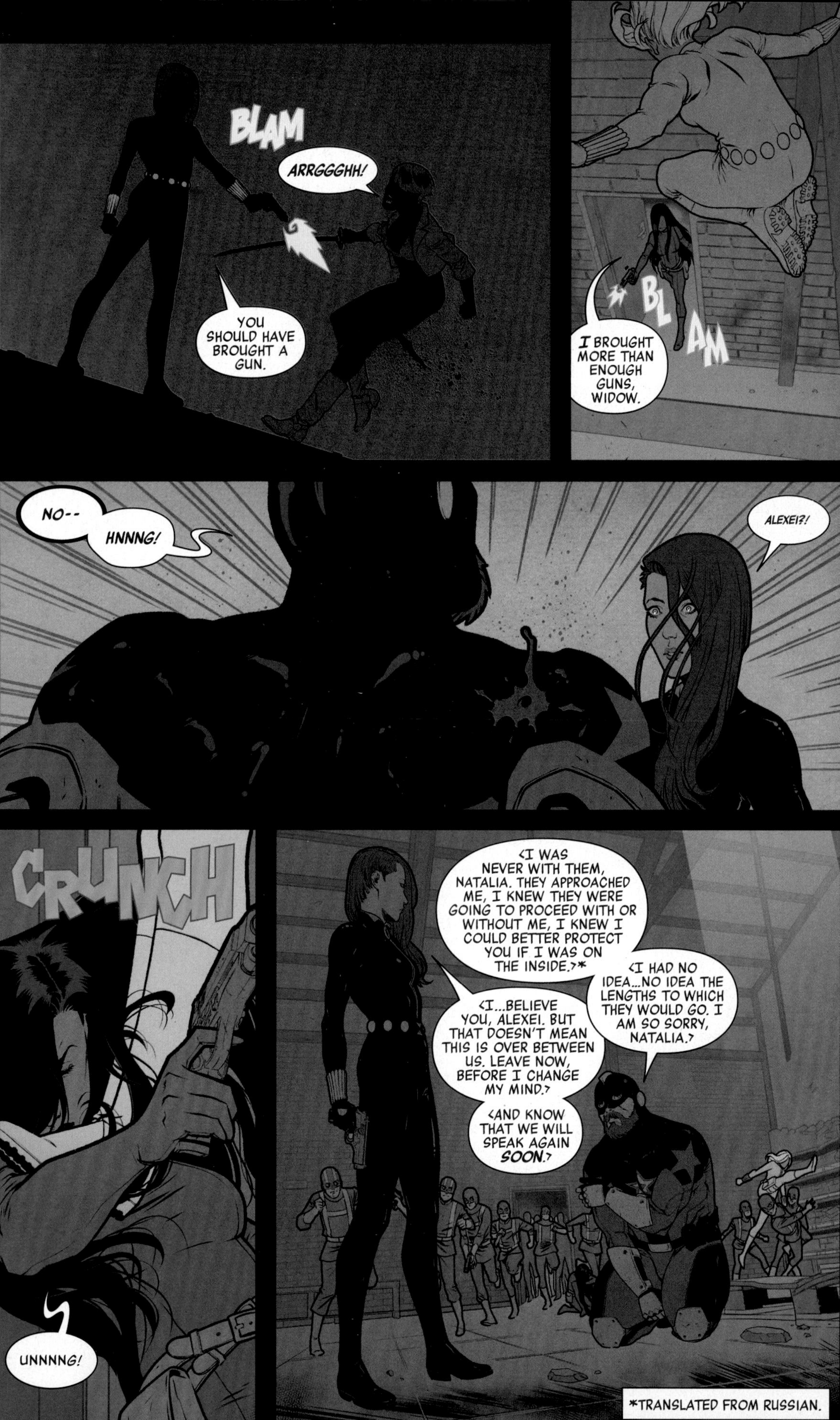
BLAM
ARRGGGHH!
YOU SHOULD HAVE BROUGHT A GUN.
BLAM
I BROUGHT MORE THAN ENOUGH GUNS, WIDOW.
NO-- HNNNG!
ALEXEI?!
CRUNCH
UNNNNG!
<I WAS NEVER WITH THEM, NATALIA. THEY APPROACHED ME, I KNEW THEY WERE GOING TO PROCEED WITH OR WITHOUT ME, I KNEW I COULD BETTER PROTECT YOU IF I WAS ON THE INSIDE.>*
<I HAD NO IDEA...NO IDEA THE LENGTHS TO WHICH THEY WOULD GO. I AM SO SORRY, NATALIA.>
<I...BELIEVE YOU, ALEXEI. BUT THAT DOESN'T MEAN THIS IS OVER BETWEEN US. LEAVE NOW, BEFORE I CHANGE MY MIND.>
<AND KNOW THAT WE WILL SPEAK AGAIN SOON.>
*TRANSLATED FROM RUSSIAN.

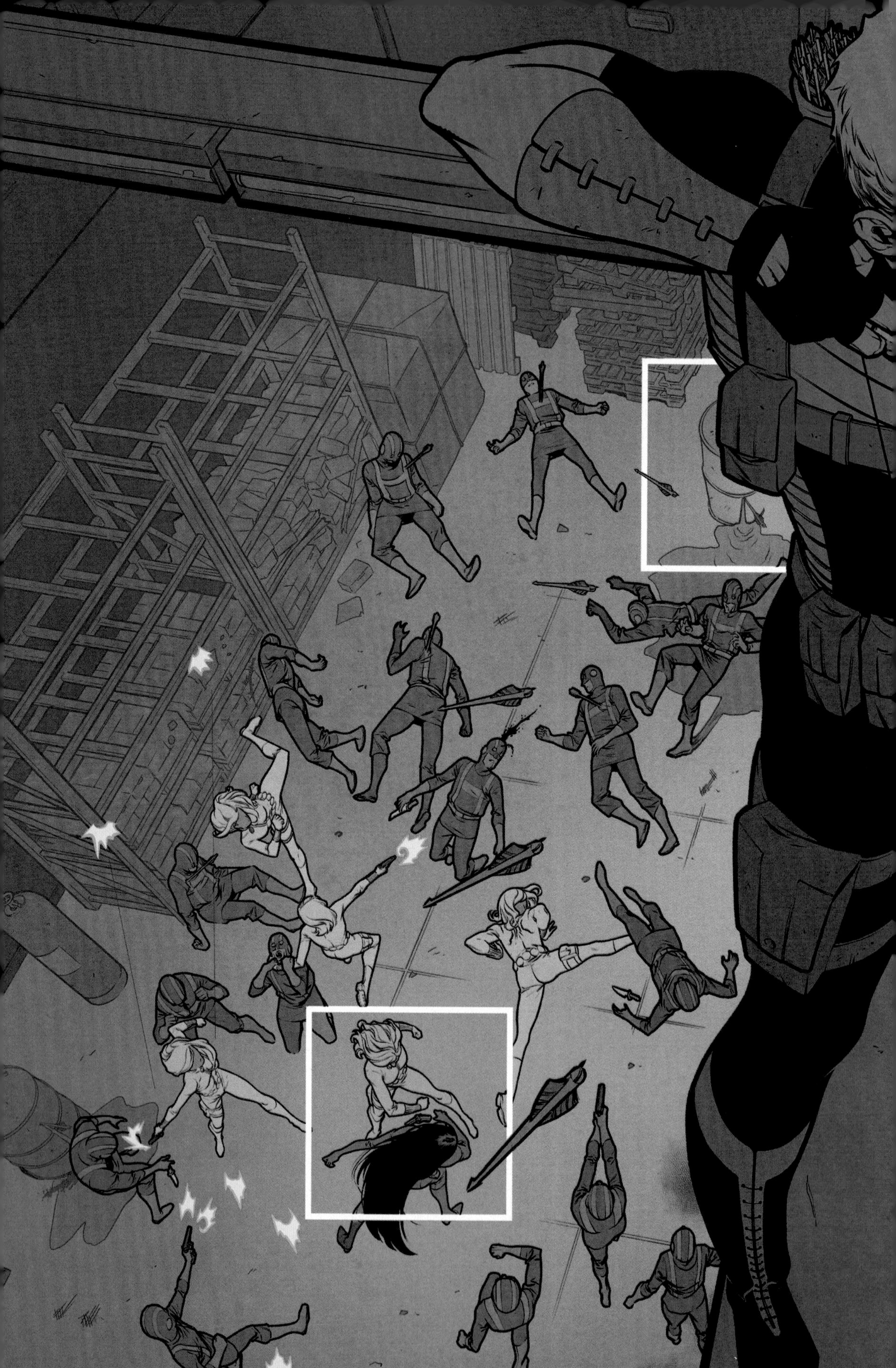

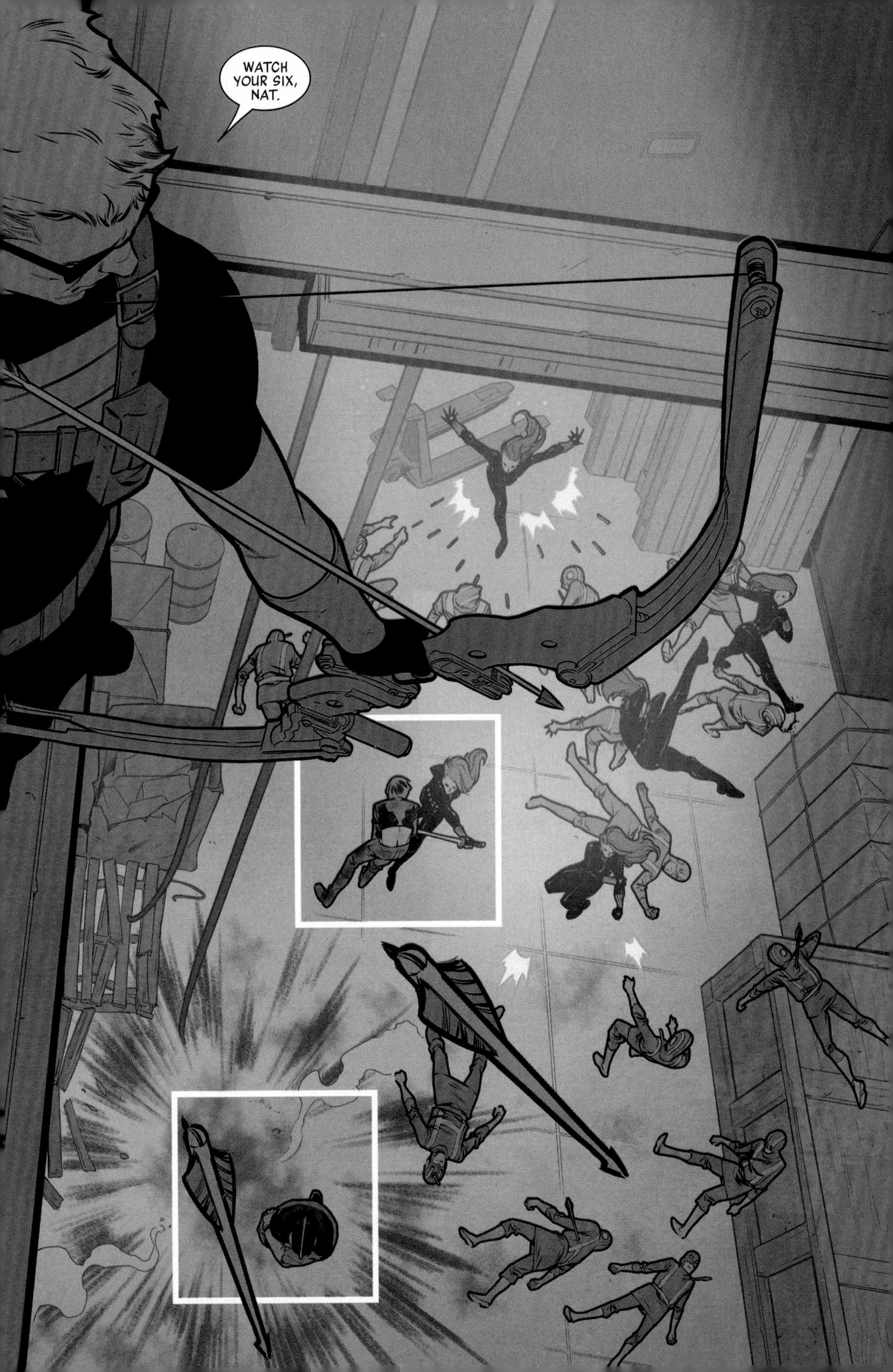
WATCH YOUR SIX, NAT.

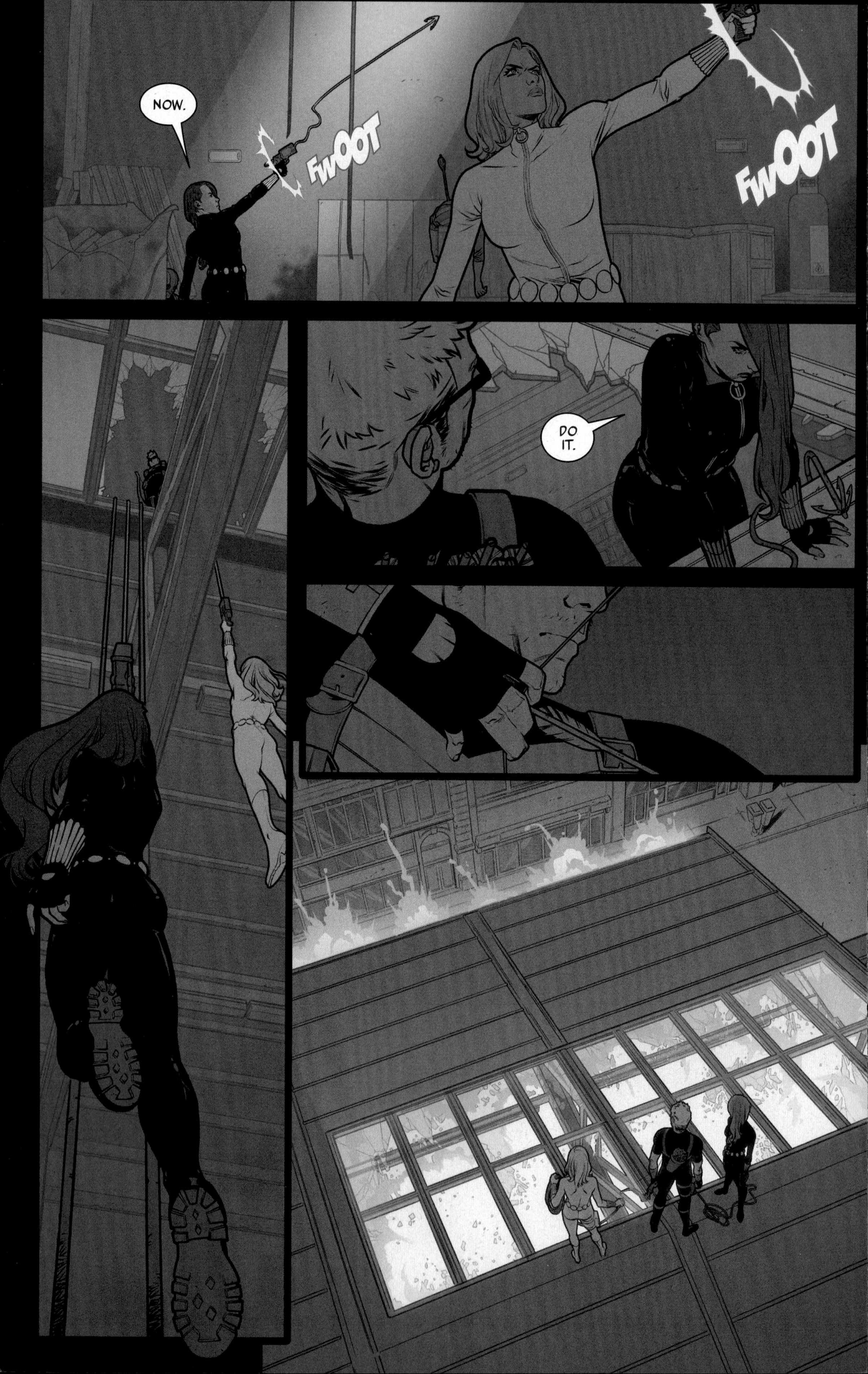
NOW.
FWOOT
FWOOT
DO IT.

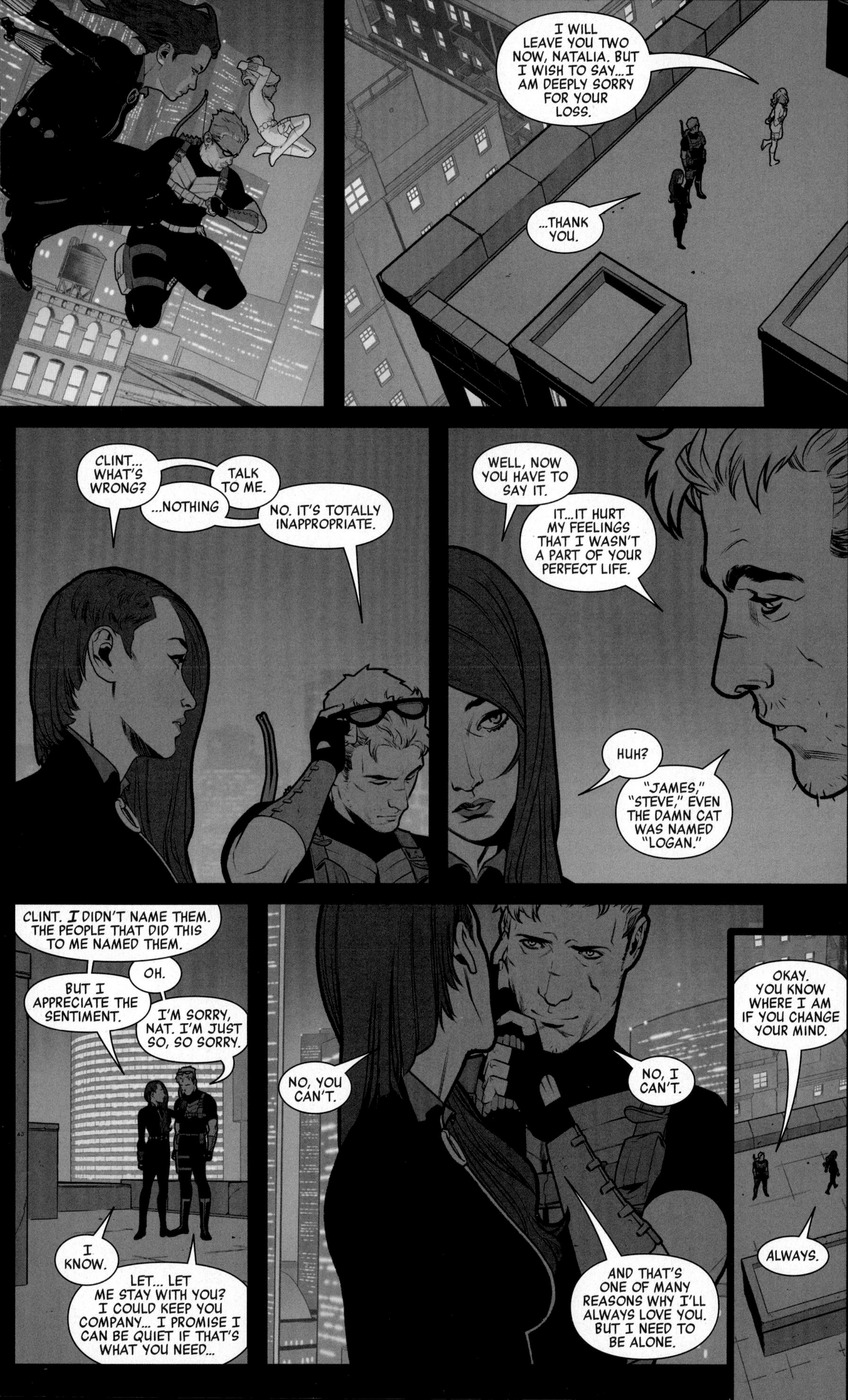

I WILL LEAVE YOU TWO NOW, NATALIA. BUT I WISH TO SAY...I AM DEEPLY SORRY FOR YOUR LOSS.
...THANK YOU.
CLINT... WHAT'S WRONG?
...NOTHING
TALK TO ME.
NO. IT'S TOTALLY INAPPROPRIATE.
WELL, NOW YOU HAVE TO SAY IT.
IT...IT HURT MY FEELINGS THAT I WASN'T A PART OF YOUR PERFECT LIFE.
HUH?
"JAMES," "STEVE," EVEN THE DAMN CAT WAS NAMED "LOGAN."
CLINT. I DIDN'T NAME THEM. THE PEOPLE THAT DID THIS TO ME NAMED THEM.
OH.
BUT I APPRECIATE THE SENTIMENT.
I'M SORRY, NAT. I'M JUST SO, SO SORRY.
I KNOW.
LET... LET ME STAY WITH YOU? I COULD KEEP YOU COMPANY... I PROMISE I CAN BE QUIET IF THAT'S WHAT YOU NEED...
NO, YOU CAN'T.
NO, I CAN'T.
AND THAT'S ONE OF MANY REASONS WHY I'LL ALWAYS LOVE YOU. BUT I NEED TO BE ALONE.
OKAY. YOU KNOW WHERE I AM IF YOU CHANGE YOUR MIND.
ALWAYS.

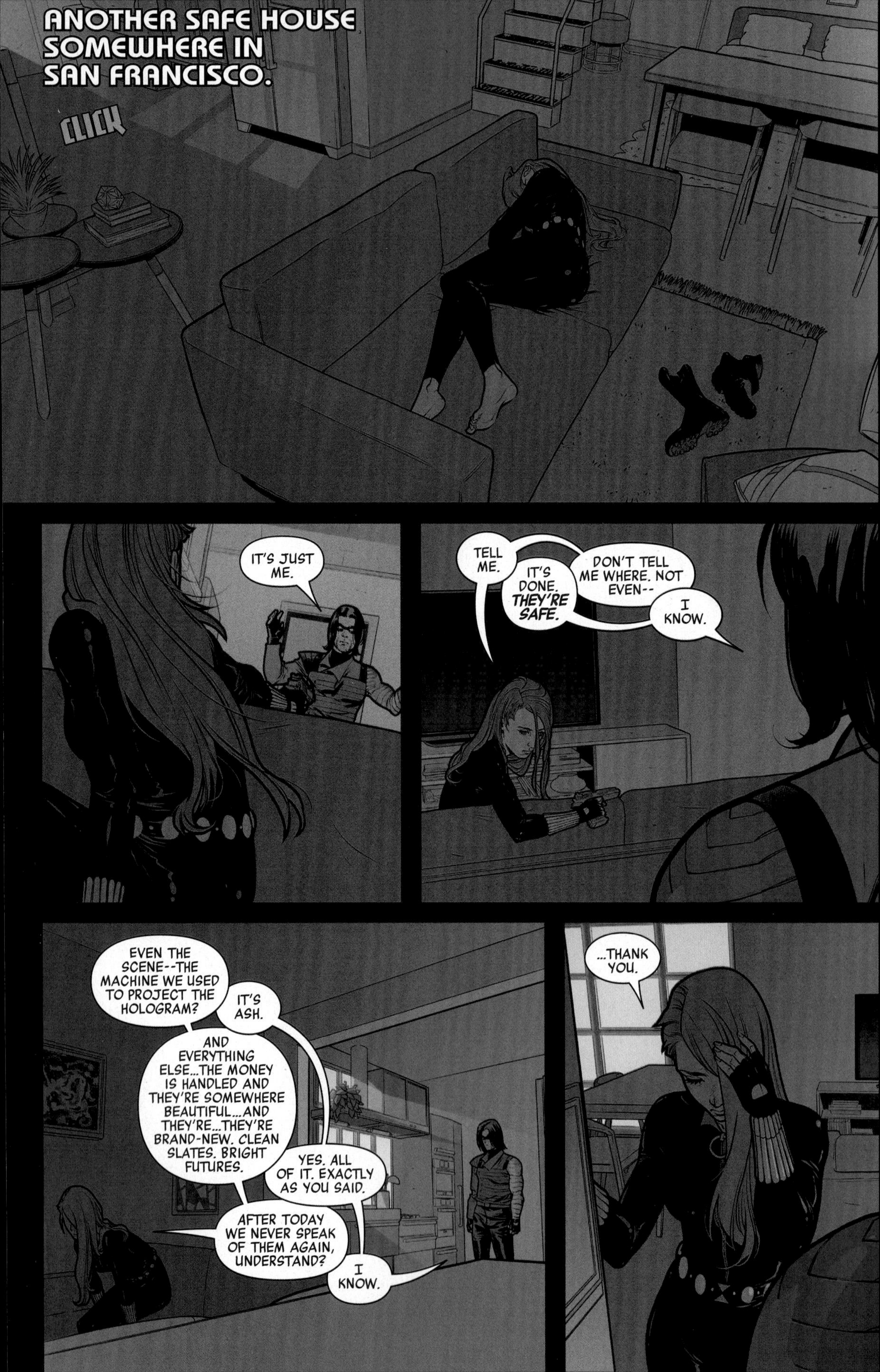

ANOTHER SAFE HOUSE SOMEWHERE IN SAN FRANCISCO.
CLICK
IT'S JUST ME.
TELL ME.
IT'S DONE. THEY'RE SAFE.
DON'T TELL ME WHERE. NOT EVEN--
I KNOW.
EVEN THE SCENE--THE MACHINE WE USED TO PROJECT THE HOLOGRAM?
IT'S ASH.
AND EVERYTHING ELSE...THE MONEY IS HANDLED AND THEY'RE SOMEWHERE BEAUTIFUL...AND THEY'RE...THEY'RE BRAND-NEW. CLEAN SLATES. BRIGHT FUTURES.
YES. ALL OF IT. EXACTLY AS YOU SAID.
AFTER TODAY WE NEVER SPEAK OF THEM AGAIN, UNDERSTAND?
I KNOW.
...THANK YOU.

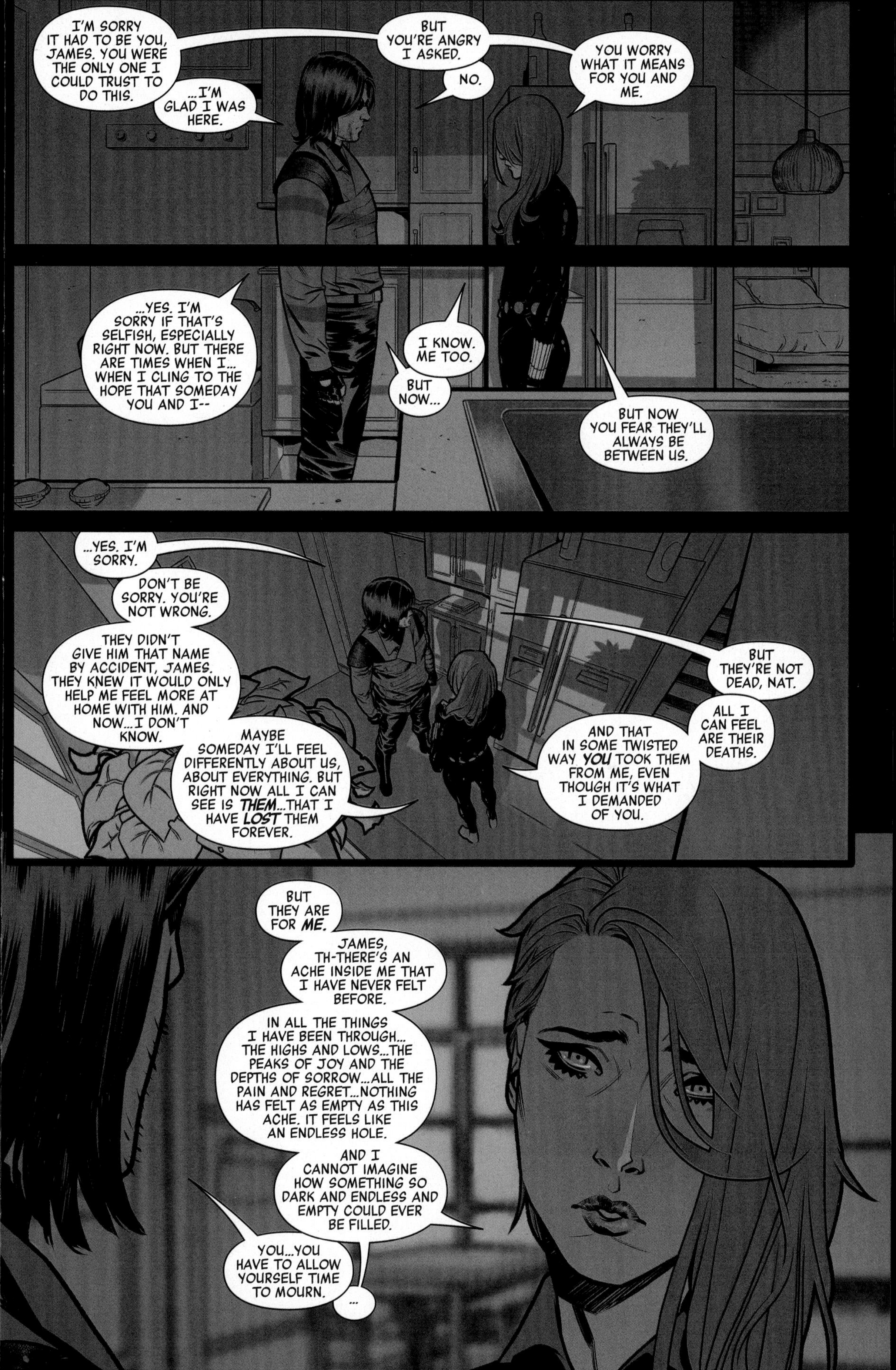
I'M SORRY IT HAD TO BE YOU, JAMES. YOU WERE THE ONLY ONE I COULD TRUST TO DO THIS.
...I'M GLAD I WAS HERE.
BUT YOU'RE ANGRY I ASKED.
NO.
YOU WORRY WHAT IT MEANS FOR YOU AND ME.
...YES. I'M SORRY IF THAT'S SELFISH, ESPECIALLY RIGHT NOW. BUT THERE ARE TIMES WHEN I... WHEN I CLING TO THE HOPE THAT SOMEDAY YOU AND I--
I KNOW. ME TOO.
BUT NOW...
BUT NOW YOU FEAR THEY'LL ALWAYS BE BETWEEN US.
...YES. I'M SORRY.
DON'T BE SORRY. YOU'RE NOT WRONG.
THEY DIDN'T GIVE HIM THAT NAME BY ACCIDENT, JAMES. THEY KNEW IT WOULD ONLY HELP ME FEEL MORE AT HOME WITH HIM. AND NOW...I DON'T KNOW.
MAYBE SOMEDAY I'LL FEEL DIFFERENTLY ABOUT US, ABOUT EVERYTHING. BUT RIGHT NOW ALL I CAN SEE IS *THEM*...THAT I HAVE *LOST* THEM FOREVER.
BUT THEY'RE NOT DEAD, NAT.
ALL I CAN FEEL ARE THEIR DEATHS.
AND THAT IN SOME TWISTED WAY *YOU* TOOK THEM FROM ME, EVEN THOUGH IT'S WHAT I DEMANDED OF YOU.
BUT THEY ARE FOR *ME.*
JAMES, TH-THERE'S AN ACHE INSIDE ME THAT I HAVE NEVER FELT BEFORE.
IN ALL THE THINGS I HAVE BEEN THROUGH... THE HIGHS AND LOWS...THE PEAKS OF JOY AND THE DEPTHS OF SORROW...ALL THE PAIN AND REGRET...NOTHING HAS FELT AS EMPTY AS THIS ACHE. IT FEELS LIKE AN ENDLESS HOLE.
AND I CANNOT IMAGINE HOW SOMETHING SO DARK AND ENDLESS AND EMPTY COULD EVER BE FILLED.
YOU...YOU HAVE TO ALLOW YOURSELF TIME TO MOURN.
...

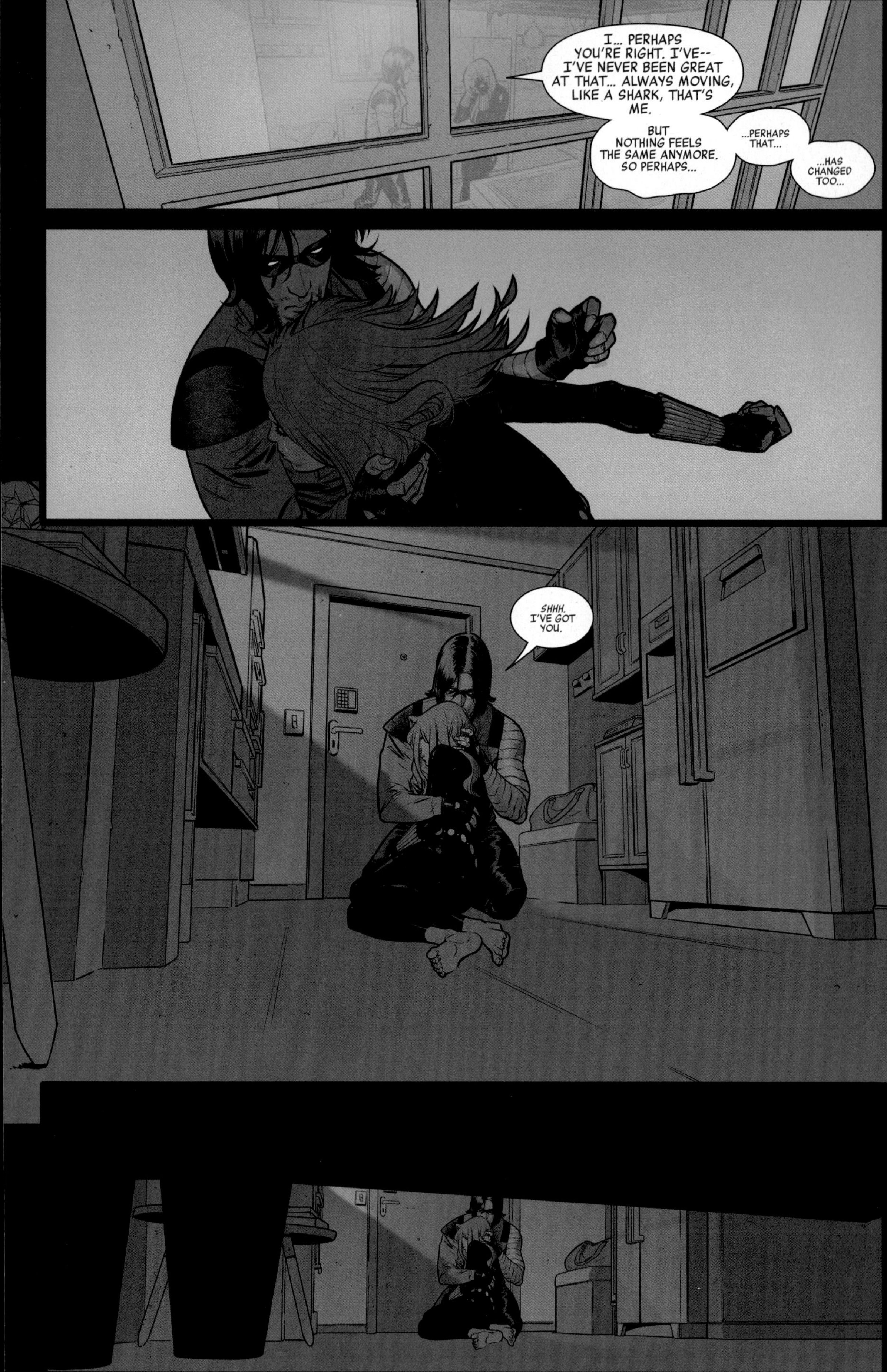
I... PERHAPS YOU'RE RIGHT. I'VE-- I'VE NEVER BEEN GREAT AT THAT... ALWAYS MOVING, LIKE A SHARK, THAT'S ME.
BUT NOTHING FEELS THE SAME ANYMORE. SO PERHAPS...
...PERHAPS THAT...
...HAS CHANGED TOO...
SHHH. I'VE GOT YOU.

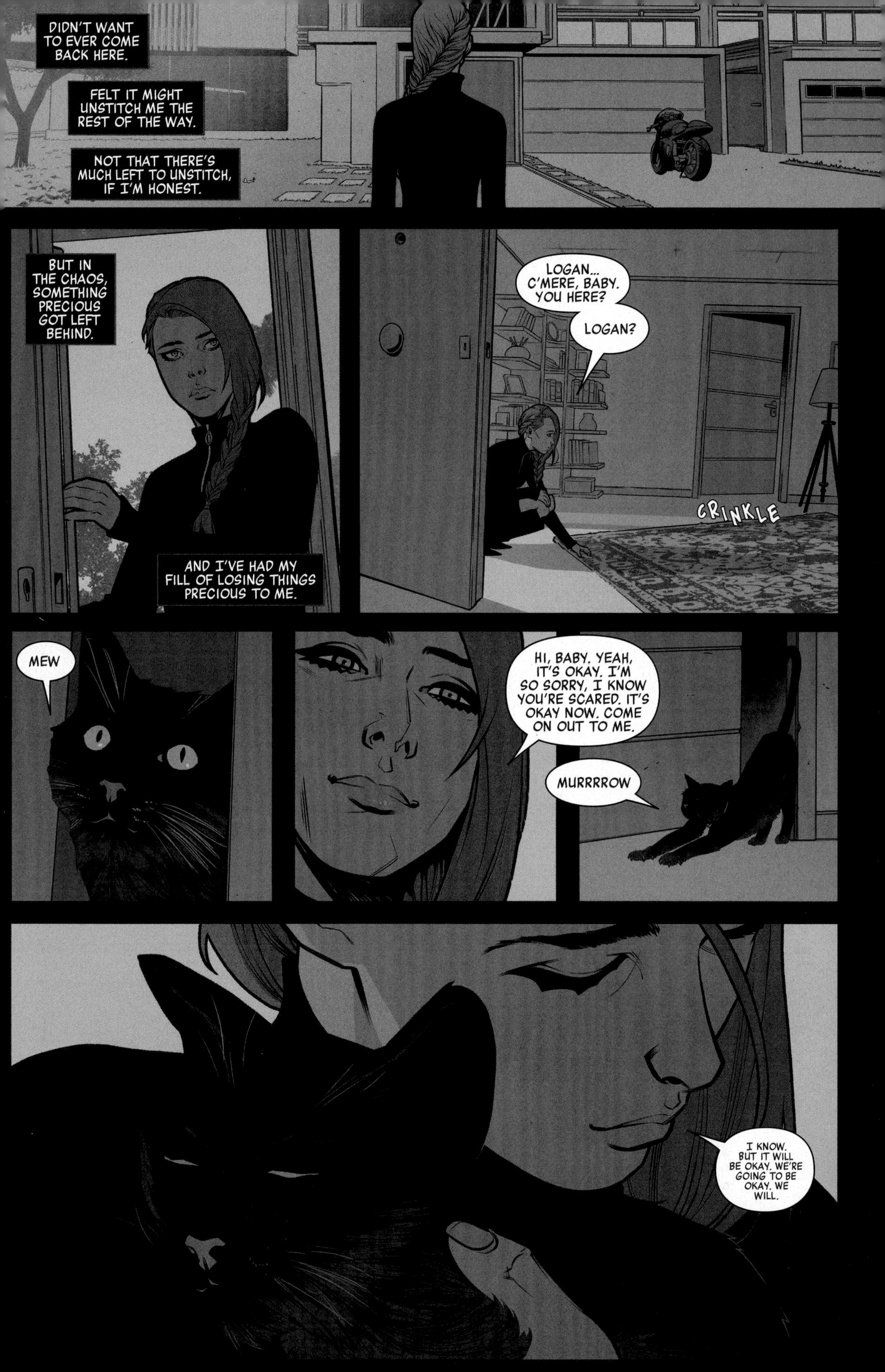
DIDN'T WANT TO EVER COME BACK HERE.
FELT IT MIGHT UNSTITCH ME THE REST OF THE WAY.
NOT THAT THERE'S MUCH LEFT TO UNSTITCH, IF I'M HONEST.
BUT IN THE CHAOS, SOMETHING PRECIOUS GOT LEFT BEHIND.
AND I'VE HAD MY FILL OF LOSING THINGS PRECIOUS TO ME.
LOGAN... C'MERE, BABY. YOU HERE?
LOGAN?
CRINKLE
MEW
HI, BABY. YEAH, IT'S OKAY. I'M SO SORRY, I KNOW YOU'RE SCARED. IT'S OKAY NOW. COME ON OUT TO ME.
MURRRROW
I KNOW. BUT IT WILL BE OKAY. WE'RE GOING TO BE OKAY. WE WILL.

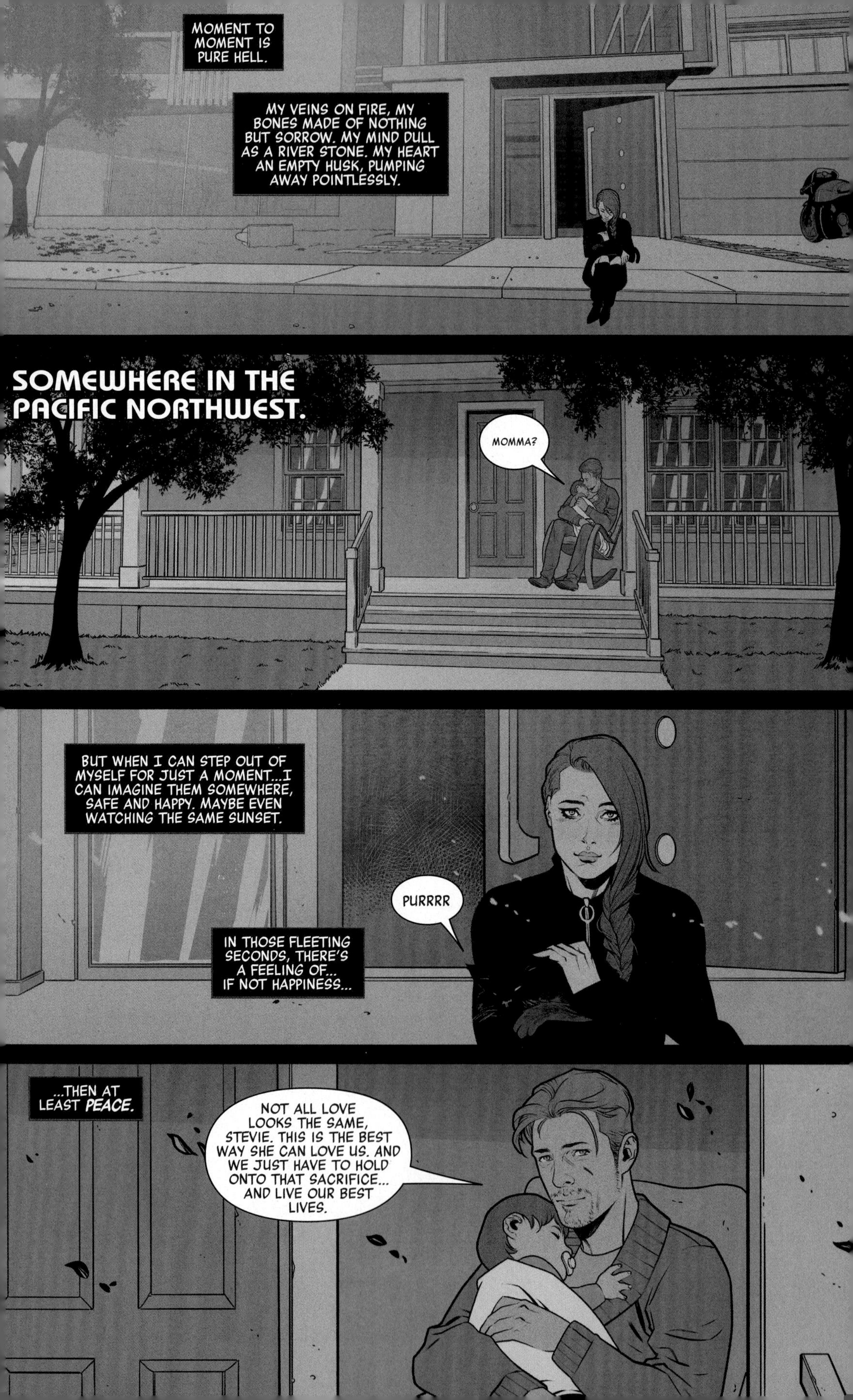
MOMENT TO MOMENT IS PURE HELL.
MY VEINS ON FIRE, MY BONES MADE OF NOTHING BUT SORROW. MY MIND DULL AS A RIVER STONE. MY HEART AN EMPTY HUSK, PUMPING AWAY POINTLESSLY.
SOMEWHERE IN THE PACIFIC NORTHWEST.
MOMMA?
BUT WHEN I CAN STEP OUT OF MYSELF FOR JUST A MOMENT...I CAN IMAGINE THEM SOMEWHERE, SAFE AND HAPPY. MAYBE EVEN WATCHING THE SAME SUNSET.
PURRRR
IN THOSE FLEETING SECONDS, THERE'S A FEELING OF... IF NOT HAPPINESS...
...THEN AT LEAST *PEACE.*
NOT ALL LOVE LOOKS THE SAME, STEVIE. THIS IS THE BEST WAY SHE CAN LOVE US. AND WE JUST HAVE TO HOLD ONTO THAT SACRIFICE... AND LIVE OUR BEST LIVES.

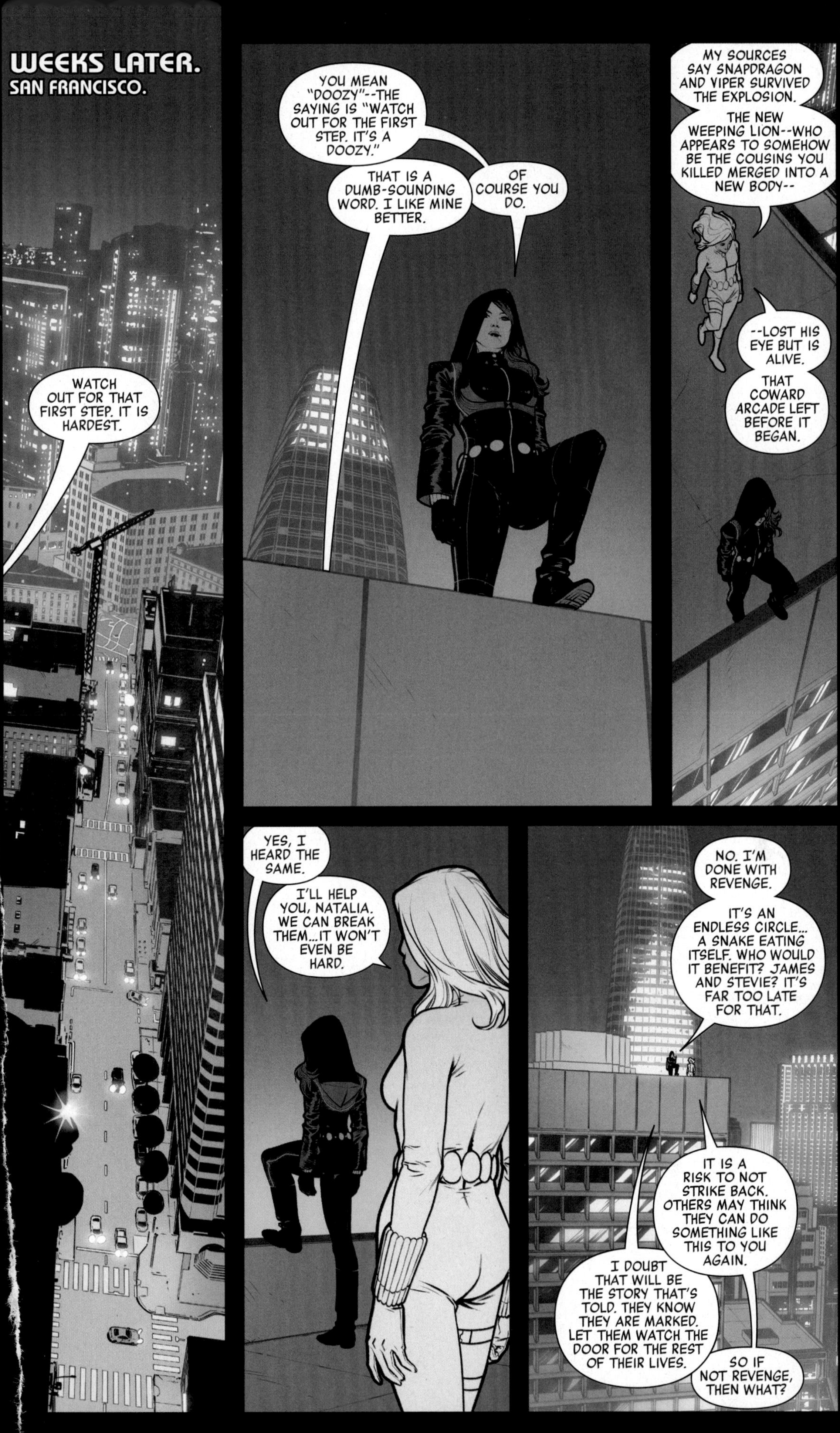
WEEKS LATER.
SAN FRANCISCO.
WATCH OUT FOR THAT FIRST STEP. IT IS HARDEST.
YOU MEAN "DOOZY"--THE SAYING IS "WATCH OUT FOR THE FIRST STEP. IT'S A DOOZY."
THAT IS A DUMB-SOUNDING WORD. I LIKE MINE BETTER.
OF COURSE YOU DO.
MY SOURCES SAY SNAPDRAGON AND VIPER SURVIVED THE EXPLOSION.
THE NEW WEEPING LION--WHO APPEARS TO SOMEHOW BE THE COUSINS YOU KILLED MERGED INTO A NEW BODY--
--LOST HIS EYE BUT IS ALIVE.
THAT COWARD ARCADE LEFT BEFORE IT BEGAN.
YES, I HEARD THE SAME.
I'LL HELP YOU, NATALIA. WE CAN BREAK THEM...IT WON'T EVEN BE HARD.
NO. I'M DONE WITH REVENGE.
IT'S AN ENDLESS CIRCLE... A SNAKE EATING ITSELF. WHO WOULD IT BENEFIT? JAMES AND STEVIE? IT'S FAR TOO LATE FOR THAT.
IT IS A RISK TO NOT STRIKE BACK. OTHERS MAY THINK THEY CAN DO SOMETHING LIKE THIS TO YOU AGAIN.
I DOUBT THAT WILL BE THE STORY THAT'S TOLD. THEY KNOW THEY ARE MARKED. LET THEM WATCH THE DOOR FOR THE REST OF THEIR LIVES.
SO IF NOT REVENGE, THEN WHAT?

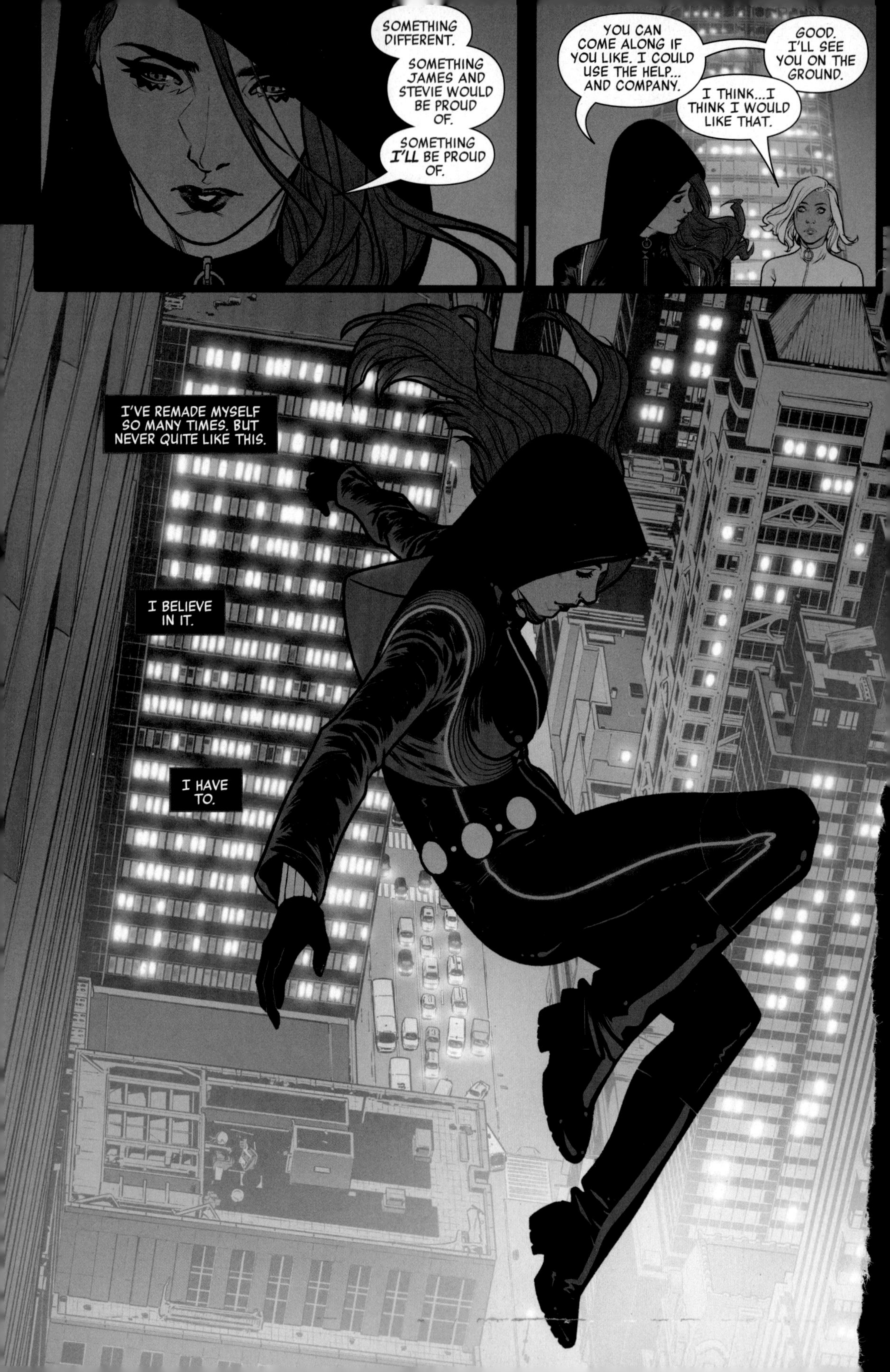
SOMETHING DIFFERENT.
SOMETHING JAMES AND STEVIE WOULD BE PROUD OF.
SOMETHING *I'LL* BE PROUD OF.
YOU CAN COME ALONG IF YOU LIKE. I COULD USE THE HELP... AND COMPANY.
I THINK...I THINK I WOULD LIKE THAT.
GOOD. I'LL SEE YOU ON THE GROUND.
I'VE REMADE MYSELF SO MANY TIMES. BUT NEVER QUITE LIKE THIS.
I BELIEVE IN IT.
I HAVE TO.